Anthony Dardis

Mental Causation

THE MIND-BODY PROBLEM

COLUMBIA UNIVERSITY PRESS *NEW YORK*

Columbia University Press
Publishers Since 1893
New York   Chichester, West Sussex
Copyright ©2008 Columbia University Press
All rights reserved

Library of Congress Cataloging-in-Publication Data
Dardis, Anthony.
    Mental Causation : the mind-body problem / Anthony Dardis.
       p. cm.
    Includes bibliographical references and index.
    ISBN 978-0-231-14416-2 (cloth: alk. paper) —ISBN 978-0-231-14417-9
(pbk.: alk. paper) —ISBN 978-0-231-51351-7 (e-book)
      1. Philosophy of mind.   2. Mind and body.   3. Causation.   I. Title.

    BD418.3.D37   2008
    128′.2—dc22

                                      2008006152

For Marla and Eli, and for Jane Buckelew
and for the memory of Thomas Anthony Dardis

Contents

THAT THINKING should make things happen—cause things—seems both necessary and impossible.

If thinking didn't make things happen, the foundations of how we think about ourselves would collapse.

Here are some of the things I make happen. I choose cereal rather than eggs for breakfast. I walk to the train rather than take the bus. I stand up to let someone sit on the train. I make certain to schedule my evening around my wife's plans, around my son's plans. I conveniently forget to wash the dishes.

My actions come from my self, my consciousness, my feelings, my experience, my choices, and, most important, my values. I make things happen by thinking about and feeling for the best way to live. If I act for the good, then I have done well, and I am proud of my actions. If I act unkindly or selfishly or thoughtlessly, then I have done badly, and I regret or feel anguish over my actions. But if *I* didn't make them happen, then I shouldn't feel these things. If these good and bad things flow from something other than my thinking, then what's the point of saying that I am good or bad? Putting value to one side, it is nearly impossible for me to so much as imagine that I am not making these things happen. *I* reach for the cereal; *I* make the box move.

But, on the other hand, it seems impossible for me—my consciousness, my feelings, my experience—to make anything happen. We are physical beings with physical bodies and physical brains. Our minds, our consciousness, our experience, our sense of values, all these things are completely physical. The physical world operates according to the laws of nature. The laws of nature govern each change in us, as they govern each change at every point in space and time. The physical properties of things are what matter. The mental properties don't: they are like labels for complex but arbitrary assemblies of physical things with physical properties.

The mental causation problem is the problem of resolving this apparent contradiction.

This book argues that the contradiction is only apparent. The world does proceed according to the laws of physical nature. But parts of it also proceed according to the laws of mental nature. The laws of physical nature don't rule out laws of mental nature, so long as the two are coordinated in a certain way.

My argument takes the form of a model of what the laws of mental nature are like and how they are related to the laws of physical nature. The model is presented in the last chapter of the book, chapter 9. It is developed against a background of ideas about physical laws, about causation, and about properties and how they are connected with laws and causation. Chapters 5 through 8 describe and argue these background ideas.

The mental causation problem is that mental properties and physical properties appear to be competitors for being the causes of things, and physical properties are the obvious winners. The solution is to set out how mental properties and physical properties are related in such a way that it will no longer make sense to say that mental properties and physical properties are competitors with one another in the same struggle for causal relevance.

If they are not competitors in the same struggle, then the possibility opens up of a conception of causal relevance according to which properties are causally relevant when they are the most successful competitors *in their own proper competitions*, competitions *at their level*. Physical properties are causally relevant because they are the most successful competitors at the level of fundamental physics. Mental properties can also be causally relevant if they are the most successful competitors at the psychological level. (Assuming, that is, that there is a psychological level; if science somehow shows that thinking isn't what makes behavior happen, then it clearly can't be causally relevant. But then, as Jerry Fodor wrote [1989: 156], "If it isn't literally true that my wanting is causally responsible for my reaching . . . then practically everything I believe about anything is false and it's the end of the world.")

Chapters 1 though 4 examine the history of the problem. Plato thought minds or souls are radically different from bodies, and Aristotle thought souls and minds are ways that bodies are organized (chapter 2). Each way of thinking leads to distinctive problems for mental causation. Aristotle's philosophy of mind is especially interesting and useful: a crucial difficulty for his view (the problem of connecting by definition mental states with perception and action) haunts twentieth-century philosophy of mind. Yet his distinction between form and matter provides a key to the solution to the problem of mental causation.

Descartes (like Plato) argued that the mind is really distinct from the body and consequently struggled (in the end, fruitlessly) to explain how they could interact causally. Thomas Huxley argued that everything that bodies do is physically explicable and hence that conscious experience is causally irrelevant (chapter 3). Huxley's contemporaries called this position "automatism." To get rid of the misleading connotation that we are automata, just simple robots, the term "epiphenomenalism" was soon pressed into service: mental occurrences are epiphenomena, caused by physical things but themselves not causing anything.

The struggle to make sense of how we can possibly make things happen (how our minds can possibly cause changes in the world) intensified in the twentieth century as science became ever more confident that things that happen in the physical world have physical causes that completely suffice to explain them (chapter 4).

Following a path opened up by Kant, Wittgenstein and Ryle argued that mental things aren't causes at all (and so there couldn't be a mental causation problem). Philosophy of mind since then almost unanimously assumes that minds are physical and that reasons are causes. Central state identity theory is the most successful with mental causation: since mental things and mental properties are just physical things and physical properties, mental things and properties must be just as much causes as physical things and properties. The trouble is that mental properties aren't physical properties. Functionalism and anomalous monism argue for this claim, yet each has distinctive difficulties with mental causation.

* * *

I wrote this book partly out of a sense of frustration over the contemporary conversation about how natural science (physics, biochemistry, neuroscience, cognitive science) understands the mind and its place in nature. If you are convinced that you are a free agent—that what you do is at least sometimes up to you—then you are likely to be convinced that there is something about the mind (or soul or spirit) that cannot ever be understood by natural science. Conversely, if you believe that the truth about the mind will emerge from natural science, you are likely to think that free will is an illusion and that you never make anything happen.

I think this is a false dichotomy. I think it can be shown that, even if natural science demonstrates that minds are purely physical, your choices at least sometimes make things happen. If you can make things happen, then it may be that some of your actions are done freely.

This book is for those who find this problem as frustrating and as compelling as I do, whether or not you have training in philosophy. I have attempted to lay out some of the historical origins of the problem and to show how it lives and breathes in contemporary discussions of the mind-body relation. The solution I offer depends on taking stances on controversial issues in contemporary metaphysics. I have attempted to keep the discussion of these issues as accessible as possible. Each chapter ends with suggestions for further reading that provide some guidance for the interested reader or student venturing into the thickets of recent debate on these issues. For newcomers to the problem, I want to show how the problem is connected up with contemporary philosophy of mind. But I also want to make a serious and original proposal about how the problem may be solved.

Acknowledgments

I OWE a very great intellectual debt to Kirk Ludwig and to Noa Latham. The ideas this book describes arose out of countless conversations with them about causation and the mind.

I've had a lot of help with this book. I want to thank Akeel Bilgrami, Jim Bogen, Mark Brown, Elwood Carlson, Randy Cartwright, Carol Cleland, Andrew Cortens, Thomas Dardis, Martin Davies, Donald Davidson, Stephen Demby, Crawford Elder, Mylan Engel, Carrie Figdor, Carl Gillett, Saul Gilson, Richard Grandy, Reinhard Grossman, Ariela Lazar, Jim Levine, Barry Loewer, Brian McLaughlin, Pete Mandik, Cei Maslen, Gene Mills, George Myro, Paul O'Grady, Gretchen Ostheimer, Dugald Owen, Philip Percival, Ullan Place, Piers Rawling, Greg Ray, Creighton Rosental, David Rosenthal, Marcelo Sabatés, Dion Scott-Kakures, Eric Steinhart, Kurt Torell, Bruce Vermazen, Susan Vineberg, and Gene Witmer.

My colleagues at Hofstra University, especially Chris Eliot, Warren Frisina, Terry Godlove, Bob Holland, Amy Karofsky, Ira Singer, and Kathleen Wallace, have read various parts of this project and have provided a supportive and critical environment in which to work.

I thank the National Endowment for the Humanities for the opportunity to attend John Heil's summer 1996 seminar "The Metaphysics of Mind," held at Cornell University. Thanks also are due to the participants of the seminar for their vigorous inquiry into the metaphysics of the mind: Lenny Clapp, Randy Clark, Jim Garson, Heather Gert, Muhammad Ali Khalidi, David Pitt, David Robb, Eric Saidel, Steven Schwartz, Nigel Thomas, Amie Thomasson, Michael Watkins, and Jessica Wilson—and, of course, John Heil.

I am grateful to Hofstra University for providing me with the time and opportunity to complete this book. My students, particularly Douglas Baena, Brook Rosini, Bryan Vetell, and Austin Walker, have worked through issues about mental causation, mind/body dualism, and free will in my classes and have provided very useful criticism and comment.

The Cognitive Science Symposium of the CUNY Graduate Center hosted two presentations based on chapters 7 and 9. The participants' success at killing a slide during a PowerPoint presentation led to a substantial revision of chapter 7.

Finally, thanks to Marla Carlson and Eli Dardis for making lots of things happen without which I could not have written this book.

* * *

Permission has been granted to use material from my previously published article "Against Sparse Properties," *Acta Analytica* 12, no. 2 (1997): 97–115. Sections of chapter 7 are based on my "Sunburn: Independence Conditions on Causal Relevance," *Philosophy and Phenomenological Research* 53, no. 3 (1993): 577–598.

Mental Causation

Why Mental Causation?

If cause forever follows,
In infinite sequence, cause—where would we get
This free will that we have, wrested from fate,
by which we go ahead, each one of us,
Wherever our pleasures urge?

—LUCRETIUS, ON THE NATURE OF THINGS, 2.255, IN LUCRETIUS 1969

WHY SHOULD you care about mental causation? What is it, anyway?

1.1 So What Is Mental Causation?

Stop reading. Look at the cover of this book.

What just happened? Light reflecting off the page caused changes in your eyes. These changes began a causal process that reached into your brain. This process caused you to understand the words on the page. Your understanding caused you to decide to take up my invitation. This decision, together with your understanding of how to take up my invitation (that is, by exercising your skill in manipulating medium-sized physical objects like books) led—caused—you to close the book and reopen it.

Mental causation isn't telekinesis. It's not bending spoons; it's not mind over matter. It's what happens when you walk down the street, when you drive, when you talk, when you see a traffic light. It's with us all the time. Whenever we perceive anything, whenever we think or reason or change our mind, whenever we do anything—make something happen—mental causation is involved.

Mental causation is ubiquitous.

1.2 What's the Problem?

What makes mental causation mysterious is how it fits with our picture of our place in the natural world. That picture is called materialism: the thesis that everything in the world is made of physical matter and that everything does what it does because of the laws that govern physical matter.

Materialism is a milder position than physicalism. Physicalism says every thing is physical and every property of every thing is a physical property. Materialism agrees that all things are physical, but disagrees about properties. Many things—thoughts, for instance, and picnics—have nonphysical properties. What makes a property physical is that it features in the laws of physics. Since the laws of physics don't talk about thoughts or picnics, picnic and thought properties are not physical. That doesn't make them spooky or out of this world: picnics are completely physical, even though they have nonphysical properties.

What does the world look like, according to materialism? The natural world includes living things and inanimate objects, some independent of us (rocks, rivers, galaxies), others created by us (furniture, roads, books). All these things are physical objects. Physical objects have parts. The parts have parts. Eventually we get to the elements from the periodic table: hydrogen, oxygen, carbon, molybdenum, and so forth. These have parts as well: electrons, neutrons, protons. And those parts have parts. This process of decomposition ought to stop at some ultimate level of completely simple parts (although it may not—it's not logically incoherent to say that the process of decomposition just goes on forever).

Living things are no different from inanimate objects. They are physical objects as well, composed of the elements.

The elements (and all the things made of them) obey the laws of physics. If anything has mass, then it obeys the law of gravity:

$$G = K(m_1 m_2)/r^2$$

where m_1 and m_2 are masses of two physical objects, r is the distance between them, and K is the gravitational constant. Two massive objects will obey Newton's Second Law,

$$F = ma$$

and accelerate toward one another through time, if nothing else acts on them. If anything has an electrical charge, then it obeys a similar law governing the interaction of charged particles. Further laws govern the building blocks of atoms. No physical object ever breaks any of the laws.

Right now physicists tell us there are five fundamental physical forces: electromagnetic, strong, weak, electroweak, and gravity. They hope that a theory of how the physical world works can be figured out based only on these forces. Of course, we may well be wrong about how the world works. Aristotle's physics was wrong, Descartes's was wrong, Newton's was too: ours probably is as well. But that's not a reason to give up hope that we can discover a grand unified theory of everything: a GUT.

If we had a GUT, then we would be able (at least in principle [Weinberg 2001]) to explain things that happen in the natural world. We would be able to explain exactly what a certain particle did in a cloud chamber in a physics laboratory in California on a particular day. We would not, however, be able to predict what that particle would do. This would be true even if we had perfect information about everything (which we never do). Much of what happens at the level of particles is probabilistic. What will happen to a given particle is never absolutely determined by how it is earlier. Rather, there are specific probabilities (which physical theory describes) that various things from a specific range of possibilities will happen.

Even if the world were not probabilistic at its core—even if the world were completely deterministic—a completed physics would not allow us to predict or even to explain all that much. Throw a rock down a hillside. Where will it go? How chipped will it be when it gets there? To get the answer with absolute precision and absolute certainty, we would have to know everything about every elementary particle on the hillside. Send a thirteen-year-old out to buy milk. When will she get back? What path will she follow? Will she come back with milk? She is a constantly changing physical object, interacting with lots of other living things, all of which are constantly changing. Plotting the interactions of all the particles that make up all those living things, plus the environment in which they interact, is just too hard.

Actually the problem is much harder than tracking a thirteen-year-old. Suppose we want to be as certain as possible of what will happen to a particular stone at a particular time and place. We would have to be able to rule out the following possibility: there are mischievous Martians in a spaceship on the far side of the moon whose idea of fun is to mess up our physical experiments by zapping them with their highly advanced weapons, for instance, adding just a nick here and there to the stone. In other words, to be absolutely certain, we need to be able to rule out all possible influences, and to do that we would need absolute certainty about huge stretches of time and space. That is just way more information than we could ever hope to get.

So even if physics were completed, it couldn't be used to predict what people are going to do. It couldn't be used for mind control, either. In principle it should be possible to make extremely specific changes in what someone thinks by making exactly the right microalterations to her brain. But the practical difficulty is even more enormous than predicting what a thirteen-year-old will do for the next forty-five minutes. It is often said that the brain is the most complex physical object we know about: it contains on the order of one hundred billion neurons, and many of these have tens of thousands of connections with other neurons. We could never know enough about someone's brain actually to use such a technique.

So: What happens in the physical world is completely determined by physical law. We are part of the physical world. Thus what happens to us is completely determined by physical law. What makes things happen in the world is the physical properties of physical matter.

The physical properties. Here is the mental causation problem: mental properties do not (apparently) ever make anything happen. All causation happens because of the physical properties of things; nothing (apparently) ever happens in virtue of things having mental properties.

1.3 Is the Mind Physical?

Shouldn't we, though, deny that we are through-and-through physical? Shouldn't we say that our souls or spirits or minds lie outside the reach of the natural sciences? And if we say this, can we not then say that the soul or spirit or mind is an independent causal principle?

I will return to this question several times in this book, particularly below, in chapter 3. But for the moment, consider the consequence of removing the soul or spirit or mind from the causal order of the physical world. If we aren't physical, we can't make physical things happen. The soul would then be unable to make anything happen in the physical world. So if we deny that we are physical, then the mental causation problem has no solution; our wills are never the cause of our actions. Assuming, that is, that physics is closed, that whatever happens in the physical world has a physical cause. Until fifty years ago it might have seemed reasonable to doubt that physics is closed. But no longer (Papineau 2001). The scientific evidence for the closure of physics is overwhelming.

Suppose I pour a cup of coffee. That is a physical event: something that happens in the physical world. Since physics is closed, that event has physical causes. Since physics is closed, nothing more than those physical causes contributes to making there be coffee in the cup.

If my choice is something nonphysical (because it comes from my mind or my spirit or my soul), then it cannot make coffee be poured. It cannot cause anything physical.

Opting for dualism, the idea that the mind or soul or spirit is nonphysical, just makes the problem impossible to solve. If we make anything happen, the mind is physical.

1.4 Related Problems

This problem derives from tensions in the most basic categories we use to understand ourselves and the world around us: the categories of minds, bodies, the natural world, causation, and laws of nature. It is no surprise, then, that the mental causation problem is at the center of several profoundly puzzling philosophical questions about human agency.

1.4.1 Free Will

If I do something freely, then what I do is up to me. If my action is up to me, then I cause it.

But that isn't enough. If my action is caused by my reasons, and materialism is true, then what makes the action happen is the littlest bits of physical stuff that make up my reasons, the physical particles of which I am composed. I have nothing to do with it. The fact that my reasons are reasons has nothing to do with what they cause. All that matters is the fact that my reasons are physical structures with physical properties that enter into physical laws.

So free action requires not just that reasons cause actions but that reasons cause actions because they are the reasons they are. So if there is any free action at all, then there has to be mental causation. If there is no mental causation, then there cannot be any free action.

1.4.2 The Mind-Body Problem

The mental causation problem is the heart of the traditional mind-body problem: explaining how the mind and the body are related.

By itself the mental causation problem is one of the three great puzzles that make it so hard to explain the mind-body relation. If the mind is something distinct from the body, then it is impossible to explain how you (your decisions) make anything happen. If the mind is the same thing as the body, then it's not you that is making things happen, it's your body.

Consciousness is the second great puzzle about the mind-body relation. Frank Jackson argued that someone could know all the physical facts there are and yet not know what it is like to see something red. Jackson (1982, 1986) concluded that what it is like to see something red is not a physical fact and therefore, again because of the closure of physics (section 1.3 above), that conscious experience never makes anything happen. Jackson's argument makes the connection between the problems of consciousness and mental causation explicit and vivid: if facts about consciousness are not physical facts, then they can't make anything happen, if, as materialism assumes, whatever happens is caused by physical facts.

Intentionality is the third great puzzle. Intentional states are ones that are about or directed at something other than themselves (Searle 1983), such as beliefs, desires, and intentions. Mental causation clearly involves causation by intentional states. But some theories of intentionality make this impossible. For instance, if intentionality relates you to nonactual things (like Santa Claus), but causation always depends on what is actual, then intentionality isn't involved in causation at all ("Appendix: Why There Still Has to Be a Language of Thought," in Fodor 1987). Here's another argument that disconnects intentionality and causation (Horwich 1980; Field 1986). Truth and intentionality are intimately connected, since what an intentional state is about is what it would be true of. But truth—so this argument goes—is not a causal explanatory property. If you say, "what he said is true," you aren't saying that what he said has a distinctive property; really, all you are doing is endorsing what he is saying, without actually saying it. So, the argument concludes, intentional mental properties do no causal work.

1.4.3 Mind, Body, and Health

Most people, perhaps all, have had some experience of their thoughts being out of their control. Sometimes you can't get a song out of your head. Or you can't seem to focus on what you know you need to do.

When things go seriously enough awry, we lose confidence that the causation is mental. We say that some pathological physical state is causing what happens to the person rather than what she thinks being responsible for what's going on.

There is an ever-present temptation here. Suppose psychiatry works out an explanation for, say, schizophrenia, that doesn't depend on mental causation. All the causation is based in physical properties of the brain. If that's the case, then—we might be tempted to conclude—surely all the causation in normal action must be purely physical as well? The temptation is to give in to the mental causation problem. (Psychiatrists, by the way, are not the only scientists prey to this temptation: physicists regularly succumb, and psychologists, whose business it is to uncover the mechanisms of human—and animal—behavior are especially susceptible.) Each discovery of a physical mechanism underlying some aspect of human behavior is taken as another nail in the coffin of the ideas that we are free and that we freely make things happen. One of the goals of this book is to remove that temptation. Just because there's a physical mechanism underlying my making something happen, that doesn't mean that I don't make it happen.

There is a tempting and equally fallacious argument in the reverse direction. What our minds do is often a scientific mystery. People often respond well to treatments that certainly have no effect, like sugar pills: the placebo effect. Somehow, believing that you will get well can make you get well. (Unfortunately, only sometimes.) This is taken as proof of mind over matter and, by extension, evidence that materialism must be incorrect. But it is extremely likely that the placebo effect is ordinary physical causation. The body and brain have resources that we do not understand yet, but they are all physical mechanisms.

1.4.4 Ethics

Harman (1977) argues against the reality of moral properties. For a property to be real, it must enter into physical explanations of phenomena. But surely the laws of physics do not refer to the moral properties of actions? All the causation that is going on in these situations is physical causation. There's no room for moral facts to do any causing. So, conclusion: morality is subjective. The argument is very similar to arguments against mental causation: since the causation is physical, it couldn't possibly involve moral properties.

1.4.5 Color

Democritus held that things do not have colors. "By convention [or custom], sweet; by convention, bitter; by convention, hot; by convention, cold; by convention, color; but in reality, atoms and void" (Sextus Empiricus, *Against the Mathematicians* 7.135, cited in Cohen, Curd, and Reeve 1995:68). Galileo gives essentially the same argument: how the world works depends only on certain physical properties of things and the laws of physics. The rest must (somehow) just be in us.

So what you experience—the rich world of colors—is a product of how things really are in themselves together with a complex neural machine designed by nature to coordinate sensing light with useful behavior. As Locke puts it (1975:2.8.9–10), colors "in truth are nothing in the Objects themselves, but Powers to produce various Sensations in us by their *primary Qualities*." Colors "in truth are nothing": once we see that the underlying causal mechanism is physical, we decide that color isn't real and that it never causes anything.

1.5 Metaphysics

I've just presented repeated instances of the following pattern of reasoning. We become convinced that there is a causal mechanism at work underlying various familiar phenomena. The mechanism then seems to usurp causal responsibility from consciousness, thought, value. Yet our most ordinary, our most intimate, experience convinces us that our consciousness, thought, and evaluative attitudes have causal powers.

So it must be—we feel, very strongly—that the mind has a nature different than the nature of material things.

If the mind has a nature different from the nature of material things, then it may not decay and degenerate as do material things. If the mind has a nature different from the nature of material things, then there is a fundamental metaphysical split. There are two kinds of reality, material and mental. Perhaps mental reality is an ideal reality. Perhaps God is involved in the ideal reality.

This is an appealing course of reasoning. The argument of this book, if it is successful, will undercut this reasoning. Mental causation is special in various ways but not in ways that require us to say that it is radically different from material reality. Spirituality and religion are simply different issues from the mental causation problem.

1.6 Further Reading

For further readings specifically on the mental causation problem, see the end of chapter 9.

Probably no one has been more instrumental in pressing the mental causation problem than Jaegwon Kim, most recently in his *Mind in a Physical World* (1998) and *Physicalism, or Something Near Enough* (2005). Heil and Mele's *Mental Causation* (1993) is an excellent collection of essays on the problem of mental causation. Neil Campbell's *Mental Causation and the Metaphysics of Mind* (2003) is a collection of primary texts (historical and contemporary) on the mental causation problem.

Thomas Kuhn's *The Copernican Revolution* (1957) is an account of how the atomic account of physical matter has become the reigning world picture. A beautiful book on how physicists think of the laws of nature is Feynman's *Character of Physical Law* (1965). The philosophical problem of the laws of nature was first set by David Hume in his *Treatise of Human Nature* (Hume 1978: book 1, sec. 3). David Armstrong's *What Is a Law of Nature?* (1983) challenges Hume's view. Philip Kitcher's *Abusing Science* (1986) is an introduction to scientific method and the question of the credence we should attach to scientific theories.

Ted Honderich's *How Free Are You?* (1993) is a lively introduction to the free-will problem. Gary Watson's anthology *Free Will* (2003) is a clear and accessible collection of essays on free will.

For background on the philosophy of mind and the mind-body problem, see Paul Churchland's *Matter and Consciousness* (1984) and Kim's *Philosophy of Mind* (1996). Three excellent anthologies of contemporary papers on philosophy of mind are volume 1 of Ned Block's *Readings in Philosophy of Psychology* (1980a), David Rosenthal's *Nature of Mind* (1991), and David Chalmers's *Philosophy of Mind: Classical and Contemporary Readings* (2002).

Five good recent books on consciousness are John Searle's *Rediscovery of the Mind* (1992), David Chalmers's *Conscious Mind: In Search of a Fundamental Theory* (1996), Charles Siewart's *Significance of Consciousness* (1998), Joseph Levine's *Purple Haze: The Puzzle of Consciousness* (2001), and David Rosenthal's *Consciousness and Mind* (2006).

A good recent introduction to metaphysics is Michael Jubien's *Metaphysics* (1997). Frank Jackson's *From Metaphysics to Ethics: A Defence of Conceptual Analysis* (1998) begins with a discussion of the core principles of metaphysics centered around the mind-body problem and illustrates the way they work in the cases of ethics and colors. Nicholas Sturgeon's essay "Moral Explanations" (1985) and Gilbert Harman's book *The Nature of Morality* (1977) present two sides of the question whether ethical properties could be real causal properties.

C.L. Hardin's *Color for Philosophers* (1988) argues that colors are not real; David Hilbert's *Color and Color Perception: A Study in Anthropocentric Realism* (1987) argues that they are, as does Michael Watkins's *Rediscovering Colors: A Study in Pollyanna Realism* (2002).

2

Immortality and the Body

> What they say is like saying that carpentry gets inserted into flutes; in fact a craft must use suitable instruments, and equally the soul must use a suitable body.
>
> —ARISTOTLE, *DE ANIMA*, 407B22–26, IN ARISTOTLE 1941

PLATO AND Aristotle were both deeply curious about the mind and its causal relations to the physical world. Neither saw the mental causation problem quite the way we do, since neither conceived of the physical world in quite the way physics does now. But as this chapter will show, their (distinctively different) views lead very naturally to puzzles about how the mind can cause things. Neither view quite makes it past the Scylla of dualism or the Charybdis of monism: dualism takes the soul too far away from physical things to cause them, while monism seems to make all the causation exclusively physical.

2.1 Plato: Immortality

2.1.1 The Causal Theory of Action

Plato and Aristotle both talk confidently about thoughts causing actions. While this idea has been challenged (see below, chapter 4), its roots are deep in our conception of ourselves and how we relate to the world around us.

We are all familiar with battles between reason and desire. Socrates asks whether there are thirsty people who don't wish to drink (*Republic* 438c,

Plato 1992). Indeed there are. (A sign on a faucet that reads "nonpotable water, do not drink" won't take away a person's thirst, but she won't want to drink there.) Yet there is something paradoxical about this: the word "thirsty" means "wishes to drink." So we are imagining people who wish to drink and do not wish to drink. How could that be? "It is obvious that the same thing will not be willing to do or undergo opposites in the same part of itself, in relation to the same thing, at the same time. So, if we ever find this happening in the soul, we'll know that we aren't dealing with one thing but many" (436b). In other words, since no one thing can both wish to drink and not wish to drink (in the same way at the same time), no one thing can have both of those two characteristics; we thus manage this by being more than one: one part of the soul wishes to drink, and another does not wish to drink.

Plato uses the word "*psyche*" for this entity that has more than one part. This word is usually translated as "soul." His word is far more general—covers a far wider range of phenomena—than does our word "soul." *Psyche* is that part of us that takes in perceptions from the world around us, desires things, reasons about things, has battles with itself about things. This is essentially what we now call the mind.

Thus Socrates uses a simple observation to discover something surprising about the soul (the mind), that it has parts: "We'll call the part of the soul with which it calculates the rational part and the part with which it lusts, hungers, thirsts and gets excited by other appetites the irrational appetitive part, companion of certain indulgences and pleasures" (438d). There is one further part of the soul, the "spirited" part. The form of the argument is the same: two people who are exactly similar in both the rational part and the appetitive part may nevertheless do different things. Socrates recalls Leontius, who (a) had an appetite to gaze on corpses but (b) thought that it would be rational not to: "For a time he struggled with himself and covered his face, but, finally, overpowered by the appetite, he pushed his eyes wide open and rushed towards the corpses, saying, 'Look for yourselves, you evil wretches, take your fill of the beautiful sight!'" (439e–440a). Socrates' suggestion is that the appetitive part wins, aided by another part of the soul that stirs it on. This Socrates calls the "spirited" part (*thymos*). Sometimes the spirit acts in defense of reason, sometimes in defense of appetite; hence we should (according to Socrates) infer that it is a part different from either.

The three-part soul enables Plato to explain evil in a flexible and persuasive way. Sometimes people do bad things out of ignorance; but often they know full well what they are doing. This is weakness of will, or *akrasia*: intentionally doing one thing, even though convinced that one would prefer doing something else. Plato's explanation is that one acts akratically when one's action comes from a part of the soul with which one is not fully identified. (I express this in terms somewhat foreign to the way Plato or Aristotle thought about the issue. Aristotle thought that the akratic action must always be the worse action. But if *akrasia* is simply acting against one's own best judgment, it could happen that what one ends up doing is, objectively, the better action [Davidson 1970a].)

The terms Socrates uses to describe Leontius—"struggle," "overpowered," and even "pushed"—are all causal terms. Psychological struggle, then, is what happens when various parts of the soul interact causally. Equally, when one part of the soul wins out, that part, "victorious," causes its favored action. Leontius's spirited part is causally responsible for his eyes widening ("pushed his eyes wide open") and for his rushing headlong toward the corpses.

If that is what happens in conflicted action, it would seem to be what happens in unconflicted action as well. Even if Leontius had remained serene, averted his gaze, and walked away, his reasoning part would have done that causal work, that is, caused his actions. Hence the perfectly familiar experience of doing (or failing to do) as you choose shows that your actions are always caused by your reasons.

2.1.2 The Soul Is Not the Body

If "like causes like" (Makin 1991), then, since reasons cause physical things to happen, reasons must be physical. Perhaps the most natural way to understand how reasons could be physical is to suppose that they are, like other natural things, subject to growth and decay. Plato's *Phaedo* is mainly concerned with the question of the indestructibility of the soul—perhaps a solace for Socrates on the day of his execution—hence with an extended argument that reasons, and the soul, are not like other natural things. The argument is based on considerations about causation, explanation, and the soul.

The conversation begins with the distinction between the mind and the body and the distinction between thinking and sensing. Socrates claims that the soul reasons best when it is free of the senses and the body, and hence the best state for a soul is to be disembodied—in other words, dead. The fundamental distinction between thinking and sensing is invoked to argue that each of our souls must have existed before our bodies came into existence. Consider "sticks or stones or some other things that are equal" (*Phaedo* 74b, Plato 1977). We know they are roughly the same in size or length. But we don't ever sense that they are perfectly equal in length, since our senses are too coarse (and the world is too varied) to detect perfect equality. How, then, do we know equality itself, since nothing in our experience is really and truly equal? Socrates' answer is that the senses are not the only way to know things.

The soul can know the Forms: eternal unchanging universals. Our very first acts of sensing anything presuppose knowledge of equality itself, since we can tell that things are unequal even when we are infants. So we must have had knowledge of the Forms from before birth.

Then, since "like is known by like" (*De Anima* 404b20, Aristotle 1941), the nature of the soul must be more like the nature of the Forms than like things that grow and decay. So, apparently, our souls are eternal and unchanging just like the Forms, and hence there is no reason to fear death.

Socrates' interlocutors are not fully persuaded. What if, Simmias asks (*Phaedo* 85e–86d), the soul is just the body and is "scattered and dissipated by the winds" (84b) with the decomposition of the body? Even if it outlasts the body, Cebes asks (87b–88b), might it only outlast it for a time, and hence we still have reason to fear death?

Simmias points out that the arguments in favor of the separability of the soul—that the soul, unlike the body, is invisible, beautiful, partaking of the divine—should work equally well to show that the harmony of a lyre is separable from it. Harmonies, indeed, are special in the natural world in having distinctive mathematical properties, hence they too are more like the Forms than many other things subject to decay and destruction. Yet we know that the harmony is destroyed when the lyre is destroyed. Whatever its Formlike properties may be, lyres and harmonies are ordinary sensible objects. So maybe the soul is like that. Maybe the soul is just another item like the things we see every day, and maybe the characteristic features of the soul come from special ways that ordinary sensible objects are arranged: "We really do suppose the soul to be something of this kind; as the body is stretched and held together by the hot and the cold, the dry and the moist and other such things, and our soul is a mixture and harmony of those things when they are mixed with each other rightly and in due measure" (86b). Simmias's picture of the relation between the soul and the body is very similar to the way the contemporary materialist sees it, particularly contemporary functionalists (chap. 4, sec. 4.3). The mind or soul is something that has a material nature. And the material nature of a thing—what it is made of and the arrangement or mixture of those elements—determines what it is like and how it behaves.

Socrates' Replies

Socrates responds in three stages. The first stage makes specific objections to the idea that the soul is a harmony. The objections are not very convincing.

Souls themselves can be harmonious or disharmonious. A disharmonious soul would fail to be a harmony and hence would fail to be a soul, if the harmony theory were correct. But this objection overlooks the complexity of harmonies. Play a chord, say a C major chord on a piano or a guitar. Three strings will vibrate harmoniously together. Each string will vibrate at its primary or lowest frequency and also at other frequencies, the overtone series. Depending on what the strings are like, different strings will resonate more strongly at different places in the overtone series. Hence it is possible for three strings to resonate harmoniously together and yet at the same time resonate disharmoniously together.

Socrates, Cebes, and Simmias agree that the soul rules the body and can make it do things that otherwise it would not do. So—Socrates argues—the soul must be something different from the body. Again, this objection overlooks how complex a structured system can be. Steam engines, for instance, have governors: one part of the system controls how other parts are behaving.

Here are two more tempting objections to the harmony theory (not considered by Socrates and his friends, though). Socrates hasn't told us how a harmony amounts to a soul. Since we don't have that structural story, we can't see how a harmony would do it. Sometimes we know enough about some class of things that we are pretty confident we know what kind of explanation would work for it. (If you know roughly how circulation works in humans, you won't find circulation mysterious in, say, aardvarks.) But sometimes we lack even that much insight into how things work: 150 years ago, it was so mysterious how life works that scientists could seriously maintain that it must be a nonphysical phenomenon. So, lacking even the beginnings of a theory of how a harmony could add up to a soul, one might, not unreasonably, think that a harmony couldn't possibly add up to being a soul. (Compare the contemporary debate about consciousness between David Chalmers and the Churchlands; see Chalmers 1996; Churchland 1996.)

But we wouldn't want to rest on this form of argument: just because we don't know how the mind might be a harmony, we can't conclude that the mind can't be a harmony.

Second objection: if human beings were (merely) structured systems of ordinary physical stuff, wouldn't they all act the same? Wouldn't we just be a bunch of physical robots?

The answer is surely no. Our physical natures are vastly complex. There is more than enough complexity, and more than enough difference from one physical body to the next, to account for the differences among us.

Kinds of Cause

The second stage (96a–101e) of Socrates' response is more fundamental, an "investigation into the cause of generation and destruction." Socrates reports, "When I was a young man I was wonderfully keen on that wisdom which they call natural science," which investigates the causes for why things come to be and perish. It became clear to him that the natural science way of investigating things doesn't work for mathematics. We might say that 1 and 1 are somehow parts of 2, but it doesn't make sense to say that 2 is causally generated out of 1 and 1—"made out of 1 and 1"—or that 1 results from the destruction of 2. Socrates learned from Anaxagoras that there is an alternative to causal explanation: "It is Mind that directs and is the cause of everything . . . in the way that was best" (97b–c). This seems to be different from the kind of causation involved in coming-to-be and perishing, since Mind directs action in light of the goodness of the end result: in some peculiar way, what lies in the future is the cause of what Mind does in the present.

Anaxagoras himself, by Socrates' report, didn't develop this insight and continued to seek causes in the constituents of things. Socrates suggests that Anaxagoras might have given the following explanation for why he, Socrates, was now sitting in the jail cell:

> The reason that I am sitting here is because my body consists of bones and sinews, because the bones are hard and are separated by joints, that the sinews are such as to contract and relax, that they surround the bones along with flesh and skin which hold them together, then as the bones are hanging in their sockets, the relaxation and contraction of the sinews enable me to bend my limbs, and that is the cause of my sitting here with my limbs bent.   (98c–d)

Socrates thinks the explanation in terms of Mind would have been much better; in fact, the causal one is patently absurd: "For by the dog, I think these sinews and bones could long ago have been in Megara or among the Boeotians, taken there by my belief as to the best course, if I had not thought it more right and honorable to endure whatever penalty the city ordered rather than escape and run away" (98e–99a). Socrates diagnoses the error as a failure to distinguish "the real cause from that without which the cause would not be able to act as a cause" (99b).

What exactly Socrates means by "the real cause" he does not say. The third stage of the argument of the *Phaedo* develops a very different conception of explanation from what we would call causal explanation, different also from what we might have thought Anaxagoras was suggesting.

Necessary Connections

According to Socrates in this dialogue, the simplest possible answer to the question "why is that?" is the Form of whatever is indicated. I point to my dog and ask, "why is that?" (why is he a dog?), and the answer is, he participates in the Form of Dog. The next, more complex answer to a "why is that?" question supplies necessary connections among things that are guaranteed by the

Forms. Dogs are animals, and animals move; hence he moves. Doing proofs in number theory is learning about the structure of the absolutely necessary connections among numbers. Equally, a proper answer to a "why?" question about, say, dogs should display the absolutely necessary connections between being a dog and the subject of the question. That is what Socrates says he came to think we really mean when we say we want to know the cause of things. We want it to become absolutely intelligible, rationally lucid, why things are the way they are. Knowing that is knowing the Forms of the particular things.

Socrates then uses the necessary connections guaranteed by the Form of Soul to argue that the soul is immortal. Necessarily, the soul brings life to whatever has it (105c–d). And life is the opposite of death. So whatever has a soul necessarily excludes death and is hence deathless. Hence, Socrates concludes, when death approaches, only the body dies; the soul lives on.

This is a dazzling argument. It has the same core as the so-called ontological arguments for God's existence in St. Anselm's *Proslogion* and Descartes's Fifth Meditation, a move from the nature of something to the existence of something. Socrates' argument seems particularly unconvincing. One could in the same way argue for the immortality of anything that could be said to bring life to a thing. For instance, hearts bring life to things—consider the heart transplant—but hearts are not immortal.

The problem stems, I think, from confusing individuals and Forms. Forms are distinct from individuals, and that distinction needs to be rigidly enforced. Forms delimit how individual things may be, if they exist and share in the Form. It is true that anything that shares the Form of soul is alive, and so it is true that, necessarily, any living thing is not dead. So we could put Plato's point this way: whatever has a soul is indestructible *so long as it is alive*. But that is most definitely not the same thing as immortality.

Despite this confusion, Plato is on to an important distinction in kinds of explanation. Take a particular action, such as waving your arm at a particular moment. We can ask, "why is that?" and get an answer in terms of reasons: you saw your friend, and you wish to greet her. We can ask Socrates' "simple" question, "why is that?" and get his simple answer: it is an action of greeting, because it is an instance of the Form of actions of greeting. We may also ask, what makes that movement of your arm into an action of greeting: "why is that an action of greeting?" Here we could be asking why "that" (the arm moving) merits the description "an action of greeting." Plato's "necessary connections" strategy supplies an answer: "it was an action of greeting because it was caused and rationalized by your desire to greet someone." Here we are exploiting the logically necessary structural connection between actions and reasons. As Plato pointed out, this kind of explanation is not the kind of causation involved in coming-to-be and perishing that apparently interested Anaxagoras, since it describes necessary connections among the natures of reasons, causes, and actions. This is true despite the fact that the explanation refers to the fact that the action was caused by your reason. (More on this theme below, in chapter 7.)

Socrates does not, however, put the point in terms of different kinds of explanation. He talks about what the real cause is. When he points out the absurdity of Anaxagoras's bones-and-sinews explanation for why he, Socrates, is in jail, he says Anaxagoras fails to distinguish "the real cause from that without which the cause would not be able to act as a cause." And when Socrates describes his own preferred kind of explanation, the one involving the Forms, once again he seems to think that here he has finally found what we really mean by "cause."

Socrates does not explain why one kind of cause is the true cause while the other is not a cause. He also does not explain why it is not possible for both to be true causes.

But there really are several kinds of explanation. The auto mechanic's cause has to do with masses and materials and forces. The biologist's (functional or teleological) cause has to do with ends and goals and values. And the philosopher's definitional cause has to do with how concepts are hooked together. Not distinguishing kinds of cause can lead to philosophical confusion: perhaps to Plato's idea that the soul is immortal.

2.1.3 Dualism

Whether the arguments succeed or not, Plato is clearly on the side of dualism: the view that the soul/the mind is fundamentally different from the body and indeed fundamentally different from any of the things that come to be and perish. Dualism is the view that the soul, or the mind, is something nonphysical, something crucially not part of the world that we see and touch. Plato's investigation into the Forms provides a model for what the soul might be like (or a "place" for a nonphysical soul): the soul (or the mind) is like the unchanging Forms.

This is a very difficult view to understand. Our minds are not unchanging; on the contrary, they change constantly. I turn my head, and my perception of the things around me changes steadily and completely (even if I fix my gaze on, say, the coffee cup before me, as my head moves, the place it appears in my visual field shifts, however slightly). As I wonder what to do next, memories and feelings and ideas come and go; finally, I form an intention, for instance, to pour a cup of coffee. Hence things in my mind come to be and perish. They do so under the influence of things in the world that come to be and perish. When I make things happen, I bring something to be that did not exist before, something that will itself perish sooner or later, for instance an action of greeting.

Clearly my body is an ordinary thing that is part of the natural world. The natural world, by way of my senses, causally sculpts my conscious experience: I see and hear and smell the things that are actually here before me. My will sculpts the path of my body through the natural world. As I discussed at the beginning of this chapter, Plato thinks of action in causal terms: when someone acts akratically, somehow the wrong part of the soul gains control over the body and makes something happen in the world around us. How could my soul do these things if it is radically different in kind from anything in the natural world?

Socrates holds that the aim of philosophy is the separation of the soul from the distractions of the body. But even when Plato describes what happens to the soul after death (*Phaedo* 110b–115a and *Republic* 614b–621d) the description is of a physical world. He remarks (*Phaedo* 114c): "Those who have purified themselves sufficiently by philosophy live in the future altogether without a body; they make their way to even more beautiful dwelling places which it is hard to describe clearly, nor do we now have the time to do so." But Socrates needs more than time to "describe clearly" this beautiful place. What would it mean to "dwell" in such a place if one didn't have a body? How could one open or close the door or sit by the fire? Assuming that the most beautiful places have dogs, how could one scratch one's dog?

If dualism were true, if the soul/the mind were a different kind of thing from the body, then it may survive the death of the body. It is exceedingly painful, both intellectually and emotionally, to think how the person is no longer here when the body is evidently dead. Yet intellectually it is far more difficult to see how the person could ever do anything—make anything happen—if she isn't physical at all, if she doesn't have a body. Physical things have physical causes; how can something that isn't part of the physical world at all make any difference to it? This problem becomes acute with the rise of modern materialism, as I'll explore further in chapter 3, below.

2.2 Aristotle: The Form of the Body

In two famously obscure passages (*De Anima* III.5, 430a10–26, and *Metaphysics* XII), Aristotle argues that souls (or a certain kind of soul) must be able to exist without matter and must be immortal. But in most of the rest of his writings he argues that the soul is not something distinct from the natural world. The soul is the form of a living body. Hence Aristotle's view does not have dualism's difficulty explaining mental causation. But his view does lead quite directly to several distinctive problems about mental causation, problems also experienced by contemporary accounts of the mind-body relation.

2.2.1 Hylomorphism and the Four Causes

Aristotle develops his view of the soul against a metaphysical framework that is much more suitable for giving explanations of natural phenomena than is Plato's. The two most important elements of the framework are his hylomorphism and his doctrine of the four causes. (Unless otherwise noted, I quote the texts of Aristotle in Aristotle 1996.)

Hylomorphism: Form and Matter

Every man-made thing—every artifact—has three basic features: (a) what it is made of, its material; (b) its form (this might simply be a matter of shape, or it might be a dynamic disposition to do various things in various circumstances); and (c) its function, what it is for. The form and the matter together explain the characteristic behavior of an artifact and hence explain how the artifact performs its function (*Physics* II.1, 192b8–193b21).

Everything else in the world, according to Aristotle, is also a hylomorphic entity—some *hylê*, matter, in a certain form, *morphê*. Cats, for an example of a living thing, (a) have flesh of various kinds (fur, bones, sinews, and so forth), (b) arranged in a shape that is disposed to do various things, which (c) contribute to the function of the cat (primarily, to make more cats and, secondarily, to do the various things—hunting, eating—that enable it to perform that primary function). Nonliving things also have matter and a form. A stone, say, a piece of limestone, has a certain kind of matter arranged in a certain form and (according to Aristotle) has a function.

The form/matter distinction has levels. The parts of an animal are organs. Each organ has a form and a matter. The matter (tissues, cells) in turn has its own form and a matter. And so on all the way down. Aristotle did not endorse the atomic conception of matter (although he knew of the basic idea, from Democritus) but rather thought of all things as composed of the four elements earth, air, fire, and water.

The Four Causes

Aristotle and Plato share the idea that a cause is an explanation: something you could give in answer to the question "why is that?" Thinking of objects as hylomorphic entities generates different kinds of answers to "why" questions. Ask "why is that?" pointing to my cat Grushenka, and you get different answers as you focus on different aspects of that one cat: (a) she's made of cat

flesh of various kinds, (b) she has the typical form of a cat, (c) she is for making more cats, and (d) this cat got set into motion by her cat parents.

Thus Aristotle's four causes (*Physics* II.3, 194b17–195a27): the *material*
cause is the matter of which a hylomorphic entity is composed, the *formal*
cause is the form, the *final* cause is the end or goal of the thing, and the *efficient* cause is what sets a thing in motion.

Aristotle is very clear that all four answers are perfectly legitimate (*Physics*
II.3, 195a5–27). There is no reason to think that one is more nearly the right
answer than any of the others. They are different causes, but they are not in
competition.

Aristotle does see a kind of competition elsewhere. We can specify a particular kind of cause (one from the four) in more or less detail or precision.
"A man, for example, is building because he is a builder, and he is a builder
insofar as he has the building craft; his building craft, then, is the prior cause,
and the same is true in all cases" (*Physics* II.3, 195b23). Aristotle says we must
always seek the "most precise" cause, the explanation that picks out the cause
in the most complete detail. That cause is prior. But he does not say that the
prior cause is the only cause, even within a category of causes. That leaves
open the possibility that Aristotle could permit more than one cause within
a category of causes. He could say that the causes of the man's building are
(a) that he is a builder and (b) that he has the building craft: the first is a less
prior, the latter a more prior efficient cause.

2.2.2 Soul as Form

Aristotle's theory of the soul is expressed in the following formula: "the
soul is the first actuality of a natural body that is potentially alive" (*De Anima*
412a27). Consider a ten-day-old fetus. It has the potential to grow eyes. It
does not have eyes now, but if it develops normally, it will have eyes. Once it
has eyes, much of the time the child will not see (when it closes its eyes or
sleeps). When the child actually sees things, the potential to see is fully actu-
alized: that is the second actuality of vision. When our eyes are closed or
we are asleep, our eyes only have the first actuality of vision. The fetus has
what we might call the "zero-th" actuality of vision, the mere potential to develop eyes.

So the first actuality of a thing is the state in which it has the ability to perform a characteristic activity but isn't now performing it. The second actuality is the thing actually doing what it is able to do. The second actuality of a
living body is the body actually doing the things characteristic of living. The
first actuality of a living body is its power to do those things: what it is about
the body that permits it to act in the manner characteristic of living things.

The soul, according to Aristotle's account of the tradition (*De Anima* book I), is what explains the characteristic activities of living things (notably, motion and knowledge). Hence the soul is the first actuality of a living body. Finally, the form (the arrangement of the parts) of the living body is what explains how the body is able to do these things: hence the soul is the form of a living body.

Since the form is simply the arrangement of the parts and the fact that they interact in a certain way, the soul is not a thing in addition to the body. As Aristotle puts it: "Hence we need not ask whether the soul and the body are one, any more than we need to ask this about the wax and the seal or, in general, about the matter and the thing of which it is the matter. For while one and being are spoken of in several ways, the actuality <and what it actualizes> are fully one" (412b6–9). Since the soul is what explains the characteristic activities of any living thing, Aristotle is perfectly comfortable with the idea that dogs and goldfish and geranium plants all have souls. His use of the concept of soul is thus even broader than Plato's. Since all the activities of what we would call the mind are also characteristic activities of the living human being, Aristotle's conception of the soul is broad enough to encompass our conception of the mind. Consequently, he needs to explain the mind in hylomorphic terms. I will look at his explanation of sensation and his explanation of belief, desire, intention, and similar states.

Sensation: Form Without Matter

When we sense things (when we see, hear, smell, etc.), we get information about those things, information about properties or characteristics of those things. Aristotle understands the properties of things to be the forms of those things.

Aristotle proposes (*De Anima* II.5, 416b33–418a7) that sensation is the sense organ coming to have the very same form as the perceived object (but of course with its own matter). A "pin art" impression toy similarly takes on the form of an object but in a different matter.

To illustrate: Your eye is able to see white. When you aren't seeing white—when your eyes are closed or you are looking at something nonwhite—the form of your eye is the first actuality of a body able to see white. The same goes for the white thing: unless it is being seen, it isn't producing any visual perceptions, so its form is the first actuality of a body able to be seen as white. When your eye turns to the white thing in good light, and you are attending to what it looks at, both first actualities go to their second actuality states: the white thing is being seen, and the eye is seeing. (In fact, Aristotle held [425b26] that the second actuality of the object of perception and the second actuality of the sense are the very same thing.) That is: you see white.

Thought: Form Without Matter

It is not so clear how to extend this idea to belief and desire. Take the belief that the New York Yankees won the World Series in 1999. For someone to have this belief is for the cognizing part of the soul to take on the form of the fact that the Yankees won the World Series in 1999. The matter of the cognition and the matter of the actual fact are different, but they share a form. But what is the form of the fact? and what would it be for a soul to take on that form?

The form of something can be dynamic—that is, involve characteristic activities (in addition to static shape). We can in parallel think of believing—thought taking on the form of a state of affairs without the matter of that state of affairs—in terms of characteristic activities. Having the form of something in one's soul might be having the ability or disposition to engage in various activities that are related in special ways to that thing. If a person has a belief that somehow involves the number 1999, then that person should be able to count. If a person believes things about the Yankees then she should be able to engage in baseball-related activities: she should be caused to form baseball-related beliefs by baseball-involving events, and her beliefs should be able to motivate baseball-related actions. (For example, if she sees the words "Go Mets!" she forms the belief that a Mets baseball fan wrote those words, and if she's offered a ticket to a Yankees game, she is grateful.) My suggestion, then, is that taking on the form of a fact, without the matter, is taking on a disposition to behave in a certain way, in particular, to behave in various ways in relation to that fact. (I intend for this suggestion to echo recent work on psychosemantics, or causal accounts of the content of mental representations, as, for instance, in Dretske 1988 or Fodor 1987. These theories begin with causally maintained isomorphisms between the way something in the world behaves and the way something in the organism behaves.)

2.2.3 Aristotle and Mental Causation

Aristotle thus believes that the soul, and perceptions, and thoughts are all completely physical. Hence he does not have Plato's problem of explaining how a nonphysical soul can cause things. Yet Aristotle's materialism has its own difficulties explaining mental causation. In this section, I will look at three ways Aristotle might respond to Socrates' puzzle, in the *Phaedo*, of whether our thoughts or our bones and sinews are the cause of our motions through the world. The first of the three is the core of the solution I will develop in chapter 9 to the contemporary mental causation problem. The second and third are tempting but ultimately unworkable.

"That Without Which the Cause Would Not . . ."

Socrates thinks the real cause of his sitting in the cell is his conviction that it is best to remain. The bones and sinews are "that without which the cause would not be able to act as a cause" (*Phaedo* 99b). Socrates appears to be invoking mind/body dualism at this point. The mind, and the conviction, are things that are distinct from the bones and sinews and could exist without them, but without them would not be able to act as causes.

Aristotle lampoons the idea that the soul is something distinct from the body: "They speak as though it were possible, as in the Pythagorean stories, for just any old soul to be inserted into any old body, whereas in fact each body seems to have its own distinctive form and shape. What they say is like saying that carpentry gets inserted into flutes; in fact a craft must use suitable instruments, and equally the soul must use a suitable body" (*De Anima* 407b22–26, Aristotle 1941). The precise character of your soul and the precise character of your body are two sides of the same coin.

But the question remains, what causes the body—a moving arrangement of parts—to sit in the cell? One explanation is an efficient-cause explanation: the way the body was moving earlier is what causes the body to move now. According to the hylomorphic account of particular states of mind offered above, Socrates' conviction that it is best to remain in the cell is part of the structure (the form) of his body, since it is a part of his soul, and his soul is the form of his living body. So we can think of his conviction as some part of his body (nowadays we think it is part of his brain) that has the right kind of form to cause the behaviors characteristic of having such a conviction. Hence when he acts on this conviction, this part of his body—a certain portion of matter, with a certain structure—is the efficient cause of what the body now does.

Suppose Aristotle had argued that the matter of the conviction—its parts—is the efficient cause of the present motion of the body, rather than the conviction itself. Then there is a short argument that the only efficient causes are the four elements. The matter of large things like people is typically more hylomorphic things. Bones are a certain structure of the matter of bones. So the argument that undercuts the claim that the conviction has to be the cause of the action would also undercut the bones as a cause and in fact any hylomorphic entity. So the only causes are the things that are not further hylomorphic entities: the four elements.

But he need not get on to this slippery slope. He can instead simply say that both the conviction and the parts of which it is made (in their structured arrangement) are efficient causes of the body sitting in the cell. In chapter 9, I will show how to flesh out this idea.

Category Confusion?

Aristotle pays careful attention to the differences among the fundamental categories of things and, in this case, the differences among the four kinds of causes. Since they are so different, and so fundamental, it's clear that getting the category of a thing wrong leads to real philosophical confusion. Teleological explanation only looks problematic, for instance, if one thinks that the final cause is an efficient cause (since, typically, efficient causes occur before and final causes occur after things done for an end).

So Aristotle could, apparently, say that there is a category confusion (Ryle 1949) involved in asking whether both the bones and sinews *and* Socrates' conviction cause him to remain in the cell. He could say: The bones and sinews are efficient causes of the movement of the body. The fact that Socrates has this conviction is the fact that these elements (this matter) are arranged in a certain way. But—he can say—it is not true that the conviction is another efficient cause of motion. Rather, the conviction is a form, not matter. Just as the soul is not another thing of the same kind as the matter that is arranged in the form of the soul, the conviction is not another thing of the same kind as the matter that composes it.

The problem with this line of thinking about the causes of action is that Aristotle does think that Socrates' conviction is an efficient cause of action. He has to, since (as Plato showed) our everyday experience of making things happen is experience of our reasons as efficient causes of action. The bones and sinews are material causes of the conviction as well as efficient causes of his action. And the conviction too is an efficient cause of the action. Hence the category confusion move won't help Aristotle stay off the slippery slope of the last section: the temptation to say that the bones and sinews are the real efficient causes or, rather, that only the four elements are the ultimate real causes.

Second-Order Properties and Mental Causation

Aristotle points out that there are different "sciences" of aspects of the soul: "The student of nature and the dialectician would give different definitions of each of these affections—of anger, for instance. The dialectician would define it as a desire to inflict pain in return for pain, or something of that sort, whereas the student of nature would define it as a boiling of the blood and of the hot <element> around the heart. The student of nature describes the matter, whereas the dialectician describes the form and the account: for desire, for instance, is the form of the thing, but its existence requires this sort of matter" (403a29–403b5). The student of nature studies things like the boiling of blood and the hot regardless of their connection with psychology. The psychologist is the scientist who studies the "account," or definition, of psychological things.

The Aristotelian psychologist's account of reasons might look like this: A particular person's belief that the Yankees won the World Series in 1999 is the matter of that person taking on a certain dynamic form, namely, the disposition to behave in the familiar ways that people do when they have that belief. This behavior involves a causal pattern: the belief has certain typical causes (perception, testimony) and certain typical effects (speech behavior, action). This account of belief defines belief in terms of its causal connections to other things (just as the dialectician defines anger as a desire to inflict pain in return for pain). Hence to have a belief one must have a state that stands in the causal relations called for by the definition. In other words, beliefs are second-order states: the state of being in some (first-order) state or other that is capable of standing in certain causal relations.

Now, if being a belief is by definition being a state that is caused in a certain way and typically causes certain things, then, it would seem, Aristotle has a straightforward solution to the problem. The conviction, just like the belief, must by definition be a cause of actions based on that conviction. So it has to be that the conviction causes Socrates to remain seated in the cell. (And, presumably, so do the bones and sinews.)

The trouble is that when we define belief (or conviction) in this way, belief turns out to be something that has certain causes and effects. But it's the "something" here that is doing the causing, not the thing that (by definition) is the pattern of causing and being caused. In other words, all the causing is done by the first-order states (in this case, the bones and sinews, that is, the body), not by the second-order states. The second-order states constitute a sort of office, a job description; the first-order states are the holders of the office, the things that actually do the job.

This problem for Aristotle—below, in chapter 7, I will call it "the new logical connections argument"—is serious, and it infects contemporary philosophy of mind, particularly the behaviorism of Ryle and contemporary functionalist accounts of the mind. The problem is bad enough to justify rejecting certain versions of functionalism altogether (chapter 7, sec. 7.6).

2.3 Conclusion

Plato and Aristotle are interested in questions about the causing and the explanation of action but not in the contemporary mental causation problem.

Plato thinks of the kind of causation involved in coming-to-be and perishing as a species of the kind of explanation we seek in mathematics and in the analysis of meanings and concepts. He uses that model of explanation to argue that the soul is indestructible. This account of the soul has two serious difficulties from the perspective of mental causation. First, souls (minds) change constantly as they perceive and think different things, but if they are more like Forms than like vegetables (changeable natural things), they cannot change. Second, perception and action demand ordinary causation between things in the natural world and thoughts. But if souls are fundamentally different in kind from natural things, then they can't have causal relations with natural things—hence no mental causation.

Aristotle keeps as much as he can in the natural world. The soul is the form of a living body, hence it is an aspect of a thoroughly natural object. There are various kinds of causal relations that natural objects enter into, but they are all relations in the natural world. Aristotle thus appears better situated to explain how mental causation is possible than is Plato. Still, there are difficulties. The parts of a structured object, working together, cause the same things as the whole structured object, hence there is a reason to think that only the unstructured parts of hylomorphic entities ever cause anything. And there is a danger in defining the soul, and defining particular mental states, as a dynamic form, that is, as standing in causal relationships with other things. The danger is that the dynamic form picks out a pattern of things interacting causally. Then the causing is done by the elements of the pattern rather than the whole pattern.

Neither Plato nor Aristotle considered the precise version of the mental causation problem I described in chapter 1, section 1.2: that for anything you or I do (anything we make happen), there is an explanation in terms of the physical properties of our bodies and the physical laws. Neither Aristotle nor Plato (especially Plato) thought that physical matter explains very much. Both knew of the atomist theories of the world of Democritus and Leucippus. Both thought that the order and purposefulness of the world could not possibly arise out of the unguided interactions of unthinking matter (see particularly Aristotle, *Physics* 2.8).

Since the seventeenth century and the rise of modern physics beginning with Galileo and Newton, it has become ever more plausible that the order and purposefulness of the world could be produced simply by the interactions of blind physical matter (blind to the order and purposefulness that emerges). It wasn't unreasonable for Plato and Aristotle to doubt this, given that the atomism of their contemporaries had very little systematic empirical support. (Equally, it wasn't unreasonable to think that matter-in-motion could produce all the phenomena there are: Lucretius, three hundred years later, a Democritean materialist who had no more empirical support than did Democritus, proposed exactly that; see Lucretius 1969.) Only with the depth and power of contemporary physical theory are we compelled into the mental causation problem in its present form: since physics, in principle at least, explains everything, there is no room for the mind to make anything happen.

2.4 Further Reading

Christopher Bobonich's "Akrasia and Agency in Plato's *Laws* and *Republic*" (1994) describes Plato's evolving account of weakness of will. Some useful articles on the *Phaedo* and causes and the soul include Gregory Vlastos's "Reasons and Causes in the *Phaedo*" (1969), Christopher Byrne's "Forms and Causes in Plato's *Phaedo*" (1989), Gareth B. Matthews and Thomas A. Blackson's "Causes in the *Phaedo*" (1989), and Sean Kelsey's "Causation in the *Phaedo*" (2004).

A good source of articles on Aristotle's *De Anima* is *Essays on Aristotle's De Anima* (Nussbaum and Rorty 1992). In that collection, Burnyeat's "Is an Aristotelian Philosophy of Mind Still Credible?" and the article by Martha Nussbaum and Hilary Putnam, "Changing Aristotle's Mind," deal with the question of how close Aristotle's view is to contemporary functionalism.

3

Dualism and Automatism

> The consciousness of brutes would appear to be related to the mechanism of their body simply as a collateral product of its working, and to be as completely without any power of modifying that working as the steam-whistle which accompanies the work of a locomotive engine is without influence upon its machinery.
>
> —THOMAS H. HUXLEY, "ON THE HYPOTHESIS THAT ANIMALS ARE AUTOMATA, AND ITS HISTORY" (1874:240)

THE MENTAL causation problem became acute in the seventeenth century. Galileo had seen the moons of Jupiter revolving around something other than the center of the universe. Clearly their Aristotelian natures were not drawing them to the center of the stationary earth. Things out there work according to principles that are not sensitive to our sense of the order and moral value of the world. Descartes and other natural philosophers of the seventeenth century argue that all natural phenomena are to be explained on the basis of a very small number principles governing the motions of tiny indivisible bodies (corpuscles). But how, then, can our choices make any difference to what happens?

This chapter recounts some of the responses that philosophers made to this conundrum from Descartes's time up to the beginning of the twentieth century. Descartes famously argued for mind/body dualism and equally famously could not explain mind-body causal interaction. D'Holbach argued that since materialism is true, freedom is an illusion. Kant argued that freedom is possible only if the self is different in kind from the things of the natural world. Thomas Huxley argued (on essentially Cartesian grounds) that both animals and people are machines, or automata: the working of the machine causes conscious experience, but conscious experience never causes anything in return.

3.1 Descartes: Dualism and Causal Interaction

3.1.1 The Real Distinction

Descartes argues in several places for "the real distinction" between the mind (a *res cogitans*, a thinking thing) and the body. He claims that this shows that the human soul does not die with the body (at the beginning of his prefatory letter to the deans and doctors of the Faculty of Theology at the Sorbonne [1964:7:1–2; 1984:2, 3]). Two of his arguments for the real distinction are particularly important for my purposes.

The Limits of Mechanical Explanation

Descartes is one of the first philosophers able to exploit the corpuscular conception of matter at many levels to get powerful explanations for natural phenomena. In part 5 of the *Discourse on Method*, he writes of Harvey's explanation for blood flow and concludes that the bodies of animals and men are mechanical in nature. His reason for describing Harvey's explanation in such detail is interesting. Contemporary Aristotelians had grown up on Aristotle's arguments (*Physics*, book 2) that blind causes cannot produce regular, orderly, goal-directed patterns of events. But forcing his contemporaries through the details of how it all actually works should, Descartes thinks, make them recognize that Aristotle was simply wrong about this.

He also argues (1964:6:56–57; 1984:1:139–140) that despite the power of mechanical explanation, it nevertheless gives out. There is something about man that transcends mechanical nature, namely, speech and reason. The difficulty isn't simply that a future Harvey of the mind hasn't yet arrived to figure out the mechanism. Rather, there are principled reasons why thought and consciousness cannot be understood in mechanical terms.

An Argument from the Concepts of Mind and Body

Descartes's most subtle and complex argument for the real distinction occurs in the Sixth Meditation (1964:7:78; 1984:2:54). The concept of mind and the concept of body pick out distinct "principal attributes" (*Principles of Philosophy*, part 1, sec. 53, Descartes 1964:8a:25; 1984:1:210–211) of things: the principal attribute of a mind is thinking, and the principal attribute of a body is "extension," that is, taking up space. The principal attribute of a thing is what enables it to be a "substance," a thing capable of independent existence. Descartes argues that no one thing can have more than one principal attribute. It seems to follow, then, that the mind is a substance that is distinct from any body whatsoever. Hence the mind must be something that does not share any characteristics with bodies: it has no place in space, and it has no physical properties at all. Consequently, a puzzle: how can I make things happen, if I am nowhere?

3.1.2 Mind-Body Union

In the Sixth Meditation, Descartes presents a straightforward mechanical model for how mind and body interact. There are fine fibers (your nerves) running throughout your body. When someone steps on your foot, the pressure tugs these fibers. This motion is transmitted along the length of the fiber and is eventually communicated to the brain. The paths of the fine fibers end at the pineal gland in the center of the brain. A signal reaching that termination causes something to happen in the (nonphysical) soul. Your soul is like a carillon: a bell in your soul—the sensation—is rung by the pull of the rope in your body. When we act, the causal path goes in the opposite direction. Choice causes a change in the pineal gland, which causes a signal to propagate along the nerves, and that signal then causes the relevant part of the body to move.

Clearly, that is not the way it feels to suffer pain and to act: as Descartes writes, "Nature teaches me by these sensations of pain, hunger, thirst and so on, that I am not merely present in my body as a sailor is present in a ship" (1964:7:81; 1984:2:56; unless otherwise noted, I quote the translation in Descartes 1984). I do not note information that comes from my fingertips. I touch things and feel them. Thus two core philosophical difficulties: (a) the carillon model doesn't cohere well with our actual experience of mind-body interaction, and (b) it doesn't explain how causal interaction between a physical body and a nonphysical soul is possible.

In his letter to Princess Elisabeth of May 21, 1643 (1964:3:663–668; 1984:3:217–220), Descartes says that there are "very few" primitive notions on the basis of which all others are formed. There are exactly three primitive notions "as regards body in particular" (1964:3:665; 1984:3:219): the notion of mind, the notion of body, and the notion of the union of the mind and body together. The last is not simply a composite of the first two (see Radner 1971 and Broughton and Mattern 1978 for discussion). We are not just a composite entity, a soul glued to a body. We are a substantial union of a mind and a body. Corresponding to the special metaphysical connection between the mind and body, there is a special kind of experiential relation we have of substantial union (1964:3:691–692; 1984:3:227): "What belongs to the union of the soul and the body is known only obscurely by the intellect alone or even by the intellect aided by the imagination, but it is known very clearly by the senses." Substantial union thus explains how it feels to be a soul joined to a body in this special way. The union of soul and body is not a causal union: it is not a matter, as it were, of two distinct entities or items being wired up together in a particular way (as the processor of a computer is wired up to the rest of the computer in a peculiarly intimate way). It is, rather, a basic metaphysical connection, not to be explained in terms of other metaphysical categories. Descartes can then say that the union has as one of its special features that sensation causes changes in the mind and that decision causes action. Since the causation would not be a matter of two things interacting mechanically, there is no need to explain how such mechanical interaction could take place.

3.1.3 Mind-Body Causal Interaction

This much, unfortunately, looks flatly question-begging, and Elisabeth didn't buy it.

The Problems
On May 6, 1643, she had written,

> So I ask you please to tell me how the soul of a human being (it being only a thinking substance) can determine the bodily spirits, in order to bring about voluntary actions. For it seems that all determination of movement happens through the impulsion of the thing moved, by the manner in which it is pushed by that which moves it, or else by the particular qualities and shape of the surface of the latter. Physical contact is required for the first two conditions, extension for the third. You entirely exclude the one [extension] from the notion you have of the soul, and the other [physical contact] appears to me incompatible with an immaterial thing.
>
> (SHAPIRO 2007:62; DESCARTES 1964:3:661)

Unsatisfied with his response (the letter of May 21, 1643), she wrote back on June 10 that she is unable to understand how the soul is unable to move the body and says, "I admit that it would be easier for me to concede matter and extension to the soul than to concede the capacity to move a body and to be moved by it to an immaterial thing" (68; 3:685). She is particularly concerned with the question of how a soul that was able to reason well "can lose all of this by some vapors" (68; 3:685). Two years later (August 16, 1645) she is still concerned that "there are diseases that altogether destroy the power of reasoning . . . others that diminish the force of reason" (100; 4:269).

There are perhaps four distinct problems that we might list for Descartes.

Causation Only Between Substances of the Same Kind
The principal attribute of the mind is thinking; the principal attribute of the body is extension. If *a* causes *b*, then the principal attributes of *a* and *b*

must be the same. Therefore no soul can determine the motion of any material thing.

Contact

Elisabeth notes that for one thing to determine the motion of another thing, the first thing must be in contact with the second thing. Yet souls, if they are immaterial, are never in contact with any material thing. Hence no soul can determine the motion of any material thing.

How Does It Work

Elisabeth was unimpressed by Descartes's claim that the substantial union of mind and body is best conceived by the senses. She writes (July 1, 1643): "I also find that the senses show me that the soul moves the body, but they teach me nothing (no more than do the understanding and the imagination) of the way in which it does so" (72; 4:2) There are two complaints here. First, if we lack even the barest outline of a reasonable story about how, for instance, bodily vapors can suppress reason, then we cannot say that substantial union explains how the body moves the mind or that the soul can determine the motion of any material thing. Second, experience shows us that our mental state depends in complex and detailed ways on our physical state, and that our physical state depends in complex and detailed ways on our mental state. If Descartes's account of mind-body interaction cannot make sense of this datum from experience, then that datum counts as a serious objection to the account.

Conservation

Leibniz wrote: "Descartes recognized that souls cannot impart a force to bodies because there is always the same quantity of force in matter. However, he thought that the soul could change the direction of bodies. But that is because the law of nature, which also affirms the conservation of the same total direction in matter, was not known at that time. If he had known it, he would have hit upon my system of pre-established harmony" (*Monadology*, 80, in Leibniz 1989:223). Souls cannot cause changes in the direction of the movement of bodies (for instance, the pineal gland, where Descartes supposed that mind-body interaction takes place) since that would violate the law of conservation of momentum.

Descartes's Responses

None of these arguments is knock-down. There are things Descartes did say in response, and things he could have said. But in the end it comes down to a judgment about whether physics has to treat minds as separate kinds of things from bodies. And the answer seems to be, no, it does not.

Causation Only Between Substances of the Same Kind

Any claim that the world divides into fundamentally different realms (for instance, the physical and the mental) has to depend on a clear principle stating the basis for dividing the world. One such principle is causal. We might say that what makes a substance part of one realm rather than another is that it is possible for the substance to interact causally with items in its own realm, but it is not possible for the substance to interact causally with items in any other realm. If Descartes had subscribed to this principle and assigned mental things to one causally isolated realm and physical things to another, then his view would entail that mental things and physical things could not possibly interact causally.

A different principle of realm division might begin with Descartes's "principal attributes" (those attributes that enable something to be a complete self-standing thing, a substance [*Principles of Philosophy*, part 1, sec. 53]). Two things belong in different realms if they have different principal attributes. One could go on to argue for a causal principle about principal attributes, leading back to the causal division among realms. Again, causal interaction between mental things and physical things would be impossible.

But Descartes does not endorse either of these principles governing realms and causation. Since he clearly believes in causal interaction between mental things and physical things, the best course for him is to divide realms by principal attributes but to deny the additional causal principle barring causation between things that have different principal attributes.

Contact, and How It Works

In his first response to Elisabeth's questions, his letter of May 21, 1643 (1964:3:663–668; 1984:3:217–220), Descartes invokes the three "primitive notions," patterns on the basis of which we form other conceptions of body in particular (see sec. 3.1.2, above) and writes, "So I think that we have hitherto confused the notion of the soul's power to act on the body with the power one body has to act on another" (3:667; 3:219). Trying to conceive of how one kind of thing has the power to act, in terms suited for another kind of thing, can only lead to confusion (an echo of Plato's criticism of Anaxagoras). He offers an independent example of this sort of confusion. Gravity appears to work without any contact between the heavy thing and the earth. Scholastic physics explained gravity as a matter of the heavy object possessing a "real quality" (3:667; 3:219) of heaviness. This real quality "carried bodies towards the centre of the earth as if it had some knowledge [*cognitio*] of the center within itself" (1964:7:442; 1984:2:298). The real quality makes the heavy body strive to reach the earth, even though no contact is moving it. Descartes in effect says to Elisabeth that the Scholastics were wrong to apply this primitive notion to the case of gravity, but they were right that there is such a primitive notion and that it does permit action without contact.

Again Elisabeth might well have objected that Descartes is begging the question. The difficulty is how causation can work without contact. This response consists in asserting that it does.

Gravity is, however, a particularly well-chosen example. (The following argument is based on Garber 1982 and Bedau 1986.) Obviously there is no question that gravity operates on things. To this day, though, gravity continues to be a mystery, and we still don't know whether it operates by contact. So the facts that mind-body causation apparently doesn't involve contact and that we don't understand how it works cannot constitute an objection to mind-body causation.

It is easy, in a sense, to explain the workings of things that have a complex and easily accessible structure. You just have to know the detailed structure of the things involved and their particular causal contributions. How does sunlight cause plants to flourish? Electromagnetic radiation of a certain wavelength causes changes in chlorophyll molecules. How does that causation work? Photons of a certain energy interact with certain portions of the molecules. How does that causation work? Well, that depends on whether those interactions still have structure. If they do, then we continue explaining in terms of the ever-finer structure. But there comes a point at which structure is exhausted. The things that interact have no more structure. The causation is brute. There is nothing more to say than "this is what happens."

Brute facts are the facts in terms of which other facts are explained (Fahrbach 2005). They themselves cannot be explained. Explanation must stop somewhere, and hence some facts must remain brute.

So Descartes can answer Elisabeth's question in the following way: there is mind-body causation. There is no explanation for it. But that is not a difficulty for Cartesian interaction. Every account of the world must have a place for kinds of causation for which there is no explanation. Roderick Chisholm (1964) made the same response to the question, how does "agent causation" work? We have no idea how causation of any kind works, so it cannot be an objection that we have no idea how agent causation (or mental causation) works.

So there is, I think, no a priori objection to Descartes saying, in effect, "this is how it works—there is no further explanation to be had." But there remain two very high level empirical objections to saying this, one Leibniz's, the other Elisabeth's.

Conservation

Since Descartes already argues for a law of conservation of motion, there isn't any principled reason why he should resist introducing a law of conservation of momentum. The difficulty is that momentum is defined in terms of properties of extended bodies (it is the product of mass times velocity, and velocity is defined as distance—through space—divided by time). Hence minds can't have momentum.

However, in principle, anyway, Descartes could have insisted that the whole story about the movement of bodies requires the concept of "momentum+," not just momentum. This would be a quantity that has two components, one the momentum we are familiar with and the other related to minds. When ordinary physical objects interact, the mental component of their momentum+ is zero, and hence the conservation law looks just like the actual conservation of momentum law. But when minds interact with bodies, the mental component of the momentum+ is not zero. And the conservation law for momentum+ differs in some appropriate way from the conservation law for momentum. This new conservation law would be part of a more comprehensive physics that would include mental events as well as what physicists call physical events. If there could be such a physics, then mental events would turn out to be perfectly physical—just not in space.

In principle this could be done. But neither Descartes nor anyone since has shown that physics needs such a quantity. Worse, there is a good general reason to resist the idea of such a quantity.

The Vapors Again

Elisabeth asks how vapors in the brain could lead to loss of rationality: how diseases can reduce or destroy the force of rationality. She asks how our rationality can be sidetracked or degraded by passion. If the soul were a self-contained distinct substance from the body, with only a single channel of communication with the body, it is mysterious how passions, and diseases of the body, could alter the operations of the soul in such complex and graduated ways.

There would appear to be two possible explanations for this systematicity. One is that the nature of the mind-body connection is so constituted that this just is how it works: God arranged it that way for the well-being of the whole person (Sixth Meditation). The other explanation is that thought, rationality, and consciousness have a systematic, complex, graduated, and consistent dependence on the operations of the body.

This second explanation appears to be much more in keeping with the program of the *Discourse on Method*. The details there were wrong: the heart does not distribute fire throughout the body. But the program of explanation was right: decompose the mechanisms of the body into simpler mechanisms until we can understand how the whole works on the basis of knowledge of how the parts work. How, for instance, does alcohol work on the mind? Presumably, by altering the chemistry and operation of the nervous system. Why does alcohol have the effects on the mind that it does? Presumably, because the mind just is the nervous system.

So the objection is a very high level empirical objection. We see various systematic and complex patterns of correlations between changes in the body and changes in the mind. We know that if we saw patterns of correlations like this between two kinds of changes elsewhere, the best explanation for the patterns would be a systematic and complex physical linkage. This is a fundamental methodological principle that is supported by its history of successes. Why, then, should we not use the same principle in understanding mind-body interaction?

3.2 Freedom and Kant's Transcendentalism

The answer to this question was obvious to eighteenth-century philosophers: because if the world were purely physical then we could never make anything happen. And we could never act freely. Philosopher and pre-Revolutionary French intellectual Paul-Henry Thiry, Baron d'Holbach wrote, "Thus man is a being purely physical; in whatever manner he is considered, he is connected to universal nature, and submitted to the necessary and immutable laws that she imposes on all the beings she contains, according to their peculiar essences or to the respective properties with which, without consulting them, she endows each particular species. Man's life is a line that nature commands him to describe upon the surface of the earth, without his ever being able to swerve from it, even for an instant" (2001:1.11.97–98). D'Holbach accepts that we are not free; other responses to the apparent incompatibility of freedom and natural causation were even more radical.

Immanuel Kant argued that the self is not involved in causation at all. Kant's Copernican revolution was to relocate metaphysical categories, like space and time and causation, from the world to the mind. For example, Kant held that it is necessary that events have causes. But he agreed with David Hume that we couldn't know this on the basis of experience, and he further agreed with Hume that the necessity does not derive from the concepts of event and cause; as Hume put it (1978: sec. 1.3.3), it is not "demonstrable" that every event has a cause. Kant's way out of this puzzle is to say that the principle that every event has a cause is part of the structure of the mind. It is a part of reason that makes coherent experience possible.

If causation is in the mind, then the mind isn't in the causal nexus. Kant's idea is not simply a new sort of Cartesian dualism, where the mind inhabits a realm that is different from the realm of the physical but still causally interacts with it. Kant has causation only in the world of experience, the "phenomenal" world. The world as it is in itself, the "noumenal" world, is not causal. So if the mind is an inhabitant of the noumenal world, it is not a causal inhabitant, since nothing in the noumenal world is causal at all. (This is one solution that can be found in Kant's texts. Meerbote 1984 urges that Kant argues for something quite different: that descriptions that involve reference to mental states are "anomalous" even though they describe things that are subject to laws. Meerbote proposes that Davidson's anomalous monism [see chap. 4, sec. 4.4, below] is the best model for understanding Kant's thinking on this issue, or at least a plausible part of it.)

This is an attractive solution to worries about freedom and mental causation. If the mind isn't in the business of causing at all, then there's no problem about causation. In the mid-twentieth century Wittgenstein and Ryle exploited this Kantian suggestion and argued that it is a fundamental confusion to say that minds are causes (Wittgenstein 1953; Ryle 1949; see also chap. 4, sec. 4.1, below). In a recent work on freedom and responsibility, Bok (1998) follows Kant in arguing that there is a fundamental difference between reasoning about matters of fact and reasoning about what to do. One upshot is that reasons aren't causes in the same way that rocks are causes of window breakings. So we solve the mental causation problem by denying that reasons are causes.

But it can't work. The reason is simple. Scratch your nose. Now ask: why did those fingers do that? The answer is, because your thinking made it so. Suppose a wicked neuroscientist had managed to slice just the right spinal nerve just when you chose to move your arm. Your arm wouldn't have moved. Why not? Because the causation between your thinking and your arm would have been interrupted.

3.3 Huxley's Automatism

The science of the nineteenth century only made the difficulty worse. The more we learn about the causal mechanisms underlying human behavior, the more we are inclined to downgrade the causal efficacy of thought.

Thomas Henry Huxley was a Victorian biologist and essayist. He is best known for his defense of Darwin (he was called "Darwin's bulldog") and Darwinian evolutionary theory (and for being the grandfather of Aldous Huxley).

Descartes, following William Harvey, had argued that animals are machines. When animal bodies are opened up and explored, you can see that they are intricately constructed devices. So human behavior can be explained just as the operation of a machine can be explained—but, according to Descartes, only up to a point (*Discourse on Method*, part 5). He thought that no machine could speak or reason. So he concluded that some part of us, namely, the mind or the soul, must be something other than a natural machine.

Huxley took the same argument and turned it on its head. He begins by fully endorsing Descartes's conception of the methods and aims of physiology. He shows that Descartes had already stated and argued for five methodological principles accepted by physiologists of the later nineteenth century. We've got a better grip on the factual details than did Descartes, but that is surely nothing to fault him for.

Descartes had criticized his contemporaries for drawing the wrong conclusion from the science of physiology. Animals and humans are alike, they had reasoned, in being mechanical beings. We have consciousness. Therefore consciousness and mind must be present in animals as well. Descartes thought the argument should go the other way around. The behavior of animals is completely explicable in mechanistic terms. But we can speak and reason, and no machine can do that; hence we are conscious, and animals are not.

Huxley defends Descartes's contemporaries. He reasons that animal bodies and human bodies are extremely similar. He agrees with Descartes that the motions of animal bodies are produced mechanically by their organic machinery. So, Huxley concludes, the motions of human bodies are precisely as mechanically produced. Human beings and other animals are natural automata. We are conscious; each of us knows that from our own experience. Hence consciousness has nothing to do with the causal engine of motion. Instead, consciousness is a by-product of certain kinds of mechanical biological processes. It is caused by those processes, but it has no causal role beyond that. In particular, it cannot cause anything.

Huxley describes a wide variety of experimental evidence that animals can engage in complex behaviors even when they are not conscious. Perhaps the most striking is a sergeant of the French Army, F—. During his service, a bullet fractured the parietal bone of his skull, leaving a lasting syndrome of effects. Periodically he underwent peculiar episodes that lasted some fifteen to thirty hours. He seemed not to be conscious and for the most part unable to smell or see things. Nevertheless he behaved in approximately normal ways.

> Sitting at a table, in one of his abnormal states, he took up a pen, felt for paper and ink, and began to write a letter to his general, in which he recommended himself for a medal, on account of his good conduct and courage. It occurred to Dr. Mesnet to ascertain experimentally how far vision was concerned in this act of writing. He therefore interposed a screen between the man's eyes and

his hands; under these circumstances he went on writing for a short time, but the words became illegible, and he finally stopped, without manifesting any discontent. On the withdrawal of the screen he began to write again where he had left off. The substitution of water for ink in the inkstand had a similar result. He stopped, looked at his pen, wiped it on his coat, dipped it in the water, and began again with the same effect.

On one occasion, he began to write upon the topmost of ten superimposed sheets of paper. After he had written a line or two, this sheet was suddenly drawn away. There was a slight expression of surprise, but he continued his letter on the second sheet exactly as if it had been the first. This operation was repeated five times, so that the fifth sheet contained nothing but the writer's signature at the bottom of the page. Nevertheless, when the signature was finished, his eyes turned to the top of the blank sheet, and he went through the form of reading over what he had written, a movement of the lips accompanying each word; moreover, with his pen, he put in such corrections as were needed, in that part of the blank page which corresponded with the position of the words which required correction, in the sheets which had been taken away. If the five sheets had been transparent, therefore, they would, when superposed, have formed a properly written and corrected letter.

(HUXLEY 1874:232–233)

3.3.1 Huxley's Argument

On the face of it, the case of Sergeant F— does not show that consciousness plays no causal role in explaining behavior. When undergoing one of his episodes, Sergeant F— does not speak, his reasoning is impaired, and his behavior is decidedly odd. Why isn't his lack of consciousness the cause (assuming, with Huxley, that he is not in fact conscious)?

Huxley has an answer to this worry. Descartes says there is a radical discontinuity between human beings and other animals: we can speak and reason; they cannot. Huxley gives the following very general empirical argument against this radical discontinuity.

The doctrine of continuity is too well established for it to be permissible to me to suppose that any complex natural phenomenon comes into existence suddenly, and without being preceded by simpler modifications; and very strong arguments would be needed to prove that such complex phenomena as those of consciousness, first make their appearance in man. We know, that, in the individual man, consciousness grows from a dim glimmer to its full light, whether we consider the infant advancing in years, or the adult emerging from slumber and swoon. We know, further, that the lower animals possess, though less developed, that part of the brain which we have every reason to believe to be the organ of consciousness in man; and as, in other cases, function and organ are proportional, so we have a right to conclude it is with the brain; and that the brutes, though they may not possess our intensity of consciousness, and though, from the absence of language, they can have no trains of thoughts, but only trains of feelings, yet have a consciousness which, more or less distinctly, foreshadows our own.   (1874:237)

As he states it, the "doctrine of continuity" only supports the idea that animals as well as humans are conscious, not the further idea that consciousness plays no causal role in explaining their behavior. But Huxley can use the doctrine of continuity in a different way, this time up from nonconscious processes rather than down from our consciousness to that of animals.

Clearly, some biological processes are purely mechanical, unaccompanied by consciousness. There isn't any consciousness involved in digestion or in my heart's beating. There isn't any consciousness involved in the operations of the immune system. Each of these processes is very complex (particularly the last). So processes of very widely varying levels of complexity are possible without consciousness. But—the argument continues—animal and human behavior is just the movement of biological bodies through space and time. Movement has mechanical causes. So—we conclude—it is possible that any animal or human behavior has a fully sufficient mechanical cause. The biological machinery is enough to account for anything that could possibly happen in the natural world.

So Huxley concludes that consciousness is an epiphenomenon: caused by the normal mechanical workings of animal brains but itself not causing anything. Consciousness, according to Huxley, is like the sound of a steam whistle on a locomotive: just as the whistle does not affect the machinery of the locomotive, consciousness is completely unable to influence the operations of the body. William James writes (in response to Huxley):

The theory maintains that in everything outward we are pure material machines. Feeling is a mere collateral product of our nervous processes, unable to react upon them any more than a shadow reacts on the steps of the traveler whom it accompanies. Inert, uninfluential, a simple passenger in the voyage of life, it is allowed to remain on board, but not to touch the helm or handle the rigging.

The theory also maintains that we are in error to suppose that our thoughts awaken each other by inward congruity or rational necessity, that disappointed hopes *cause* sadness, premises conclusions, etc.; The feelings are merely juxtaposed in that order without mutual cohesion, because the nerve processes to which they severally correspond awaken each other in that order.   (1879:1)

3.3.2 Automatism Makes Freedom Impossible

As outrageous as this is, there is worse to come. Huxley recognizes that his theory poses a threat to human freedom. His response is to give a definition of that elusive word "freedom" that permits pure material machines to act freely: "an agent is free when there is nothing to prevent him from doing that which he desires to do" (1874:240).

Suppose I want an ice cream and the desire is conscious. So it is an epiphenomenon. It is caused by the workings of my body. But it doesn't cause anything. Now suppose my body reaches for an ice cream. Nothing prevents me from getting it, and I do. So I have done exactly what I want. So, according to Huxley, I am free.

But in truth I am not. My action doesn't happen because I desire it. The action happens because it is produced by mechanical causes, namely, the mechanical operations of my biochemical parts. My conscious experience is no better than a self-deceived onlooker, generated by the machine but itself doing nothing. That is flatly inconsistent with freedom: if I am a free agent, then I cause my actions. If not a single one of my mental states causes any of my actions, then neither do I. So Huxley's automatism (epiphenomenalism) entails that we are never free.

3.4 Conclusion

Descartes is right that there is something special about human thought and consciousness. But we don't know exactly what it is that makes it special. Even though we have not succeeded in producing a machine capable of reason and speech, we have made progress. There are theories of consciousness that make it a perfectly respectable physical phenomenon. So perhaps the difference is not one of fundamental ontological category but merely a difference in how physical matter is arranged.

Dualism really won't help us here. If the mind or soul is part of a nonphysical realm, then mental causation would require a special sort of transrealm causation, and we have really no good empirical reason to believe in any such thing. Huxley's automatism is a particularly vivid and explicit admission of this fact. He thinks that everything we do has a perfectly physical explanation. Consciousness is special, though. So it turns out to have no effects—no "efficacy," as William James called it—in the world. Despite Huxley's efforts at defining the word "freedom," such a view entails that human freedom is an illusion, since the mind isn't making anything happen.

So the only hope for freedom and mental causation is some kind of materialist account of the mind. Let us now turn to the materialism of the twentieth century. Just as Aristotle's materialism didn't quite escape the problem of mental causation, neither does twentieth-century materialist philosophy of mind. Indeed, the problems are virtually identical.

3.5 Further Reading

Three good books that treat Descartes's overall thought and his philosophy of mind are Margaret Wilson's *Descartes* (1978), Janet Broughton's *Descartes's Method of Doubt* (2002), and Marlene Rozemond's *Descartes's Dualism* (1998). Lisa Shapiro (1999) discusses the interaction between Descartes and Elisabeth on mind-body union. Shapiro's *The Correspondence Between Princess Elisabeth of Bohemia and Rene Descartes* (2007) contains the complete correspondence.

Hilary Bok's *Freedom and Responsibility* (1998) argues that freedom and determinism are compatible, along Kantian lines. Dana Nelkin's "Two Standpoints and the Belief in Freedom" (2000) criticizes the Kantian strategy that says there is no conflict between claims made from the standpoint of theoretical reason and claims made from the standpoint of practical reason.

Charles Blinderman and David Joyce of Clark University maintain a Website of materials on Thomas Henry Huxley, including the full text of "On the Hypothesis That Animals Are Automata and Its History" (1874): alepho.clarku.edu/huxley/.

4

Ghosts and Machines

That everything should be explicable in terms of physics (together of course with descriptions of the ways in which the parts are put together—roughly, biology is to physics as radio-engineering is to electro-magnetism) except the occurrence of sensations seems to me to be frankly unbelievable.

—J. J. C. SMART, "SENSATIONS AND BRAIN PROCESSES" (1959:142)

TWENTIETH-CENTURY PHILOSOPHY of mind is dominated by this question: assuming that everything is physical, where—how—does the mind fit in?

This chapter briefly surveys the main materialist models of the relation between thought and the physical world: behaviorism, identity, functionalism, anomalous monism, and externalism. I'll focus on how well the models handle mental causation. The identity theory has the most straightforward response to the problem: if mental properties are identical to causally relevant physical properties, then they are causally relevant. The problem with the identity theory is that mental properties are not identical to physical properties. So we are still faced with the question of how mental properties as well as physical properties could be causally relevant.

In addition, behaviorism and functionalism face the problem we saw for Aristotle (chap. 2, sec. 2.2.3): if mental properties are "second order," then they are causally irrelevant. As chapter 7 will describe in more detail, this means that any acceptable materialist philosophy of mind has to allow that mental properties are independent of (not defined in terms of) the things they causally explain.

Let's begin with behaviorism.

4.1 Ryle's Behaviorism

I know what I am thinking and feeling from moment to moment, and I don't have to do any special investigations to learn these things. But my knowledge of other people's minds isn't like that: I know my own mind because it's me, but I can't be you in that way. Instead, I have to use evidence and inference: you say something, in a particular context, looking a certain way, doing various things, and from this evidence I infer that you think we should get together next week.

If Cartesian dualism were true, and our minds were altogether distinct from our bodies, this inference would be extremely shaky. The mind's interactions with the body happen in some way that is hidden from plain view. So how can I be at all sure whether my surmise about Suzy's state of mind is correct? Indeed, how can I be certain that Suzy has any conscious experience like mine at all? How do I know she isn't (as the philosophers would say) a zombie?

Gilbert Ryle (1949) thought it was perfectly obvious that we know a great deal about what other people think. (Consider: would it be rational to drive on a highway if you didn't know a lot about what other drivers were thinking? How could you buy anything if you didn't know, at least approximately, what the seller is thinking?) If mental states were inner, Cartesian states, he thought, we could never know what another person is thinking or even whether the person is thinking at all: "One person could in principle never recognize the difference between the rational and the irrational utterances issuing from other human bodies, since he could never get access to the postulated immaterial causes of some of their utterances. Save for the doubtful exception of himself, he could never tell the difference between a man and a Robot" (22). If mental states are not inner, Cartesian states, what are they? Well, I know things about your behavior, and I know things about your mental states. So (here's the theory) mental states are dispositions to behave in certain ways. Your intention to get together with me next week is your disposition: to tell me what you intend; to arrive on time; to not schedule other things at that time; and so forth. (Notice how similar this view is to Aristotle's hylomorphic account of thought: for the soul/the mind to take on the "form of a fact" is for it to become disposed to behave in suitable ways related to that fact [see chap. 2, sec. 2.2.2, above].)

Ryle's behaviorism may be termed "categorical behaviorism" because it focuses so sharply on the proper fundamental category for mental states. So-called logical behaviorism (Carnap 1959; Hempel 1935) holds that every sentence about mental states can be translated into a sentence about behavior. So-called methodological behaviorism (J. Watson 1924; Skinner 1953) holds that the only proper subject matter for the science of psychology is behavior. While logical and methodological behaviorism have their own problems, and their own problems with mental causation, the arguments below apply mainly to categorical behaviorism.

Dispositions seem like the right kinds of things to be beliefs and desires and intentions. You don't have to manifest a disposition, and you don't have to act on a desire in any way—it can remain entirely inert. But it's there. It's a kind of readiness to do something given other contributing factors. That readiness is part of you even when you are asleep, even when this desire is the farthest thing from your mind.

And dispositions are not, according to Ryle, any kind of hidden inner cause, some nonmaterial, ghostly entity waiting for the right triggers to leap out and produce behaviors. "Dispositional statements are neither reports of observed or unobservable states of affairs, nor yet reports of unobserved or unobservable states of affairs. They narrate no incidents . . . [rather,] they are satisfied by narrated incidents" (120). Ryle thought of statements of dispositions as connected with hypothetical statements, statements of the form, "if such-and-such were true, then thus-and-such would be true." If I say something is fragile, then in some (loose) sense I am saying that if it is struck, then it will shatter. (Loose, since some things that shatter when struck aren't fragile, and some things that are fragile don't shatter when struck.) Ryle didn't even think that hypothetical statements are true or false. Instead, he thought of them as "inference tickets," providing a rule for how we should reason, based on the pattern of things that we experience.

Consequently, according to Ryle, disposition explanations are not causal explanations. The structure of the explanations and the kinds of facts on which they are based are quite different, despite the fact that we use the words "explain" and "because" for both kinds of explanation.

> There are at least two quite different senses in which an occurrence is said to be "explained." . . . The first sense is the causal sense. . . . The "because" clause in the explanation reports an event, namely the event which stood to the fracture of the glass as cause to effect. . . . [There is] another sense of "explanation." We ask why the glass shivered when struck by the stone and we get the answer that it was because the glass was brittle. Now "brittle" is a dispositional adjective; that is to say, to describe the glass as brittle is to assert a general hypothetical proposition about the glass. So when we say that the glass broke when struck because it was brittle, the "because" clause does not report a happening or a cause; it states a law-like proposition [a hypothetical "inference ticket"].   (86)

In other words: suppose you want to know why the glass broke, and I tell you that it was unusually brittle. According to Ryle, this means (roughly) that it's the sort of thing that, if you strike it, it will shatter ("shiver"). The disposition isn't a cause or even part of a cause; it is simply the fact that this glass will break if struck. So the only cause on the scene is the stone.

4.1.1 Are Reasons Causes?

Ryle falls in with a group of philosophers who were highly influential in the 1940s and 1950s who argued that reasons are not causes. This group includes Wittgenstein (1953, 1958), Anscombe (1957), Winch (1958), and Melden (1961). They gave several sorts of arguments to explain why reasons cannot be causes. Two of them in particular are important for my purposes.

The Category Argument

Ryle writes, "When we describe people as exercising qualities of mind, we are not referring to occult episodes of which their overt acts and utterances are effects; we are referring to those overt acts and utterances themselves" (26). In the *Phaedo* Socrates stays in place because of his regard for the state. Ryle says his regard for the state just is the fact that he stays put (under circumstances such as those he is actually in). The category into which mental states fit is the category of patterns of behavior. Those patterns might themselves be composed of causes and effects. (His bones and sinews do cause Socrates to stay in his cell.) But a pattern that is built up out of cause and effect pairs is not itself a cause or an effect.

Here is a parallel example. Suppose a baseball player hits a grand slam. The grand slam doesn't cause the player on second to run for home. The grand slam consists of the man on second (along with the other men on base) being caused to run home by the batter's hit.

I want to emphasize that this really is a knock-down argument. If Rylean behaviorism were true, then reasons couldn't be causes, any more than grand slams cause the players on base to run for home.

The Logical Connections Argument

Back to Socrates: if what it is to have a high regard for the state is to stay put, then there is a logical connection between that regard and the behavior. But Hume argued that causes and effects are logically independent of one another (1978:1.3.3). So this reason cannot be a cause of this action.

4.1.2 Yes, Reasons Are Causes

Davidson (1963) and Fodor (1968) argued that reasons are causes. Davidson observed that someone could have two different full reasons for an action. Suppose Suzy wants some ice cream. She walks along the boardwalk until she reaches an ice-cream stand. She stops, waits in line, asks for a vanilla cone, receives it, pays for it. At the same time, however, she is also thinking about her little brother, who is walking with her, and she knows he really wants some ice cream, and she promised him some earlier. Which reason explains the action? "A person can have a reason for an action, and perform the action, and yet this reason not be the reason why he did it. Central to the relation between a reason and an action it explains is the idea that the agent performed the action *because* he had the reason" (Davidson 1963:9). Explanation requires a certain kind of uniqueness: one thing that happened; one thing that explains it. If there are several things available, all of which could explain what happened, then we need something additional, something to select the one that does explain it. Davidson's suggestion is that the cause is what explains the action. When we say that the agent performed the action because he had the reason, that means that the cause of the action was that reason.

Davidson's answers to the two anticausalist arguments run as follows.

The Category Argument

Ryle gets a lot right about the mind: mental states always occur in extremely rich patterns of behavior and other mental states, and we often know quite a bit about others' mental states. But these facts don't add up to a reason for thinking that mental states aren't in the category of causes. In fact, we know they have to be in the category of causes, as Plato showed us (chap. 2, sec. 2.1): whenever we explain behavior, akratic or unconflicted, we are talking about what made the behavior happen, what caused it. So it must be that we use this rich pattern of behavioral evidence in some other way than Ryle thought. We don't say another person's thinking is the very same thing as her behavior. Rather, we use the behavior as evidence for the mental states that cause the behavior.

The Logical Connections Argument

It's true that there is some sort of logical link between language for reasons and language for actions. But this is no obstacle to reasons being causes. Suppose a rock hits a window and breaks it. We can describe the rock's hitting the window this way: "the cause of the window's breaking." Then the following is true: the cause of the window's breaking caused the window to break. Uninformative, tautological, but nevertheless true.

There's more to be said. Davidson was right that the logical connections argument doesn't work to show that reasons can't be causes. But there's a similar argument—the new logical connections argument—that does show that reason properties cannot be causally relevant to action properties. I will return to this issue in chapter 7, below.

4.2 Identity

In 1956 U. T. Place wrote, "In the case of cognitive concepts like 'knowing,' 'believing,' 'understanding,' 'remembering,' and volitional conceptions like 'wanting,' 'intending,' there can be little doubt, I think, that an analysis in terms of dispositions to behave is fundamentally sound. On the other hand, there would seem to be an intractable residue of concepts clustering around the notions of consciousness, experience, sensation and mental imagery, where some sort of inner process story is unavoidable" (1956:55).

Smart (1959) echoed the same basic idea: behaviorism is a bad theory of conscious mental states like pains. Being in pain isn't merely a disposition to do various things. Smart rejects any theory that pains or other mental states are "irreducibly psychical" (1959:142) things. The reason is mental causation: such psychical things would be "nomological danglers" (ibid.), produced by the physical causes of things but themselves never causing anything, much as Huxley had thought of them (chap. 3, sec. 3.3).

The only remaining position, according to Place and Smart, is that reports of sensations are reports of brain processes. Their theory was really not that different from Ryle's behaviorism. Perhaps one way to characterize the difference is that Place and Smart wouldn't have been reluctant to say that where there is a disposition there is an internal mechanism responsible for the manifestations of the disposition.

What is later termed "identity theory" emerged as theories designed to supplant it, mainly functionalism, were articulated. Smart himself doesn't distinguish between these later theories and his original theory, calling all of them "identity theories" (2004). This suggests that to some extent these later theories criticize a straw theory. The straw theory, however, endorses one particular claim that has important consequences for the mental causation problem. So let me articulate the straw theory.

The claim concerns properties. Properties (as I'll show below, in chapter 5) are ways things are, and they are ways that several distinct particular things— "particulars" for short—may be. At the coffee shop, you can get a cup of coffee; that is a particular. The coffee shop sells many, many particular cups of coffee. They all have something in common, namely, that they are cups of coffee. That is to say: they all share the property of being a cup of coffee.

Each particular cup of coffee is the same as every other, as far as being a cup of coffee is concerned. But each particular cup of coffee also differs from every other. Some are hot, some are cold, some come in paper cups, others in porcelain, some taste good, others do not.

We can say the same about mental states. Each particular desire for a cup of coffee is the same as every other particular desire for a cup of coffee, as far as being a desire for a cup of coffee goes. Each of those particular desires shares the property of being a desire for a cup of coffee. But each particular desire differs from every other, in innumerable ways. You want a hot coffee, I want an iced coffee; you want a cup of coffee in fine china, I want a cup of coffee in a paper cup with a picture of the Parthenon on it.

So we may view mental states as particular things and a person's mind as (in some way) including a very large number of these particular things. The collection changes from moment to moment, as perception alters the particular thoughts you have about where you are, what there is around you, and your relations to those things. It changes as you think about what you know and change your mind about things; it changes as your body changes, so that your desire for coffee disappears, or becomes much weaker, after your first cup.

It's worth noting that we can also think of mental states as states of a whole person. This is a natural way to understand statements such as "she wants a cup of coffee" or "he thinks the coffee here is good." For my purposes, it is simpler to treat these statements as talking about mental particulars—a desire, in the first case, a belief in the second—and their properties, rather than as talking about whole persons. We can say that the whole person has the property of believing that the coffee here is good, when that person has a belief (a mental particular) that the coffee here is good.

According to the identity theory, each particular pain, twinge, sensation, after image, and so on, is identical to—is the very same thing as—some particular brain process. We can call each particular mental occurrence a token of a certain type. The distinction is modeled on the distinction between particular linguistic entities and the types they belong to. In the last sentence, there are three tokens of the word "the"; all three of them are tokens of one type, namely, the type "the." The distinction between tokens and types is exactly the same distinction as that between particulars and properties.

Mental tokens, then, will be particular beliefs, desires, feelings, and so forth. The mental types under which they fall will be things such as being a belief that kiwis are green, being a desire for a kiwi, being a feeling that kiwis are tart, and so on. These types are their mental properties.

A token-token theory says that each mental token is identical to a physical token. A type-type theory goes on to identify the properties as well: there is a single physical property that is shared by every instance of a given mental property; that is to say, mental types are identical to physical types. The token-token theory, by contrast, says that mental types are not identical to physical types: different individual tokens that have the same mental property could have different physical properties.

Officially, then, identity theory is a type-type theory. (Or, anyway, the straw theory is a type-type theory.) Mental properties are identical to physical properties.

Mental Causation

Identity theory seems uniquely well placed to settle any doubt about mental causation. If mental individuals and mental properties just are physical individuals, and these physical individuals cause things (and their physical properties matter to what they cause), then the mental things are just as much causes as the physical things.

What Could Have a Mind?

It would be very surprising if mental properties turned out to be identical with physical properties. It would be surprising if the property of being a cup of coffee were identical with some physical property (for instance, the physical property of involving a cup made of paper with an image of the Parthenon on it).

The identity theory holds that each and every mental property is identical to some physical property. So each and every mental property that my mental states have is identical to some physical property of my body. Now, I'm a human being, and hence I have a certain sort of body, with a certain sort of biochemical profile. The identity theory (or, at least, the straw version I am considering) must therefore hold that any creature who has any of the same mental properties as I have must also have a body that has the corresponding physical properties that my body has. A particular toothache of mine, for instance, is a brain process, a special kind of activation of systems of neurons. The identity theory is committed to saying that anything that has a toothache must have systems of neurons just like mine.

But this (as Block 1980b puts it so nicely) is a "chauvinist" view. We have no trouble conceiving of creatures that have bodies physically quite different from ours yet have minds: dolphins, science fiction Martians, angels, robots. Equally, it seems perfectly conceivable that there are small physical differences between the various tokens of a single belief type, across humans; in fact, it would not be entirely surprising if there turned out to be physical differences between my believing now that this coffee is cold and believing the same thing fifteen years ago. In other words, any given mental property can be realized in physically different ways, just as being a cup of coffee can be realized, for instance, by a paper cup, or a porcelain cup, or a steel cup . . .

This multiple realizability argument was the main argument offered by Hilary Putnam (1960, 1967) for rejecting identity theory. (See below, chap. 5, sec. 5.5, for more arguments that mental properties are not identical to physical properties.) Putnam, David Armstrong (1968), David Lewis (1966), and others went on to suggest a positive account of why and how mental properties can be realized by different physical properties. This theory—functionalism—opened up a way for mental properties to be realized by physical properties yet not be identical with physical properties, that is, for all mental particulars to be through-and-through physical things yet have properties that are not identical with physical properties.

4.3 Functionalism

Functionalism in the philosophy of mind argues that mental states should best be characterized by describing how they causally mediate between sensation and action. Each kind of mental state has a distinctive job to do (it is caused, that is, brought into existence, in a certain way, and it makes certain specific things happen). The job of a belief, for example, is to provide information about the world in order to guide successful action. The only way to get information about the world is to interact with it causally. The job of desire is (roughly) to steer action toward the satisfaction of a creature's needs. Even more roughly, the job of pain is to be caused by damage to the body and to cause us to avoid the source of the damage.

None of these mental states operates on its own. A desire for water will not cause an action, say, of reaching for water, unless the creature experiencing the desire also believes that what it is reaching for is water (and even this may not be enough for the action, for instance, if the creature thinks for some reason that drinking would be harmful to it). Often our memories and expectations affect what beliefs we form about what is going on around us. So the job descriptions for various kinds of mental states will include cooperative action with other mental states.

Functionalism need not be materialist: if there were nonmaterial angels with beliefs, then something nonmaterial would mediate between their sensations and actions. So to make a materialist view that is also functionalist, we have to add something to the bare job descriptions of the mental types: the things that actually perform these jobs of mediating between sensation and action must be physical things.

Different functionalists do two quite different things with these causal sensation/thought/action mediation job descriptions. (1) So-called functional state identity theory uses the descriptions to denote mental properties. According to this sort of theory, then, mental properties are causal pattern properties. The property of being a certain kind of pain is the property of having certain distinctive kinds of causes and effects. (2) So-called functional specification theory, by contrast, uses the descriptions to identify which physical items actually do the job of mediating between inputs and outputs.

Many artifact kinds are functional kinds. A mousetrap is something that takes bait and a mouse as inputs and outputs a trapped mouse. Functional state identity theory says there is a property some things have, the property of causing mice to be trapped under certain circumstances. Different kinds of mousetraps all equally have this single property. Functional specification theory takes the causal characterization and uses it to identify which things in the world fit it: here's a mouse trap that happens to be made of wood and wire, here's another that is made of plastic and a mouse poison, and so forth. Functional specification theory does not say that they all have a single property (being a mouse trap) in common. Instead, different mousetraps have different physical properties, and what they have in common is that they have the same causes and effects (mouse in, trapped mouse out).

The two kinds of theories are often called "role" and "realizer" functionalism, respectively. Role functionalism says that mental properties are the properties of having a certain role or job description. Realizer functionalism picks out what properties fill the role—satisfy the job description—using the input-output mediation characterization of the job.

Both role and realizer functionalism characterize the causal pattern abstractly. Here, for example, is an abstract causal pattern specification: mousetraps trap mice. A concrete specification of a causal pattern would state the exact physical properties of the things in the pattern, for instance, that the mousetrap is made of a particular kind of wood. The abstract characterization embraces more different kinds of mousetraps, while the concrete characterization tells you more about one particular way to catch mice. Just as with artifacts, what's important about mental states is what they do. What they are made of—their detailed physical characterization—mainly matters only to ensure that they can actually perform their function. There are lots of ways to pull corks out of bottles, hence lots of physically very different things that are corkscrews. A bejeweled titanium corkscrew might be significant in other ways, but it counts as a corkscrew because it can pull corks. Similarly, according to functionalism, what's important about pain is that it mediates between tissue damage and avoidance behavior. Each particular pain may perform that mediation in a different way and so have very different physical properties. Human pains are processes of neural activation of human neurons. Dog, and dolphin, and octopus pains are processes of neural activation of dog, and dolphin, and octopus neurons. Perhaps there are extraterrestrial creatures who have a biochemical nature quite unlike our own but who nevertheless have pains. Perhaps there could be sentient robots who have pains that are processes in silicon chips.

Functionalism thus appears to preserve the best of behaviorism and identity theory, while fixing the glaring difficulties of both theories. According to functionalism, mental states are inner causes (usually, although there is no reason why a functionalist theory cannot characterize a causal pattern that involves things that exist outside the body). Their types are causal pattern types, rather than specific brain-state types, hence it is possible for creatures physically very different from us to have mental lives. The causal pattern types include the rich patterns of behavior that base our knowledge of other people's thoughts. Rather than defining mental types one by one in terms of specific behaviors, functionalism defines the entire psychology in terms of the relations of all the psychological states to one another, to sensation, and to action.

Mental Causation

Mental particulars, according to all versions of functionalism, are causes. The mental causation problem concerns the causal relevance of mental properties. Role functionalism has two serious problems with causal relevance. One is a problem for any theory that distinguishes mental properties and physical properties (and hence a problem that will continue to occupy me for the rest of this book). The other is a problem distinctive to role functionalism. Realizer functionalism has neither of these problems but only because it, like identity theory, makes no distinction between mental and physical properties.

Role functionalism is the theory that identifies mental properties with causal pattern properties. Any mental event then has (among others) both its mental (causal pattern) property and some specific physical properties that enable it to stand in just that causal pattern. Mental causation becomes a problem for role functionalism for two reasons.

First, when a mental event causes something, which property explains the causation? There is apparently a choice between the causal pattern property and the property that realizes it, and the realizer property is the better candidate to be the cause. Role functionalism says that functional properties are causal pattern properties. They specify a role, a job for something to do: it has to be caused by certain things, and it has to cause certain other things. But it is the something that has the role, that does the job, that makes things happen, not the functional property. Suppose that in people what does the pain job is the firing of C-fibers. (C-fibers are involved in pain, but pain is vastly more complex than simply C-fiber firing [Melzack and Wall 1988].) So what explains avoidance behavior is the fact that the pains are C-fiber firings, not the fact that they have causal pattern properties, that is, not the fact that they are pains.

Second, it's not just that the role filler is a better candidate: worse, the causal pattern property can't explain the causation at all. The problem is that instances of causal pattern properties stand in certain causal relations by definition. But if one event causes another in virtue of having a certain property, it can't do that simply by definition. This is the new logical connections argument. I return to it below, in chapter 7.

Realizer functionalism has neither of these difficulties. It uses an abstract causal pattern description to pick out whatever it is, concretely, that actually does the job. Since it actually does do the job, there's no question that there might be something else better qualified to perform the job. And since the concrete properties are not defined in terms of the causal pattern, they aren't blocked from being causes, as the abstract causal pattern properties were.

What is troublesome about realizer functionalism is that it makes no distinction between mental properties and physical properties. When I reach for a glass of water when I'm thirsty, the causal pattern characterization of thirst could be used to isolate that part of my brain that actually performs the thirst job. But the causal pattern characterization doesn't pick out the property of being thirsty. And, as with the identity theory of mind, that gets the facts wrong: there is a property of being thirsty, some process in my brain has it now, and some process in the silicon brain of an alien life form could also have that property, despite being physically quite different from me. (Hence realizer functionalism turns out to be essentially a kind of identity theory; this explains Smart's [2004] view that functionalism and identity theory are not distinct theories.)

So the search is still on for an acceptable theory that (a) makes room for a distinction between physical and mental properties, (b) does not define the mental properties in physical terms, and finally, and most important, (c) has a way to explain how both the physical properties and the mental properties can be causes. Donald Davidson's anomalous monism offers ways to satisfy (a) and (b); the subject of this book is how to satisfy (c) as well.

4.4 Anomalous Monism

Donald Davidson's anomalous monism (1970b) shares elements of behaviorism, identity theory, and functionalism but isn't quite any of them. Anomalous monism is far and away the greatest lightning rod for criticisms based on the mental causation problem. This is no accident: the argument for anomalous monism depends on making explicit a conflict between physical law and mental causation. Many philosophers have argued that Davidson's response to the conflict is no help at all. This is somewhat ironic: the only contemporary position in philosophy of mind that doesn't have these problems is the identity theory. Hence if anomalous monism has a serious mental causation problem, so do many other positions in philosophy of mind.

Davidson begins his argument for anomalous monism by taking on Kant's problem of reconciling freedom and natural necessity (Kant 1964:113–115; 1929:A444–A446, B472–B474). Freedom and natural necessity appear to contradict one another. Kant acknowledges that if the contradiction is real, then there is no freedom, since natural necessity trumps freedom. Although Kant's concern isn't exactly the mental causation problem, there is very little distance between the two: physical properties of events explain what happens in the natural world by natural necessity and hence appear to preclude the mental properties of events from making any contribution.

Davidson expresses this apparent contradiction in three principles (1970b:208):

1. Interaction: "at least some mental events interact causally with physical events."
2. Causation: "where there is causality, there must be a law: events related as cause and effect fall under strict deterministic laws."
3. Anomalism: "there are no strict deterministic laws on the basis of which mental events can be predicted and explained."

Davidson argues that the contradiction is only apparent, on the basis of some plausible claims about events, minds, and scientific laws. (Later in the article [219], Davidson says that strict laws need not be deterministic; indeed, many of the fundamental laws of physics are not deterministic.)

Events are particulars, things that happen at a particular place and time, and cannot themselves be repeated. Events, like all particulars (people, places, things), can be described in many ways. Using the terminology of section 4.2, events are tokens, many events can fall under the same type, and each event falls under many different types. It's important to remember, though, that Davidson is talking about descriptions of events, not properties of events. Descriptions are linguistic, properties are not. (See below, chap. 5, sec. 5.4, for a detailed discussion of the relation between properties and language.)

What each of us thinks is constantly and rapidly changing. The array of things you believe about what things are like here and now changes constantly, for instance, as you walk down the hall. Every mental state of yours has a time at which you began having it, and every mental state of yours has a time at which you cease having it. Consequently, we can think of the contents of your mind as a collection of mental events: those events of beginning, and ceasing, to believe, desire, intend the things you believe, desire, intend.

Laws, according to Davidson, are sentences. Whenever a sentence is true of an event, it describes that event in one of the indefinitely many ways it can be described. Laws describe events in one way; other sentences describe events in a different way. (A car salesman describes a car in one way; an auto mechanic describes it in another.)

In light of these claims, Davidson in effect suggests that the second and third principles may be rewritten in a way that explains away the apparent contradiction:

2. Causation: If the sentence "event a caused event b" is true, then a and b have physical descriptions d1 and d2 respectively, and, under those descriptions, their relation follows from a strict law.
3. Anomalism: The descriptions used by psychology to pick out mental events are not descriptions that occur in strict laws.

We can then argue that mental events are physical events—that is, that anomalous monism is true—as follows: If a mental event causes a physical event, there must be a strict law covering those two events. Strict laws can only be expressed using physical descriptions. Hence there must be a physical description of the mental event. So the mental event is a physical event.

Davidson's defense of the of the anomalism principle depends on the idea that our use of various families of words depends on what he calls "constitutive laws." The measurement of length, for example, depends on the constitutive law that length is transitive. If it could sometimes happen that a is longer than b, b is longer than c, but a is not longer than c, then the whole idea of length wouldn't make sense. The argument for anomalism, then, goes like this. The constitutive laws governing the language of physics and the constitutive laws governing the language of psychology are enormously different. Given this enormous difference, we could never be confident that a putative strict law linking the mental and the physical really is a law. (Davidson thinks of laws as general statements that are confirmable by their instances. If we couldn't ever be confident that a given instance really does confirm a general statement, it would follow that the general statement isn't a law.)

What are the constitutive laws of psychology? Davidson, like Ryle, points out that beliefs, desires, and intentions (as well as the meanings of our words) only occur in large structured packages. Anyone who believes anything must also have many other beliefs, must want and intend many things, and must (according to Davidson) be able to use language. The structure of these packages is rationality: people must be pretty rational, mostly believe true things, and be mostly motivated to get what they think is good. A rational person, according to Davidson, is one who reasons roughly in accord with standard logic and decision theory. (Decision theory says that if you have several choices, you should pick the one that has the highest expected utility, where the expected utility of a choice is defined as the product of the benefit you expect to derive from the choice and the probability you attach to that benefit's actually arriving.) The laws of rationality, then, are the constitutive laws governing the language of psychology. Since there is "no echo" (Davidson 1974:231) of the laws of rationality in the laws of physics, there cannot be strict psychophysical laws: hence the anomalism of the mental.

This is an appealing argument. It gives a principled reason for thinking that psychology is importantly different from physics and the other natural sciences. And it is consistent with physicalism. Everything has a physical description. Some physical things behave in distinctive ways (they talk and act), and so a distinctive kind of description applies to them. This kind of description is so distinctive, in fact, that it's impossible to formulate strict laws linking these descriptions with physical ones.

4.5 Two Problems for Mental Causation

Many philosophers have argued that Davidson's philosophy of mind has problems with mental causation. There are two basic styles of problem. One stems from the anomalism of the mental. The other stems from Davidson's externalism about the mind. (Neither style of problem is unique to Davidson's philosophy of mind; any theory that rejects the identity of mental properties and physical properties has the first style of problem, and many philosophers other than Davidson have embraced externalism about the mind and so have the second style of problem.)

4.5.1 Irreducibility and Causal Relevance

Concerning anomalous monism and mental causation, Jaegwon Kim wrote recently (1998:33–34):

There has been an impressive unanimity among Davidson's commentators on just why anomalous monism falls short as an account of mental causation. Take any mental event m that stands in a causal relation, say as a cause of event e. According to Davidson, this causal relation obtains just in case m and e instantiate a physical law. Thus m falls under a certain physical (perhaps, neural) kind N, e falls under a physical kind P, and an appropriate causal law connects events of kind N with events of kind P. But this apparently threatens the causal relevance of mentality: the fact that there is a mental event—that it is the kind of mental event it is—appears to have no role in determining what causal relations it enters into. Event m's causal relations are fixed, wholly and exclusively, by the totality of its physical properties, and there is in this picture no causal work that m's mental properties can, or need to, contribute. If mental properties were arbitrarily redistributed over the events of this world, or even if mentality were completely removed from this world—possibilities apparently left open by Davidson's anomalous monism—that would not effect a single causal relation between events of this world, leaving the causal structure of the world entirely untouched. This seems to consign mental properties to the status of epiphenomena.

Davidson's causation principle (if one event causes another, then there is a strict law covering the two events) seems to imply that causation happens because of physical laws: one event causes another because the pair has properties referred to by a strict law. The anomalism principle seems to say that a strict law never refers to mental properties. It appears to follow that causation never happens because the cause event has the mental properties it has. Instead, whenever a mental event causes a physical event, it does so because it has the physical properties it has. Hence mental properties are causally irrelevant, causally inefficacious, epiphenomenal.

We can make the argument without appeal to any special features of anomalous monism. All that's really needed is (a) mental properties are distinct from physical properties (which they will be if they are irreducible to physical properties) and (b) whatever happens, happens because its causes have the physical properties they do. The argument is exactly the argument made by Baron d'Holbach in the eighteenth century (chap. 3, sec. 3.2). Ask: how does the world work? It works by the laws of physics. Whatever happens, happens because of the physical properties of things. Anything that is not a physical property of things—and here we can count things like being a belief, being a sensation of red, being a turkey sandwich, being a football game, being a tree—is just along for the ride. Things don't happen because things have the property of being trees. Things happen around trees because trees are physical objects, and all their parts have physical properties, and those parts proceed in accord with the physical laws.

So any theory that argues that mental properties are distinct from physical properties—for instance, any theory that argues that mental properties are irreducible to physical properties—appears to entail that mental properties are causally irrelevant.

4.5.2 Externalism and Mental Causation

Externalism in the philosophy of mind is the thesis that what a thought is about—its content—is not an intrinsic feature of the agent who has the thought. Instead, content is determined partly by intrinsic features of agents and partly by their relations to things around them.

Hilary Putnam argued for externalism about the meaning of words for natural kinds like water, jade, and gold (1975a). Imagine that there is, somewhere in the universe, a world just like our world. Call it Twin Earth. Since it is a twin world, it is populated with twins: people who are physical duplicates of ourselves. This world is so like our world that if you were put in your twin's place, you would be utterly unable to distinguish that situation from your current situation. There is one difference: the liquid they call "water" is not H_2O but some substance distinguishable from H_2O only by the subtlest chemical investigation. Call this stuff "twin-water." Putnam urges that their term "water" means twin-water—not water. He suggests my term "water" means the stuff, the liquid in the world around me, which is essentially the same kind of stuff as the liquid to which I learned to apply my term: namely, water.

Davidson's externalism also depends on his views about language, although from a slightly different direction from Putnam's. Since "language is a social art" (Quine 1960: ix), if your word "water" means water, it must be possible for me to figure that out. The only information I have is what I know about your behavior in your surroundings. So I look for causal connections: if you are caused to use sentences like "that's water" by seeing quantities of water, then it's reasonable to think your word "water" means water. But if I knew that you grew up around twin-water (rather than water) I might be better justified in saying that your word means twin-water.

Davidson developed this idea in a particularly startling way (1987). Suppose Melanie is out for a walk in Tilden Park. She's walking through a swamp at the end of Lake Anza. A storm comes up. She is struck by lightning and vaporized. At the same time a fallen tree is also struck by lightning—this is a thoroughgoing accident—and its molecules are miraculously assembled into a duplicate of Melanie. This creature, the swamp person, continues Melanie's walk, appears to chat about philosophy, and so forth.

Davidson holds that the swamp person's words, at least at first, mean nothing and that the swamp person has no thoughts. The reason is that the swamp person's words have no causal history, and hence there is nothing to interpret them as meaning.

The content of our thoughts depends on exactly the same relations to the environment that determine the meanings of our words. So it follows then that the thought that I express using the words "that's water" differs from the thought my twin expresses using the same words—even if from our points of view neither of us can tell the difference between water and twin-water.

So we have two recipes for showing the causal irrelevance of the mental. Take Melanie and her twin, Twin-Melanie. We stipulate that they are physical duplicates: molecule for molecule, they are (inside) physically exactly the same. Their experience is the same in the sense that if either were placed in the situation of the other, in such a way that she doesn't notice the change, neither would notice any difference at all in her experience. Now: Melanie reaches for a glass of water. Twin-Melanie reaches for a glass of twin-water. Melanie wants to drink water. Twin-Melanie wants to drink twin-water.

The two women move in the same way. Their thoughts differ. Therefore the precise content of their thoughts is causally irrelevant to their movements.

Now take Melanie and the swamp person. On Tuesday, Melanie reaches for a glass of water and drinks. On Wednesday she is replaced by the swamp person. Later on Wednesday the swamp person's arm goes out, and water is ingested in just the same way. (We can't say the swamp person reaches or drinks, since those are intentional actions. The swamp person, having no propositional attitudes, can perform no actions.)

These two move in the same way also. Melanie has thoughts; the swamp person has none. Therefore having thoughts is causally irrelevant.

4.5.3 Which Problem?

Here are two problems of mental causation. They are clearly different problems. They may well demand different kinds of solutions.

The first problem (we might call it "the problem from below" [cf. Yablo 1998]) comes from accepting that mental properties are distinct from physical properties (perhaps they are multiply realized, or perhaps they are anomalously related to physical properties) and accepting that physical properties have the more obvious claim to causal relevance.

The second problem (we might call it "the problem from without") comes from accepting that what a thought is about is determined by the person's relations to the world around her. But two people who have exactly the same internal organization will (in the same circumstances) make exactly the same things happen. Hence the internal organization has the more obvious claim to causal relevance.

Suppose we had a solution to the "problem from without." It seems that we would still lack a solution to the "problem from below." Mental properties would still be distinct from physical properties, and physical properties would still have the more obvious claim to causal relevance.

By contrast, suppose we have a general solution to the "problem from below," that is, a theory of causation according to which nonphysical properties can be causally relevant. Then we could go on to articulate, within the structures of that solution, how mental properties (understood as the externalist construes them) can be causally relevant.

So the "problem from below" seems to be the more general problem. That is the problem I will aim to solve in the rest of this book.

4.6 Conclusion

In chapter 3 I showed that unless some sort of materialism is true, mental causation—and freedom—is hopeless. This chapter surveyed the main materialist models of the mind discussed during the twentieth century: behaviorism, the identity theory, functionalism, anomalous monism, and externalism. It turns out that materialism has its own difficulties with mental causation. Identity theory is immune to these difficulties, but at the cost of insisting, implausibly, that mental properties are identical to physical properties. We are thus left with the problem of seeing how mental events could possibly cause things in virtue of or because they have their mental properties.

Solving that problem requires getting clear on what properties are, what causation is, and what it means to say that one event causes another event in virtue of some of its properties rather than others. I turn now to these basic metaphysical questions.

4.7 Further Reading

All contemporary introductions to the philosophy of mind discuss behaviorism, identity theory, functionalism, and anomalous monism. Volume 1 of Ned Block's *Readings in the Philosophy of Psychology* (1980a) is a particularly good survey; others include David Rosenthal's *The Nature of Mind* (1991) and David Chalmers's *Philosophy of Mind: Classical and Contemporary Readings* (2002).

Davidson's views on anomalous monism can be found in his "Mental Events" (1970b), "The Material Mind" (1973), and "Psychology as Philosophy" (1974). His response to the mental causation problem can be found in "Thinking Causes" (1993). The essays presented in *Donald Davidson* (Ludwig 2003) make up a good introduction to Davidson's overall philosophy. Davidson's writing is notoriously difficult; Jaegwon Kim's "Psychophysical Laws" (1985) and Brian McLaughlin's "Anomalous Monism and the Irreducibility of the Mental" (1985) are two good papers on how the arguments of "Mental Events" work. McLaughlin's "Type Epiphenomenalism, Type Dualism, and the Causal Priority of the Physical" (1989) among other things makes it clear that Davidson's problems concerning mental causation are widely shared.

Wim De Muijnck's *Dependencies, Connections and Other Relations: A Theory of Mental Causation* (2003) works out a solution to a variety of mental causation problems based on a theory of how externalistic or relational mental properties can be causally efficacious. Three seminal works on externalism are Saul Kripke's *Naming and Necessity* (1980), Hilary Putnam's "The Meaning of 'Meaning'" (1975a), and Tyler Burge's "Individualism and the Mental" (1979).

5

Properties

In its depth I saw ingathered, bound by love in one single volume, that which is dispersed in leaves throughout the universe: substances and accidents and their relations, as though fused together in such a way that what I tell is but a simple light.

—DANTE, *PARADISO* (ALIGHIERI 1975: XXXIII.85–90)

THE MENTAL causation problem is a problem about properties. Mental events are physical events. Physical events cause things because they have the physical properties they do. But mental properties are not identical to physical properties. So—apparently—mental events don't cause things because they have the mental properties they do.

To solve this problem it is necessary to investigate how properties and causation go together. We say that one thing causes another in virtue of some of its properties rather than others it has (Shoemaker 1984:206) or because it has some of its properties (and not because it has its other properties). That is to **say**: some properties of the cause are causally relevant to the effect, and others of its properties are not. The mental causation problem, then, is to explain how mental properties can be causally relevant properties.

We need a theory of causal relevance. First, this chapter says what properties are. I'll be particularly concerned to argue that there are lots of properties other than the physical: properties like being a picnic or like being a football score and, most important, mental properties like being a desire for ice cream or being a belief that it is 1:30 P.M.

Next, chapter 6 links up properties and causal relevance. If a law of nature links two properties in a certain way, then one will be causally relevant to the other. The problem then becomes: how could mental properties meet that gold standard for causal relevance?

In my discussions of Aristotle (chap. 2, sec. 2.2.3) and of (role) functionalism (chap. 4, sec. 4.3), I said that if we define mental properties in terms of causal relations, the consequence is that they don't explain how mental events cause things. (Consider Jerry Fodor's example [1968]: if Wheaties are the breakfast of champions by definition, then eating Wheaties doesn't explain what makes a champion, since you have to be a champion already in order to qualify as a Wheaties eater.) In other words, if we define mental properties in terms of causal relations, then they aren't causally relevant to other properties. Given the accounts of properties and causation I develop in this chapter and the next, chapter 7 makes this argument more precise. If mental properties are causally relevant to, say, properties of bodily movements, then they must be suitably independent of them.

Mental properties are different from physical properties and at least some of them are independent in the right way from potential causes and effects. So how are they related to physical properties? Chapter 8 shows that mental properties (if they are to be causally relevant to anything) must supervene on physical properties.

Chapter 9 then shows how to connect up supervening mental properties to laws of nature and hence shows how mental properties can meet the gold standard for causal relevance articulated in chapter 6, below. Then the mental causation problem will be solved.

5.1 What Are Properties?

Properties are strange. Dante thought it took a mystical vision to understand them. They seem very straightforward, yet (I believe) no one has succeeded in giving a perfectly satisfactory explanation of them. Nevertheless we have to talk about them in order to make sense of causation and mental causation.

Here is a particular apple. It has a certain sort of color (varying shades of red, brown, yellow, green), a shape (mainly roundish), mass (maybe a half pound); taste (sweet and acid); texture (mainly sort of crunchy); temperature (about sixty degrees Fahrenheit). It has seeds; if it's newly off the tree and stays in the right sort of environment, those seeds might germinate, perhaps even grow up into a new apple tree. This apple is on the table in my kitchen. It is not moving (relative to the table and the kitchen, anyway).

Properties are ways a particular thing is. They distinguish one particular thing from other particular things: this apple has this shape, that one has a different shape. Hence the primary job that properties have to perform is that of distinguishing things.

Properties distinguish, but they also group. These two distinct particular things are both apples. Perhaps these two have different masses, but (probably) there is some further thing that has the same mass as the first apple. So we may say that two things are the same, in some way, precisely when they share a property.

This marks the fundamental distinction between particular things and properties. A particular thing is the thing that it is, and it is not any other thing. But many distinct particular things can have the same property. As we might say: properties are repeatable; individuals are not. A particular thing might have parts that are in various distinct places. For instance, the United States has parts that are geographically discontinuous—Hawaii and Alaska—but there is only one whole United States. But the United States and France are two different countries that have exactly the same property: the property of being a country.

Many properties determine ways things behave with other things. The color of the apple determines what wavelengths of light it reflects and absorbs and the way it looks in various circumstances. The property of being a living apple seed determines that the seed may develop into an apple tree.

Concrete particular things are not the only things that have properties. The number 17 is prime. So is the number 37. Here is a way that prime numbers behave: Euclid proved that if p is a prime number that divides a product of integers ab without remainder, then p divides either a or b without remainder.

The way abstract objects behave is itself usually called a property. Euclid's lemma states a property of primes. For abstract objects, there is no distinction between having a property and exhibiting the relevant behavior. But many of the properties of concrete particular things (the familiar properties, like mass, color, temperature, chemical characteristics) behave differently depending on what is going on around them at the moment. In the dark, the apple won't reflect any light and so it won't look like it has any color at all. Hence many properties of concrete particular things are closely connected with causation: the apple's color causes me to see it in various ways. The properties of abstract objects are not involved in causation at all. The properties of prime numbers and the properties of apples are fundamentally different, but they are all properties nonetheless.

5.1.1 One Category or More?

So there are particular things—particulars, for short, another word for individual things—and they have properties that they share with other particulars. Both particulars and properties exist (see sec. 5.1.2, below). There are, however, theories of properties that reduce one of these categories to the other.

- Since each distinct particular seems to have different properties, we could say that particulars are constituted by the properties they have. It is unlikely that this will work, since there can be two particulars that have exactly the same properties (at least in principle, if not in actual fact).
- Plato distinguished between properties and property instances (*Phaedo* 102d, Plato 1977). The mass of this particular apple is an instance of the property of having that mass; the former is a particular, the latter is a repeatable. Following Williams (1966), these are called tropes. Williams, K. Campbell (1981), and Bacon (1995:23) take tropes as the only basic category. A property, then, is defined to be a class of tropes that exactly resemble in one sort of way; a particular is a class of tropes that exactly resemble in another sort of way. But it is difficult to see why we should prefer a theory of tropes to a theory of particulars that have properties (Daly 1997).
- John Locke writes, "All things that exist [are] particulars" (1975:3.3.1), and attempts to explain generality as a feature of thought and language, rather than the world. Similarly, Roscelin (1050–1125 CE) argued that this cat and that cat are the same because they are both called "cat"—that a universal was nothing but a wind of the voice: "flatus vocis." But it's hard to understand how just a word could be what's common to the cats: isn't the cat called "cat" because it has the property of being a cat, regardless of what anybody says about it?

Many other positions have also been taken. Probably the strongest motivation for wanting to get rid of the category of property is that particulars are right here, that is, they are what we encounter in experience. Intuitions differ on this point; trope theorists maintain that what is right here is the color, the shape, of the apple, its appleness. But properties aren't like that. Even the mass of the apple isn't (exactly) "right here": what's "right here" is the apple, which happens to have a mass of about a half pound.

5.1.2 Do Properties Exist?

Should we believe in properties? Should we believe they exist? The classic arguments in favor of their existence are oddly inconclusive. Bertrand Russell offered the following argument about justice (1912:90–91): "Let us consider, say, such a notion as *justice*. If we ask ourselves what justice is, it is natural to proceed by considering this, that, and the other just act, with a view to discovering what they have in common. They must all, in some sense, partake of a common nature, which will be found in whatever is just and in nothing else. This common nature, by virtue of which they are all just, will be justice itself, the pure essence the admixture of which with facts of ordinary life produces the multiplicity of just acts." The conclusion doesn't follow, though. For suppose that in fact there are no properties (or universals) that exist separately from the many just acts. Then the premise (that there are many just acts) may well be true while the conclusion (that there exists a common nature, the universal of justice) is false. Swoyer (1982) suggests that these arguments appear to be inferences to the best explanation (hence not intended to be deductively valid). "Best" here has never been by much of a margin, so the most we could expect from arguments like this is some sort of presumption in favor of the existence of properties.

There are arguments that properties are indispensable (van Inwagen 2004): any attempt to make sense of how the world works will have to say that there are properties. On the other side, there are arguments that properties are dispensable: whatever work the concept of property does can be done without it (Devitt 1980; Schiffer 2003: chap. 2).

What if there are no properties at all? We are going to go on talking about properties. We will go on saying that two apples have something in common, a way they are. We will go on talking about the properties of primes. So if there really are no properties, we'll have to have a way to translate the things we say about properties into language about something else (for instance, about words). And there will have to be a way to translate the structure of what we say about properties into this other language. So the mental causation problem (can mental events cause physical events in virtue of both their physical properties and their mental properties?) isn't going to go away even if we get rid of properties entirely.

So we might as well assume there are properties.

5.1.3 One and Many?

Properties are repeatable; particulars are not. What makes properties especially puzzling is how they are both one and many. Here are two cats: Eddy and Grushenka. They are distinct beings. Yet they are the same, both cats. One thing—the property of being a cat—in many particulars. What account can we give of the fact that two different things can (nevertheless) be the same?

There are perhaps three leading contemporary contenders for solutions to the problem of "the one over the many":

- Properties are single things (universals) that are the same in every individual instance. David Armstrong (1989:98–99) says that the universal is "wholly present in its instances" and has no existence other than its presence in the instances. (Sort of like the relation between a handrail and the brackets that hold it on the wall: one thing that extends through a multiplicity of things, and the whole handrail is present in each of the brackets.)

- Tropes are single things that are particulars; their particularity is necessarily connected with the particularity of the thing that has them. (Eddy is a particular. He is a cat. His trope of cat is essentially his.) What makes the many cats the same is the fact that their tropes of cat exactly resemble one another.
- Properties are classes or sets of their instances. The red things make up the property of being red. Properties exist (since sets exist) and are distinct from the particulars that have them.

None of these proposals works terribly well. The third contender supplies one thing to group the many together; on the face of it, however, it doesn't touch the question of what makes all the members of the one set one thing. The first two contenders quite immediately raise more questions than they answer (what does "wholly present in its instances" mean? what is a trope?). It is not even clear that they are distinct proposals: their advocates regularly note that there may be no more than a terminological distinction between them (Armstrong 1989; Martin 1996).

Here's a suggestion. Let's ask, what kind of problem is the "one over many" problem supposed to be, anyway? We start out with ordinary things like cats and apples and numbers. We see that two of them "have the same property (are somehow of the same type)" (Lewis 1983a:201). We want to give some account of this. We find ourselves talking about particulars and properties (or universals or tropes or words or . . .). The problem then seems to turn into a mysterious and intractable puzzle about the characters of these new kinds of things and how to join them together again. (What is a particular that completely lacks properties [the problem of bare particulars]? If we have to join the property to the particular, what about the relation between the particular and the property [the problem of instantiation]?) New puzzles arise about how these new kinds of things are involved in change and causation, about which theory of these things is the most economical, and so forth.

Suppose we think of it this way instead: We start out with ordinary things. There are ways they are, and these are shared by many of them; and each particular thing is what it is and is not some other thing.

Next—and this is the crucial step—we begin talking about ways things are (just as the Russell argument talks about the one thing that all just things have in common). We need to be very careful about how we do this and about what exactly we are doing. Ways things are, are not things like cats and apples and numbers.

Nor are particulars things like cats or apples or numbers, if particulars are distinct—in a special sense—from the ways they are. Clearly, this apple is distinct from its ripeness, in the following mundane sense: after a day or two, it will no longer be ripe but rather overripe. But the ripe apple isn't distinct now from its ripeness. By contrast, for instance, Armstrong's universals are distinct, in a special sense, from the particulars that have them, since the universal of ripeness still exists even when this apple is all brown and mushy.

This seems odd: how can a universal be, as Armstrong says, "wholly present" in two distinct things and survive the destruction of one of them? But the oddness disappears when we acknowledge that we are using this expression "universal" to talk about the fact, for example, that one of the ways apples can be is ripe and that that fact isn't altered by the rotting of a particular apple.

So the problem of the one over many should be: how can we keep track of the facts about how things are the same and how things differ? What are the advantages and disadvantages of different ways of doing this? One time-honored way of keeping track is to talk about individuals and their properties. So long as we keep clearly in view that the point of talking about individuals and their properties is to keep track of the ways things are (and the way the world works), we shouldn't get in trouble. It's when we slide over into thinking of individuals and their properties (or tropes or universals . . .) as special kinds of things that the discussion seems to lose its grip on reality.

My suggestion, then, about the problem of the one over many is this. We talk about things and the ways they are. Our theories of these things have various structures, and it is always worth asking how much of the structure corresponds to real features of real things. (See Matthews 1994 for an application of a similar idea in a very different context.) Most maps display bodies of water as one shade of blue, but we know that the maps are not intended to represent accurately the color of the water. Similarly with theories of properties and particulars: we should demand that the theories display enough structure so that we can keep track of the right things in the right ways. But sometimes parts of that structure may not make sense, when understood as real features of the world. If two different ways of keeping track of the facts seem to differ about some real feature of things, it's always worth asking whether the difference is in what the theories say about the things or rather in how the theories say what they say.

So, for our purposes, the word "particulars" applies to things like cats and countries, neighbors and numbers, and the word "property" applies to ways that these things are. The one-over-many problem is only a problem about describing the structure of how we talk about particulars and properties, not a problem about special kinds of things and how they behave.

5.1.4 What Distinguishes Properties?

The property of being a cat and the property of being furry are two different properties. Leibniz's law says what it is to be one thing: given any pair of things (not necessarily distinct), they are the same thing if and only if they share all properties, different if there's a property one has that the other lacks.

We can turn Leibniz's law inside out in order to say what it is to be one property (Yablo 1992): given any pair of properties (not necessarily distinct), they are the same property if and only if they are had by the same things, different if there's a thing that has one of them but lacks the other.

Why not say Leibniz's law itself, rather than the law inside out, individuates properties, thus: given any pair of properties (not necessarily distinct), they are the same property if and only if they share all properties, different if there is a property one has that the other lacks? Here's why not: If properties are distinguishers, then we can see how the collection of all the things that are distinguished includes enough distinctions to distinguish all the properties. If, by contrast, further properties distinguish the distinguishers, then we haven't yet brought forward what distinguishes these further properties. We could say "more properties." But then we wouldn't be saying what the identity and difference of properties was; we would just be relying on the fact that they are distinguishers.

5.1.5 How Many Properties?

What's important about properties, then, is that they distinguish things. The world is not one: there are many things, and they are different. Their differences constitute the properties they have.

Things are very distinguishable. Take two distinct things. They may look the same or different, they may act in the same way or differently, they may stand in the same or different relations to other things. They are distinct and so distinguishable as the particulars they are. But they also have something in common, namely, they are the two members of this pair. So here is a generous way of counting properties: to each way of grouping things (all $2^n - 1$ ways of grouping n things), there corresponds a way those things are like one another and different from everything else; hence to each way of grouping there corresponds a property. This is usually called an "abundant" conception of properties. Some arguments for an abundant conception can be found in Jubien 1989 and Taylor 1993 as well as the work of David Lewis, whose view I will consider in more detail in a moment.

There can be two different properties such that exactly the same actual things have them. Quine's famous example was the property of having a heart and the property of having a kidney. (The example doesn't quite work;

while it's true that just about every actual creature with a heart has kidneys and just about every actual creature with kidneys has a heart, nevertheless there are people with artificial hearts and people who use dialysis machines.) We need to factor in how things could have been as well as how things are: for any pair of properties (not necessarily distinct), they are the same property if and only if it is not possible for there to be something that has one and lacks the other; they are different properties if and only if it is possible for something to have one and lack the other. Or, more briefly: for any pair of properties P and Q (not necessarily distinct), P = Q if and only if necessarily, for any x, x has P if and only if x has Q. Much more is possible than is actual. But it's not so that everything is possible; what is possible must not be logically inconsistent. (Not all philosophers agree: see, e.g., Priest 1998, 2005.)

David Lewis's theory of properties is a version of this way of counting properties (1983a, 1986: sec 1.5). Properties are sets of actual and possible particulars. The set of all the actual eggs, for instance, counts as one of the properties. That's not the property of being an egg, since possible eggs can share the property of being an egg as well. (For instance, this might be true: if I had had an egg for breakfast, I would have endangered my cholesterol count. That [nonactual] egg has the property of being an egg.)

There is also the following close relative to the property of being an egg. Take two actual eggs. There is a property, rather like the property of being an egg, except it is missing one of these two actual eggs. It is the property of being an egg, except for the missing one. (Call this the property of being an egg-minus-one.)

Lewis was a modal realist who held that the possible eggs really exist in possible worlds, which also really exist just like the actual world (1986). Whether we agree with Lewis about this or not (nearly no philosopher does), it is very useful to think about possibility and properties in terms of possible worlds and possible particulars.

There are problems with identifying properties with classes of possible particulars (*possibilia*), though. Armstrong objects that it leaves particulars utterly featureless blobs (1989:38). Moreover, if properties are sets, then they are outside of the things that have them, but particular things have their properties regardless of what other things have them. So properties should be distinct from sets of *possibilia*. The simplest thing to say is that properties are represented by sets of *possibilia*.

Assuming that there is a one-one mapping between properties and classes of possible particulars, we can define certain operations on properties that yield other properties. Take two properties. We can define their conjunction as follows. Take the two sets that represent them. Then find the set that contains all elements common to both, that is, the intersection of the two sets. The property corresponding to that set is the conjunction of the original pair.

The disjunction is defined in the same way, except that the new set contains all elements in either set, that is, the union of the two sets. The negation of a property is the property corresponding to the set of all the things that do not have the original property, that is, its complement.

Properties are not linguistic entities. So even though it makes sense to define the conjunction or disjunction of two properties, it's important to remember that the result is just another property—in other words, properties are never disjunctive or conjunctive, and so on.

5.1.6 Even More Properties?

There are conceptions of properties in which there are even more properties than this. The property of being trilateral seems to be different from the property of being triangular, yet there is no possible trilateral that is not triangular. Let's distinguish them in the following way. Take two predicates A and B. If the sentence, "everything that has A has B, and everything that has B has A" could be informative for someone, then A and B pick out different properties. In other words we could correlate properties with Fregean senses (Frege 1892).

Many philosophers will have wanted to stop the increase in the number of properties some paragraphs back. For our purposes, it doesn't matter if there are more properties than sets of actual and possible particulars. It does matter, however, if there are many fewer, if it turns out that there are no mental properties at all.

5.2 Too Many Properties?

The mass, the shape, the color of the apple are ways the apple is. These properties explain what the apple does. These all strike us as ordinary—as genuine—properties.

We can draw other ways the apple is from the enormous universe of abundant properties. This apple has the property of being either an apple or a handsaw. It has the property of being itself, or Julius Caesar, or your lunch last Tuesday: since there is a perfectly respectable set with exactly those members, this is a perfectly respectable property. This apple is a member of the set of things that are red and the time is less than some time t_1, otherwise blue. (This property is modeled on the famous property grue, invented by Nelson Goodman [1954], of being green if observed before the year 2000, otherwise blue. Emeralds are, we think, green, not grue; but it's not clear, Goodman argues, what justified us in that claim before the year 2000.)

These things strike us as outlandish. They seem not to be genuine properties.

There are a couple of marks of genuine properties (Mellor and Oliver 1997:4).

1. If two things differ in a genuine property, then they differ: they are not alike. By contrast, if this egg has the property of being an egg-minus-one, and that egg is the exception that lacks that property, they aren't really different—apparently.
2. If one thing changes, there is a genuine property that the thing gains (or loses). By contrast, this green table cloth ceased to be grue at the stroke of midnight, January 1, 2000, but it did not change—apparently.

If we collect all the genuine likenesses and differences, and we collect all the occasions of really changing and all the occasions of really staying the same, it looks like we have all the real facts about everything. So we can think about genuine properties in the following way.

Suppose we work out a minimal theory of the ways the apple is. This theory is supposed to explain and account for everything that is true of the apple. It is supposed to be minimal in relying on the very least one could possibly say about how things are in order to make this explanation. We certainly wouldn't need the egg-minus-one property for a minimalist theory.

Call a theory like this a theory of sparse properties or a sparse property theory. Here are three examples of sparse property theories.

5.2.1 Properties Are Sets of Causal Powers

Shoemaker (1984) begins with conditional causal powers. A causal power is defined with respect to something it can cause: the power to cut butter is (what else?) a power something has when it can cut butter.

A property is a bundle of conditional causal powers. The property of being knife-shaped consists of the power to cut butter if made of something rigid and applied to butter in a certain definite way, the power to appear knife-shaped to people if the light is good and their eyes are healthy (and so on), and many more.

Whatever any grue thing does can be explained in terms of color and time. So (according to Shoemaker) being grue is not a property. Consider the characteristic of being a bed slept in by George Washington. No bed has causal powers in virtue of having this characteristic that it doesn't already have in virtue of various intrinsic properties it has, so this historical feature is not a property.

5.2.2 Scientific Realism About Properties

Armstrong (1978a, 1978b) argues that the job of natural science is to discover the universals that explain how the world works. Universals meet three conditions. First, things that share in a universal constitute a genuine unity. Second, things that share in a universal genuinely resemble one another. Third, it is in virtue of sharing in a universal that a thing acts causally as it does. Armstrong argues from these conditions that there are some conjunctive universals but no disjunctive or negative universals. For, supposing that F and G are universals, the group of things that have both F and G constitutes a genuine unity, those things genuinely resemble one another, and they may cause things in virtue of being F and G. By contrast, the group of things that have either F or G is not a genuine unity, they do not genuinely resemble one another, and they may cause things in virtue of being F or in virtue of being G but not in virtue of being either F or G.

5.2.3 Natural Properties

David Lewis argues that we need universals as well as abundant properties. There is a special subset of the abundant properties; Lewis calls these universals or natural properties: "Sharing of them makes for qualitative similarity, they carve at the joints, they are intrinsic, they are highly specific, the sets of their instances are ipso facto not entirely miscellaneous, there are only just enough of them to characterize things completely and without redundancy" (1986:60). Lewis holds that we need this distinction ("It is out of the question to be without it") to solve a host of problems (1983a). Take the problem of how to analyze the concept of one thing's being a duplicate of another. Given all the abundant properties, no thing is a duplicate of any other, since some property distinguishes them. But if we have a distinguished subset of the abundant properties, that is, the perfectly natural properties, then we can say that one thing is a duplicate of another when they share their perfectly natural properties.

5.3 Too Few Properties?

So what should we do? Accept abundant properties and, with them, the cost of dealing with the host of problems that Lewis solves with natural properties? Or go for sparse properties and the idea that the only properties are ones connected with a minimal explanatory base?

I could just set this problem to one side. I could finish the argument of the book that mental properties are causally relevant and then conclude that mental properties are genuine: either because they have earned their place among the sparse properties or because they are members of a particular set of the abundant properties, the ones that really figure in causation.

But there is a danger here. There appears to be a strong motivation in favor of the sparse conception of properties that is independent of the mental causation problem. The sparse conception connects properties with a picture of how the world works. It begins by connecting properties to some version or other of a minimal explanatory base (as I discussed in the last section). But the very idea of a minimal explanatory base already involves some conception of how causation works and which properties are connected up with causation.

The abundant conception of properties, by contrast, places no restrictions on what properties there may be. Some properties are intimately connected with causation; others are not. Then we have a philosophical project: to articulate what it is about a property that connects it with change and causation. Hence the abundant conception of properties gives us a framework that lessens the danger of presupposing one or another idea about how causation works.

So rather than leaving the motivation for the sparse conception of properties to operate in the background, I want to argue here in favor of abundant properties. First I criticize a very appealing intuitive argument against abundant properties. Then I describe some very general reasons of philosophical methodology that seem to favor abundant properties. Finally I connect up the theory of properties with the theory of causation and in particular mental causation.

5.3.1 The Similarity Argument

"Abundant properties are outrageous!"

In this section I will build this sentiment into an argument for sparse properties and then show (a) why it's not a good argument but (b) why it is so powerfully appealing.

How is Eddy, my younger cat, in and of himself: how are things with him? Well, things are with him, at least in one respect, pretty much the way things are with Grushenka, my older cat: they are both cats. Eddy is also a member of the set {Eddy, Lewis Carroll's writing desk}. But surely how things are with Eddy is just different from how things are, or were, with that desk.

Here is an argument. We might call it the Moorean similarity argument, in honor of G. E. Moore's catalog of facts (1925) that are supposed to be beyond rational dispute.

Preamble: imagine that I am trying to persuade you that properties are sparse. We converse. We do and say various things. Here, roughly, is what I say to you: "Here are two things: a drinking glass and a Frisbee. There's another: a raven. The first two are similar. Neither of the first two resembles the third. Conclusion: There is something about the glass and the Frisbee such that they genuinely resemble one another, while neither the glass nor the Frisbee genuinely resembles the raven."

I submit that this argument is powerfully appealing. Yet it is quite simply and straightforwardly fallacious. The glass and the Frisbee resemble one another, and they don't resemble the raven *in that way*. It doesn't follow that there is no way that they resemble the raven.

Notice that in the original conversation I didn't say how the drinking glass and the Frisbee are similar. The conversation has no persuasive force at all if one of the speakers can't see the things (some drinking glasses are square, after all). Let's represent this quasi-formally by turning the word "Here" in the original argument into "Here, under the aspect of . . . " in order to make explicit what the conversants intend one another to see:

[p1] Here, under the aspect of circularity, is a thing: Thing1.
[p2] Here, under the aspect of circularity, is another: Thing2.
[p3] Here, under the aspect of being a raven, is another thing: Thing3.
[c1] First conclusion: Thing1 and Thing2 are genuinely the same.
[c2] Second conclusion: Thing1 and Thing3 are genuinely different.
[c3] Overall conclusion: Some things are and some things are not genuinely similar.

Since circularity looks like an aspect under which two things may be genuinely similar, we can say that [c1] follows from [p1] and [p2]. It might appear that [c2] follows from [p1] and [p3] because those two premises mention two different aspects. But it doesn't follow, since there might be some other aspect under which Thing1 and Thing3 both fall.

Why does the argument seem so appealing, though? I think the explanation is that in ordinary conversation we draw on a limited range of aspects under which to think and talk about things.

How do I get my interlocutor to see an object under a particular aspect? When we talk, we have various things in mind: what we actually see and sense around us, how we think about the things we are talking about, how we think about things generally, what we are trying to accomplish. What we have in mind factors in to what we say and what we mean in a variety of ways.

Suppose the driver of the bus says, "Every seat is taken." Clearly he's talking about this bus, not every seat in every bus (or every seat in general). This sentence can be used to say, completely literally, that every seat in the entire universe is taken. We don't understand the bus driver that way, since it is clear to us, and to the driver, that we are together on this bus and that we are interested in being able to sit on this *bus*.

Suppose I'm holding a lump of wet clay that has been made into a bust of Socrates. I might say, "this can survive being squashed into a ball." Is what I say true or false? It depends on how you and I are thinking about it. If we are thinking about it as a lump of wet clay, then what I say is true. If we are thinking about it as a bust of Socrates, then what I say is false, since it wouldn't be a bust anymore if I squash it (Ray 1992).

If I get you to think of an object under an aspect, what kind of aspect will it be? Typically (although not necessarily) we will think of things under natural aspects (in roughly Lewis's sense of "natural"). I see two eggs in the refrigerator; I think of these things as eggs (not as having the property of being an egg-minus-one). We do this because the natural aspects of things group them in ways that fit our lives. Eggs are important to us. Eggs-minus-one are not.

The properties we ordinarily think about involve possibility. I could have had an egg for breakfast this morning. But I didn't. If we think of the egg I didn't eat as a possible particular, we need to count it as one of the possible eggs. There is a property—call it "actual-egg"—which is shared by all and only the actual-eggs. The egg I could have had for breakfast isn't an actual-egg. So in thinking about what I might have had for breakfast, I am thinking of things that have the property of being eggs, not actual-eggs.

So there is a good pragmatic reason why we think of objects under aspects that correspond to natural properties. This explains why the similarity argument is so powerfully appealing. Frisbees are not like ravens, because there is no natural property shared by Frisbees and ravens—that is, no property of the sort that fits well with the way our lives proceed. True enough, but it doesn't follow from this that there is no property at all shared by Frisbees and ravens.

5.3.2 Philosophical Method

My second argument for why we want an abundant property theory derives from very general considerations about philosophical methodology.

Doing Philosophical Work

One of the apparent advantages of various sparse conceptions of properties is that they solve problems; they do philosophical work (see especially the last few pages of Lewis 1983a). I think the advantage is merely apparent. I think that the distinction between properties and particulars is so fundamental, so basic, that it really should not do any philosophical work.

Suppose we have a theory of properties and particulars that decides between two otherwise acceptable philosophical theories. Each theory seems to be all right by its own lights. Each theory depends on its own conception of properties. The conceptions are slightly different, and one of these conceptions rules out the other theory.

It could be that this conception is a better theory of properties for some reason independent of the two philosophical theories under consideration. But let us stipulate that that is not so. Each conception of properties is good as any theory of properties gets. Then I think it is clear that one of the conceptions of properties is question begging; it must somehow assert that the other theory is incorrect.

Each of those theories talks about things and their properties and relations. That much should be common ground among all philosophical theories. The theory of properties and relations is obligated, we should say, to respect that common ground. The theory of properties and relations should, that is, provide an arena in which other theories can meet; it should not prevent any of the contestants from so much as entering the arena. If we arrange a theory of properties that does decide between the two theories, then that theory must be question begging.

Consider the logical theory of relations. Common sense says that, for instance, my cat Eddy and the Golden Gate Bridge aren't related at all. To be related, there has to be some substantial connection between two things. The logical concept of a relation, by contrast, is a set of sets (n-tuples) of things. Any set of n-tuples of things is a relation.

The logician's conception of a relation is simple and clear. Equally, it is simple and clear, within the framework of the logician's concept, to describe the more commonsensical substantial relations. If you want the relation "is a niece of," then you need to say that the first member of each pair has a parent whose sibling is the second member.

I submit that we should prefer the logician's conception of a relation, since it provides a framework—an arena—for discussing the details of this or that relation—whereas the common sense conception makes the shape of the framework depend on the details of whatever substantial relations turn out to be.

Abundant property theories have room for all the sparse property theorist's properties and more. Whereas the sparse property theory entails that there are no more properties than the sparse ones. Abundant property theory therefore provides a more open arena for discussions of properties.

Similarity, Unity . . .

Philosophers talk of "carving nature at the joints" following Plato's praise of a procedure "whereby we are enabled to divide into forms, following the objective articulation; we are not to attempt to hack off parts like a clumsy butcher" (*Phaedrus*, Plato 1952:265e). "Objective articulation" or "natural joints" can be understood in various ways: in terms of similarity, in terms of genuine unities, in terms of naturalness, in terms of causal powers, in terms of laws of nature, and so forth. One motivation for a theory of sparse properties is that properties should "carve nature at its joints." They should capture the real similarities and differences among things.

The trouble is that the abundant property theory does capture those differences and similarities. It captures others besides. The sparse property theory claims—correctly—that many of the distinctions made by the abundant properties are miscellaneous, heterogeneous, and arbitrary. The abundant property theory can be supplemented with accounts of which properties are heterogeneous (etc.) and which are not. That is not a reason for saying that only some of them really are properties.

5.3.3 Sparse Properties and Mental Causation

My third and final reason for preferring an abundant theory of properties is a response to another principle from Plato, often called the Eleatic Principle since it is expressed by the Stranger from Elea: "I suggest that anything has real being that is so constituted as to possess any sort of power either to affect anything else or to be affected, in however small a degree, by the most insignificant agent, though it be only once. I am proposing as a mark to distinguish real things that they are nothing but power" (*Sophist*, Plato 1935:247e). Armstrong uses the Eleatic Principle as a criterion of existence (if a property is real, then it makes some difference to the causal powers of a thing), while Shoemaker uses it as a criterion of property identity (two properties are the same property if they share the same causal powers). Both philosophers are best understood as using the Eleatic Principle to explicate properties of concrete particulars (rather than, for instance, properties of numbers).

It is not clear why we should use the idea of causal power as the touchstone of reality or of identity and difference. But even if we do endorse the idea, it is unclear whether it is any help in metaphysical inquiry. If it were uncontroversial that mental properties either do, or do not, make a difference to the causal powers of a thing, then the Eleatic Principle would straightforwardly rule that mental properties are real (or that they are not).

Our situation, however, is that the causal powers of mental properties are a problem. There are powerful arguments on both sides. So we can't rely on the Eleatic Principle to tell us whether mental properties are real.

Shoemaker asserts, for instance, that intrinsic properties are causal powers and extrinsic ones are not. He holds that having the property of having been slept in by George Washington is not a causal power. Presumably that is because what the bed will do is exactly the same as a similar bed that wasn't slept in by George Washington. But that's clearly wrong, since, for instance, its having been slept in by George Washington might cause the U.S. Congress to pass a law concerning the treatment of this bed.

Some will say that the only way causation can work is through a local mechanism. Others will say that the sciences are rife with nonintrinsic causal concepts (R. Wilson 1993). For instance, the concept of adaptedness (from evolutionary biology) is clearly a nonintrinsic concept, since we must always ask, adapted relative to what?

Armstrong asserts that disjunctions of universals do not bestow causal powers. The reasoning goes like this: if one thing causes another because it is either red or green, then surely it causes it because it is in fact one rather than the other. But we might wonder whether one thing causes another because it has a color, and it doesn't matter which color it had. (For careful discussion of Armstrong's claim, see Clapp 2001.)

The problem, then, with the Eleatic Principle is that the principle itself doesn't tell us which things have powers to affect things or be affected by things, and neither does it tell us what a causal power is. The real work we need to do here is to figure out what causal powers are and what kinds of things have them. The best framework within which to do that figuring out is one that does not build the idea of a causal power into the very idea of a property.

5.4 Properties and Language

It may seem entirely ridiculous to expect ordinary language predicates to express properties: "is a rock" looks bad. Here are more: "is red," "is bald," "is a conservative," "is good," "is a picnic," and "is a game." Properties (as described above, in sec. 5.1) are sharp edged, but these predicates are not. Is a grain of sand a rock? A big grain of sand? There are guys who are obviously bald and guys who are obviously hairy, but there are borderline cases. Many things are obviously and clearly red. But some things are orangey-red and some things are purply-red, and about some of these, it's not so clear whether they are red or not. The things that are clearly red differ wildly in their physical properties. Being politically conservative is partly a matter of self-identification, partly a matter of endorsing or championing certain kinds of views, but there is considerable unclarity about exactly what kind of views. Maybe goodness really, ultimately, is only so-called: there's no property of goodness, just our practice of calling some things good. Wittgenstein argued that many of our concepts (for instance, for games) are family resemblance concepts (1953).

Like brothers and sisters and cousins, some games resemble one another in one way, others in other ways; the collection of overlapping resemblances is much more like a rope woven of multiple overlapping strands than a set of necessary and sufficient conditions.

It may be that the language of psychology is in the same boat as the language of colors and games and all the rest. If so, then it would be absurd to expect the predicates of psychology to refer to properties, and hence the mental causation problem would be based on a mistake.

There are three kinds of issues here: many predicates apply to things by virtue of our responses to them; many predicates apply to collections of physically heterogeneous things; and, finally, many (perhaps most, perhaps all) predicates are vague, while properties are not.

5.4.1 Response-Dependence

Pistachio ice cream tastes good. Well, it does to me, but maybe not to you. So it looks like we can't say which things have the property of tasting good.

But we can say which things taste good to me. That's a way of grouping actual and possible particulars. So one thing we can say here is that the expression "tastes good" picks out a property only when the implicit relativity is made explicit. There's a similar problem about color (things look different to different people); one response (Jackson and Pargetter 1987) is to relativize colors to perceivers.

Are response-dependent properties causally relevant? That's an important question, but mental properties are not best understood as response-dependent, so this question does not bear on the mental causation problem.

5.4.2 Physical Heterogeneity

Red things are physically extremely heterogeneous (Nassau 1980): tomatoes, the red part of the rainbow, the red highlights on the back of a compact disc, rubies. . . . This fact is often taken to show that there is no property of being red (Hardin 1988). Other philosophers have argued that it shows that colors are collections of physically different properties (Armstrong 1997a).

But there is another way. We can argue that the fact that red things are physically very different shows that colors are simply different properties from the physical properties of things (J. Campbell 1993; Yablo 1995). The fact that some games don't resemble one another in the same way others do only shows that being a game doesn't reduce to one kind of resemblance. It doesn't show that there isn't one property all games have, namely, being games.

The situation with mental properties is very similar to the situation with color; indeed, there are important parallels between discussions of the causal relevance of colors and the causal relevance of mental properties (Watkins 2002).

5.4.3 Vagueness

"Rock," "red," "bald," and "conservative" are all vague expressions. Take sentences of the form "*a* is an *F*," where we put in a name for an object in place of *a* and a predicate in place of *F*. When the predicate is vague, some of these sentences will be definitely true, some definitely false, and about some we won't be sure: If Sam has 319 hairs on his head, is it true that he is bald? Or that he is not bald?

One way to handle vagueness is to say that the meanings of our words are not fully specific (Fine 1975; Lewis 1970, 1979). The meaning of the word "bald" determines that a completely hairy guy is not bald and that a completely hairless guy is bald, but it does not determine whether a guy with 319 hairs on his head is bald. Sometimes there is simply no saying whether Sam is bald or not. We can make decisions about what we want to count as bald, either implicitly or explicitly, but this is using the word with a (slightly) different meaning.

The relation between predicates and properties then looks like this. There is no single sharp-edged property of being bald. Rather, there are lots. Suppose that Yul is a bald guy. This isn't because he has a single property that all and only bald guys have. He has many properties that group him with various groups of hairless and slightly hairy guys. Most of these properties deserve the name "baldness." It's a vague matter, which ones do and which ones don't. What makes the sentence "Yul is a bald guy" true is the fact that he is hairless enough that the meaning of the word "bald" definitely counts him as bald.

5.4.4 The Picture Theory of Language

John Heil has recently articulated a principle that he sees operating in the background of a great deal of analytic philosophy of mind, which he dubs the "Picture Theory" of language:

> (φ): When a predicate applies truly to an object, it does so in virtue of designating a property possessed by that object and by every object to which the predicate truly applies (or would apply).   (HEIL 2003A:26)

Perhaps the predicate "has a mass of one pound" fits principle (ϕ): if it is true of this rock that it has a mass of one pound, then the predicate applies to the rock in virtue of designating a property of the rock that it has and every other one-pound object has, namely, the property of having a mass of one pound. By contrast, Heil urges, the predicate "is red" isn't like that: "It is not easy to think of a property that (*a*) all red things share and (*b*) in virtue of which they satisfy the predicate 'is red'" (27).

Heil is right that principle (ϕ) is false: it's not so that always, when a predicate applies truly to an object, the object has a property shared by all and only things to which the predicate applies truly. Here's an example. One textbook treatment of Descartes's argument that his mind is distinct from his body runs as follows: my body is such that I can doubt it's really there (it is not necessarily indubitable by me); my mind is such that I cannot doubt whether I have it (it is necessarily indubitable by me); therefore my mind has a property that my body lacks (necessary indubitability), and hence they are distinct things. The textbook response is to say that the predicate "is necessarily indubitable" does not designate a property. (See below, chap. 7, sec. 7.5.3, for an argument that the predicate "is fragile" does not express a property that all and only fragile things have.)

Principle (ϕ) is false for some cases, but it may well be true for others. It may be that there is a property of being bald, or of being red, or of being a picnic. Yul has many properties each of which deserves the name "bald." Many events have properties that deserve the name "beginning of a picnic," even if it is vague exactly which ones do. Red things don't, perhaps, share any interesting physical property. But they might share some uninteresting physical property. They may even simply share the interesting, and nonphysical, property of being red.

5.4.5 Metaphysics and Semantics

I suggested in section 5.1 that properties are distinguishers. This is a claim about what there is and about how things are the same and different. It is a metaphysical claim. It is not a claim about language. In particular, I have not suggested that properties should be meanings or what are sometimes called "semantic values." There might be interesting relations between properties as distinguishers and properties as meanings. If there are, it is likely that they will have to be quite complex and indirect relations. (For instance, a vague term like "bald" will not have a single property as its meaning.) So the fact that some expression or use of language looks difficult to understand in terms of properties as distinguishers will not by itself cast doubt on my theory of properties. It may indicate that there is some real work to do to figure out the connection. Or it may indicate that properties as distinguishers are just not suitable for semantic purposes (see Brogaard 2007 for an argument that properties are not the semantic values of predicates).

5.5 Mental Properties and Physical Properties

The obscurity of the connection between the language of psychology and psychological properties is, then, no argument that there are no mental properties. So it may be that there are mental properties, and it may be that there are properties other than the physical properties. So we need to ask: are mental properties different from physical properties? Here are three arguments that they are different. (By "different" I mean only nonidentical; this is not the same as entirely distinct. This distinction turns out to be of considerable importance to the argument made in chapters 8 and 9. For discussion, see chap. 6, sec. 6.3, and chap. 8, sec. 8.3.)

Against Eliminativism

Imagine a theory that says, "strictly speaking, there are no mental properties, only physical properties." Well, if that's so, then shouldn't we say that there are no mental things? And hence that we never think anything, feel anything, decide anything (Churchland 1981, 1985)? But that would be absurd. So there are mental properties.

Nonphysical Minds Are Possible

As I argued above, in sec. 5.1.5, two properties are not identical if it is possible for there to be an individual that has one and lacks the other. So in order to argue that one property is different from another, we need to show that it is possible for there to be an individual that has the one and lacks the other. The kind of possibility involved is logical possibility. It will only be impossible for something to have one property and lack the other if it is logically contradictory to suppose that that is so.

There is nothing logically contradictory in supposing that there could be a sentient creature that is not a physical being. If we think of this creature and its mental states as possible particulars, then the various mental properties will be represented by sets that include these possible particulars. Since these possible particulars are not physical, it follows that these sets represent nonphysical properties.

Notice that it is perfectly consistent to say that mental properties are non-physical yet all the actual things that have minds (people, cats, and so forth) are completely physical beings. The property counts as nonphysical because there could have been a nonphysical mind. It still could well be—indeed, I think it is so (chap. 1)—that all the actual things that have the property are completely physical.

Mental Properties Are Not Reducible

If mental properties are not reducible to physical properties, then they are different from them (Kim 2005:34). Functionalism in the philosophy of mind is often taken to entail the irreducibility of mental properties (Block 1980c). Davidson (1970b) argues that anomalous monism entails that psychology is irreducible to physics. Although Davidson himself didn't believe in properties, we may nevertheless use Davidson's considerations as reasons for holding that mental properties are not reducible to physical properties. Finally, consciousness is widely thought to be irreducible to physics (Chalmers 1996), and consciousness is widely thought to be essentially linked up with all mental properties (Searle 1992): hence mental properties must be irreducible to physical properties.

5.6 Conclusion

The mental causation problem is about properties and causation: could one event cause another because it has the mental properties it does? We could try to get out of the problem by denying that there are any properties at all (sec. 5.1.2, above). We could try to get out of the problem by denying that there are any mental properties. But neither of these strategies is plausible. Whether we say properties exist or not, the problem is still there. And there is good reason to think there are mental properties in addition to physical properties.

So we can say, for instance, that each person who is truly described by the expression "believes that Vienna is beautiful" has a mental property picked out by this expression. If such a person is moved by her belief to say, "Vienna is beautiful," her action has physical causes. The mental causation problem, then, is this: how can her belief cause her speech act because it has this mental property? Shouldn't we, rather, say that the mental event causes the action because it has its physical properties—that all causation happens in virtue of the physical properties of events? To answer this question, we need a theory of causal relevance. Let us turn, then, to causation, and how it is related to properties and laws of nature, and then to causal relevance.

5.7 Further Reading

David Armstrong's *Universals: An Opinionated Introduction* (1989) and his *Universals and Scientific Realism* (1978a, 1978b) are the best places to start reading about properties. Mellor and Oliver's *Properties* (1997) collects important recent articles on properties, with particular attention to the issue of the distinction between "genuine" and "miscellaneous" groupings. Oliver's "Metaphysics of Properties" (1996) is a comprehensive review article on recent work on properties.

Sydney Shoemaker presents the view that properties of concrete particulars are sets of causal powers in his "Causality and Properties" (1984) and "Causal and Metaphysical Necessity" (1998a). David Lewis argues for sparse natural universals among abundant properties in "New Work for a Theory of Universals" (1983a) and *On the Plurality of Worlds* (1986).

Timothy Williamson's *Vagueness* (1994) is a magisterial and canonical work on vagueness, and Keefe and Smith's *Vagueness: A Reader* (1997) is a good collection of articles.

John Heil's *From an Ontological Point of View* (2003a) makes the case that the mental causation problem as I am conceiving it here cannot be solved; what we need instead is an ontology of powers that makes no distinction of levels between physical and other kinds of powers. The true things that we say about our thought and what it causes are made true by the action of the powers.

6

Causation and Properties

When we try to pick out anything by itself, we find it hitched to everything else in the Universe.

— JOHN MUIR, *MY FIRST SUMMER IN THE SIERRA* (1911:110)

WHAT ARE we saying when we say that one event causes another "because it has" or "in virtue of" its physical properties? In this chapter I'll discuss what makes one property causally relevant to another and hence the sort of property in virtue of which one event may cause another. First I establish a link between causation and laws of nature: whenever one particular event, c, causes another particular event, e, c and e have properties C and E, and a law of nature connects those properties. I'll call this the "cause-law" thesis (Davidson 1995). Then I say that causally relevant properties are those properties of a cause that are connected by a law of nature to properties of the effect. Finally: one event causes another because it has or in virtue of certain causally relevant properties.

So here's the plan. First I set out the cause-law thesis in detail. Next I argue that the thesis is not trivial: I argue against the claim that just about any two events are connected by a law of nature. Then I take up Anscombe's famous argument (1971) that the cause-law thesis is just false. Anscombe is right that the cause-law thesis is not a logical truth. But we need its truth for a coherent picture of how the world works.

Given the cause-law thesis, one property is causally relevant to another if a law of nature connects them. This shall be the gold standard for causal relevance. If mental properties are to be causally relevant to anything, they have to be connected by laws of nature, just as laws of nature connect physical properties. Chapter 9 shows that laws of nature can connect mental properties and other properties.

6.1 What Is Causation?

6.1.1 Events

There is a rock on my desk, a piece of obsidian, black, shiny, glassy on one side, brown and opaque on the other. I found the rock at Panum Crater, near Mono Lake in California.

Causation is a matter of one thing making another thing happen. Water freezing and expanding in the tiny fissures in the rock face caused the rock to crack. My rock fell. It lay on the ground, absorbing sunlight, affecting the overall pattern of radiation reflected from that area. (That is what caused me to notice it.) As it warmed and cooled it changed slightly in size, dislodging sand now and again.

The rock causes different things at different times of its existence. What it causes at a moment depends on two things: the way it is at that moment and what it is related to at that moment. It cannot move a grain of sand if it is not itself moving; it cannot move a grain of sand if the grain is five miles away. If it were always and everywhere unchanged and unchanging, it would not cause anything.

Causation by concrete particulars (like my rock) requires change. An event is a change in what properties some object has. At one moment the object has (or lacks) a certain property, at the next it lacks (or gains) that property.

There are lots of events. Look at a field of wheat. Each particular stalk is moving at every moment; as it does, it flexes and extends, and its flexing and extending consists of huge numbers of tiny adjustments to the cellulose structure of the stalk. There are small events: one stalk bending. There are large events: the eruption of Mount St. Helens. There are very brief very small events: a single grain of sand tipping to one side. There are very long very big events that involve a lot of particular individuals: the Peloponnesian War.

Events are particulars. Like particulars, events have places and durations and have many properties. This is what is usually called a coarse-grained conception of events. There are other conceptions of events, but the differences won't matter for what I will say about the mental causation problem (J. Bennett 1988).

6.1.2 Necessary and Sufficient Conditions?

There is a long tradition of thinking of causes as being in some sense sufficient and/or necessary conditions. Water froze one winter in a tiny fissure
behind my rock. The water expanded enough to open the fissure the rest of
the way—so it was sufficient (in some sense) for the rock to break. It was, in
some sense, necessary, since my rock would not have separated from the
rock face if the water had not frozen or had not been there. But there are
compelling reasons to think that causes are neither sufficient conditions nor
necessary conditions. (Indeed, it is not even clear that it is coherent to say
that causes are necessary or sufficient conditions; see particularly Kim 1971
commenting on Mackie 1965, and Davidson 1967.)

The water freezing clearly wasn't necessary for my rock to separate from
the rock face. My rock might have been struck by another rock or pawed by
a bear.

Physical indeterminacy is one reason why causes aren't sufficient for their
effects. The following example is drawn from Anscombe (1971:101–102) who
gets it from Richard Feynman; for a fuller version of the argument, see Dowe
(2000:22–26). Radioactive lead, Pb^{210} has a half-life of about 7×10^8 seconds
(about twenty-two years). Take Pablo, a particular atom of Pb^{210}. Pablo may
never decay or it may decay in the next minute, but the probability of Pablo
decaying in the next twenty-two years is one in two. Suppose I set Pablo next
to a Geiger counter able to detect the decay, should it happen, and rig up the
Geiger counter to a bomb. Pablo's presence is not sufficient for the bomb to
go off, since Pablo may never decay. Nevertheless, should the bomb go off,
Pablo's presence in the room does cause the explosion.

6.1.3 The "Total Cause"

But there is a much simpler reason why causes aren't sufficient for their
effects. Water freezing in the cracks wasn't sufficient to cause my rock to
separate from the rock face, in the sense of guaranteeing that it would happen, making it impossible for the rock not to separate. If a tree had pressed
just so against the rock face, my rock would have stayed in place. The golfer's
swing caused the ball to fly onto the green. But clearly all kinds of things
could have interfered with the ball's flight.

Bertrand Russell generalized this argument from interference. There are,
he pointed out, no infinitesimal time intervals. That means that no matter
how close in time a cause occurs to its effect, there is still some time between
them. Hence "something may happen during this interval which prevents the

expected event" (Russell 1912–1913:181). Imagine mischievous Martians who, from their spaceship orbiting Earth, are able—say, using laser beams—to vaporize a tiny amount of the water as it freezes, just enough to keep the pressure on the rock low enough that it doesn't crack.

We can block Russell's argument if there is a way to eliminate the possibility of interference. We need to ensure somehow that things in the neighborhood of my rock stay as they are while the water freezes. That requires ensuring that there aren't playful Martians or anything else to disturb the stability of the neighborhood. So what is strictly sufficient for the rock to break off is (a) the water freezing, (b) together with enough of the rest of the world to ensure the stability of its neighborhood—that is, enough to rule out any possible interference.

How much of the rest of the world is that? Well, according to our best understanding of the world, nothing can travel faster than the speed of light in a vacuum, C, about 300 million meters per second. Suppose it takes an entire second for the water to freeze and then crack the rock. In principle, anyway, the Martians' laser light could reach this event from anywhere in a sphere about 300 million meters in radius with the rock as its center. So to guarantee how things are around the rock for that second, things have to be certain ways in that enormous sphere—for instance, they have to exclude mischievous Martians.

If the Martians have more time, they can set up camp farther away from the rock. If they have ten seconds, they can be 3 billion meters away; if they

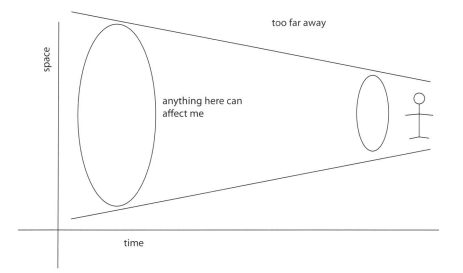

have a year, they can be as much as one light-year away. If we think of plotting this ever-expanding sequence of spheres in two dimensions, we get a cone, with the sharp end located at the rock. This is called the "light cone" for an event: relative to an interval of time, the volume of space within which an event can affect things at a point in space at the end of the interval.

What is sufficient for the rock to crack, then, is the "total cause." John Stuart Mill (1973:332, 3.5.3) calls this the "cause, philosophically speaking"; it is "the sum total of the conditions positive and negative taken together . . . which being realized, the consequent inevitably follows." The cause—the water freezing—is only part of the total cause. The total cause is the entire array of objects and their properties and relations in the time and space leading up to the water freezing, such that given that array nothing else could have happened.

So Russell was wrong: given some interval of time, and assuming that you can, godlike, fix exactly how things are in enough of the universe, you can guarantee that nothing can interfere. That completely specific and particularized array of instances of properties across an entire slice of the light cone is strictly sufficient for the effect. (Provided, that is, that how the world works in this case is deterministic; as the last section mentions, it's often true that physical causes only make certain ranges of effects probable. Even if the effect is only made probable, though, if we fix enough of the universe, nothing will be able to interfere with or alter that effect.) That total array is not necessary for the effect, since there are very many minutely different (and very many quite different) total arrays that would also be sufficient for the effect.

6.1.4 Two Problems

Now, this doesn't seem much like causation any more. When I open a can with a can opener, the cause is me, wielding the can opener. We do not ever—indeed, cannot ever—manage to talk about one of these "causes, philosophically speaking." We do not seek out such philosophical causes in ordinary life, and when the sciences seek causes (for instance, when medical researchers look for the cause of AIDS), they do not look for "causes, philosophically speaking."

Moreover, this picture of how causation works seems to entail that any two events, one in the light cone for the other, are connected by laws, not just the causes and effects (Latham 1987). For example, take any two events where the first is in the light cone for the second and it seems clear that it is not a cause of the second—maybe an otter in the Pacific Ocean off Big Sur, hundreds of miles away, cracked open an oyster a week or so before my rock fell. Then there is an exhaustive specification of a section of the light cone that includes the otter cracking open the oyster and is strictly sufficient for my rock to fall.

Hence it seems, given any two events, the first prior to the second but not outside the light cone for the second, there is a law connecting them.

So, two problems. To solve the second, we need to look at laws of nature. I'll do this in the next two sections and return to the first problem in section 6.1.7.

6.1.5 Laws of Nature

"Causes, philosophically speaking" appear to have one further vice. Causes ought to be reproducible: if water freezing in a fissure caused my rock to break off, then water freezing in fissures ought to be able to do this again. But a "cause, philosophically speaking," that is, a slice of the light cone, is virtually guaranteed to be unreproducible.

In fact, the reproducibility or generality of causes hasn't been eliminated from the story; instead, it has just been kicked downstairs to the level of the fundamental laws of nature. John Stuart Mill thought of the whole of nature as a kind of tapestry woven from separate, tiny strands of connection made by laws of nature (1973:315, 3.4.1):

> In the contemplation of that uniformity in the course of nature, which is assumed in every inference from experience, one of the first observations that present themselves is, that the uniformity in question is not properly uniformity, but uniformities. The general regularity results from the coexistence of partial regularities. The course of nature in general is constant, because the course of each of the various phenomena that compose it is so. A certain fact invariably occurs whenever circumstances are present, and does not occur when they are absent; the like is true of another fact; and so on. From these separate threads of connexion between parts of the great whole which we term nature, a general tissue of connexion unavoidably weaves itself, by which the whole is held together. If A is always accompanied by D, B by E, and C by F, it follows that A B is accompanied by D E, A C by D F, B C by E F, and finally A B C by D E F; thus the general character of regularity is produced, which, along with and in the midst of infinite diversity, pervades all nature.
>
> The first point, therefore, to be noted in regard to what is called the uniformity of the course of nature, is, that it is itself a complex fact, compounded of all the separate uniformities which exist in respect to single phenomena. These various uniformities, when ascertained by what is regarded as a sufficient induction, we call in common parlance, Laws of Nature. Scientifically speaking, that title is employed in a more restricted sense, to designate the uniformities when reduced to their most simple expression. Thus in the illustration already employed, there were seven uniformities; all of which, if considered sufficiently certain, would, in the more lax application of the term,

be called laws of nature. But of the seven, three alone are properly distinct and independent: these being pre-supposed, the others follow of course. The three first, therefore, according to the stricter acceptation, are called laws of nature; the remainder not; because they are in truth mere cases of the three first; virtually included in them; said, therefore, to *result* from them: whoever affirms those three has already affirmed all the rest.

We could view these separate strands as aspects of a single underlying super-law, but for our purposes it will turn out to be important to be able to refer to them separately. Each of the component laws relates fundamental properties, and the combination of all the tiniest parts of the world that have the fundamental properties following the component laws makes up the world as we see it.

Let us say that Mill is describing the motor of the world. I model this expression on Boethius's expression *mundana machina*, "the world machine" (*De Consolatio Philosophiae* 3p12.14); I intend the expression to be neutral on the question of how, or whether, one state of the machine makes the next occur, that is, on the dispute concerning what Hume called "necessary connexion" (see below, sec. 6.3). The idea that the unfolding of the world is like a text written in an alphabet of being goes back to Lucretius and Democritus.

Mill's account of the motor of the world goes like this: throughout space there is a distribution of things. These things have certain special properties: their physical properties. Their physical properties determine, in accord with the laws of nature, what happens next. It is as if the laws say: "if things are a certain way at a given time and place, then they will be thus-and-so a moment later." Some of these lawful relations are probabilistic: a law might say that given an instance of one property, the chance of getting an instance of another is such-and-such. Some are deterministic: given an instance of one property, it is guaranteed that there will be an instance of another.

Different philosophers tell the story of the motor of the world in different ways. Some say the instances of properties are governed by laws. Some say the laws are sentences that report the patterns of the instances of the properties. Some say that things have dispositions that (in the company of other dispositions) necessitate further instances of dispositions (so laws depend on dispositions, rather than the other way around). It does not matter which way we tell the story. It does matter (sec. 6.3, below) what we say about the relation between physical properties and mental properties and how they connect to the motor of the world; this will be key to solving the mental causation problem in chapter 9.

Properties always work collectively. When my rock broke off the rock face, there was water there, at a particular temperature. The laws of electrostatics and thermodynamics determine that liquid water at that pressure and tem-

perature will crystallize and in so doing increase in volume. The pressure on
the water is explained by the properties of the rock and further laws. All the
endlessly many instances of properties present at that time and place work
together to yield the effect: frozen water.

Mill's picture of the tapestry of the laws only has the laws working together
additively ("A B is accompanied by D E"). Most interactions are not like that,
though. Instances of two properties may interact to produce an effect quite
unlike anything they do otherwise. For instance, the Millikan oil-drop experi-
ment involved exactly balancing the force of gravity and an electromagnetic
force on a tiny drop of oil so that it was suspended motionless (Hempel 1966:
24–25).

The result of all these properties interacting according to the laws is the
world we see: the world of enduring physical objects, some quite stable, others quite changeable. The day my rock broke off the wind was blowing; the
wind moved the grass, stirred up waves in Mono Lake, ruffled the fur of a
fox. Over the short run, the rocks of Panum Crater don't change much. Rock
is pretty stable: the property interactions going on in rocks tend to keep the
rocks together.

6.1.6 Producing and Standing By

John Muir wrote, "When we try to pick out anything by itself, we find it
hitched to everything else in the Universe" (1911:110). The idea of the total
cause and the light cone seems to show that things are connected even more
than Muir had thought: for instance, everything happening at the star Alpha
Centauri five years ago is affecting everything going on here and now. Why?
Because by definition anything in the light cone for an event around here
could potentially affect it. (It takes light about four years to get from Alpha
Centauri to here.)

But this doesn't seem right. Lots of things go on around here that aren't influenced at all by what is going on at Alpha Centauri. Indeed, lots of what is
happening near me right now doesn't affect what is going on around you right
now. How can we fit this idea into the framework of Mill's tapestry of laws of
nature?

We need to make a distinction between producing and standing by. We
can see Alpha Centauri, and so its light does indeed affect how things are
around here. It positively produces changes, for instance, in my eyes. Given
the right conditions, bits of dust near Alpha Centauri could affect how things
are around here. But those conditions aren't set up. So the dust has no effect
on us at all. The dust is standing by, holding a place from which we could be
affected—but aren't.

Suppose I am looking up at the night sky at Alpha Centauri. At one moment a single photon from Alpha Centauri arrives at a single molecule of rhodopsin in my retina and switches that molecule from the 11-cis to the 11-trans form. (This is the first step in all detection of light by visual pigments in the eye.)

Several things together positively produce this change: the arrival of the photon, the temperature in my retina, the matrix of the cone cell that holds this molecule of rhodopsin, and many others.

Let's call this collection of property instances a "positive producer."

Meanwhile, lots and lots of things aren't positively producing this change. You were at your house, turning the dial on your radio. Things there could have affected what happened at my retina. Mischievous Martians could have interfered from your house. But they didn't. Nothing happening at your house is making any difference to what is happening in my retina. Hence nothing where you are is a positive producer of this change. Events at your house are standing by relative to what is going on in my retina.

To get a condition that is fully strictly sufficient for this change, we need to specify how the light cone is at every point, so as to rule out interferers. But only some of the light cone positively produces the change. So the configuration of property instances that actually produces the change at my retina is like a Swiss cheese slice of the light cone: cheese where it matters to the effect, holes where what in fact is there makes no difference to the effect. (Although what is in one of these "holes" does not in fact make any difference to the effect—for instance: your turning the radio dial makes no difference to my seeing Alpha Centauri—what is actually there is important to the effect in the sense that had something else been there, it might well have influenced the effect.)

So the positive producer is a spatially structured array of property instances. It occurs a moment before an event. Given the laws of nature, if instances of these properties are present, and nothing interferes, then an effect of this type will happen. (Or: if the transition in this case is indeterminate, there is some definite probability that it will happen.)

Positive producers are spatially structured arrays of property instances. Each component property instance itself had a positive producer. That means there is a two-step causal thread extending from each part of that positive producer to the change in my retina.

In general, then, let a causal thread be any such sequence, of however many steps, of instances of properties that together positively produce effects. Let us say that when there is a causal thread between two property instances, then the earlier causally influences the later.

Clearly the number of causal threads eventuating in this tiny change in my retina is enormous. (The most salient is the thread constituting the path of the photon from Alpha Centauri to my eye.) As we look back in time before the event, there is an ever-growing web of causal threads. But equally there is an enormous number of property instances that are not connected to this change in my retina by any causal thread. Your turning the radio dial has no causal influence on this change in my retina.

Think of the otter cracking its oyster at Big Sur a week before my rock fell to the ground. There was a sound. Sound travels a lot faster than otters do. But as it travels it gets softer and softer, since it takes energy to compress air to make sound. Cracking the oyster shell didn't move the air with all that much energy. So even though the otter's cracking the shell is in the light cone for the event of my rock breaking off the rock face, its sound has no effect on the rock. The causal thread initiated by the crack of the shell causing compression waves in the air peters out. It makes changes up to the point where the compression wave no longer has enough energy to make any further change, and then that causal thread just stops. It could have caused changes that affected things at my rock—but it didn't.

The reach of most causal threads is much less than that of a sound. There are electrostatic forces holding together the glassy structure of the rock. These don't extend very far beyond the molecules in which they originate. So how things are at one point in the rock doesn't affect how things are in the rock even fairly close by.

Muir was right that the otter is hitched to my rock. The water that cracked my rock may well have been rainfall from moisture that came from the Pacific Ocean, and indeed the very molecules of water that froze and broke the seam in the rock may have passed through that otter. That is: there are connections, many more than we might have thought. But that doesn't mean that everything is connected with every other thing in every possible way.

6.1.7 Solving the Two Problems

Back to the two objections to the idea that when one event causes another, the first event is part of a light-cone-wide array of property instances that is strictly sufficient for the second event. The objections were that these things don't look like ordinary causes and, trivially, laws connect any two events, as long as one is in the light cone for the other.

I've just described how to respond to the second problem. Even though everything in the light cone for an event could interfere, only parts of the light cone positively produce the event (the rest are standing by). Stringing positive producers together yields causal threads. Laws only connect those property instances connected by causal threads. Others property instances are—relative to a given actually occurring event—only bystanders.

What about the first problem? Mill leads us along a path from ordinary causes, to what he calls the "cause, philosophically speaking" (the total cause, whatever is in fact strictly sufficient for the effect), and then finally to the image of the "tissue of connexion" made from the threads of the laws of nature. Many authors have argued that causation has nothing to do with laws of nature at all. In the next section, I will tackle the most radical version of this claim (Anscombe 1971). Whether or not that version is true, it still seems extraordinarily unlikely that laws have much of anything to do with causes. When I bake bread, I want to know what to do in order to make good bread; I don't care about laws of nature. When scientists try to figure out why bees are dying, they want to know what is causing the bees to die and what we can do about it; they don't care about laws of nature.

There are two kinds of intertwined issues at work here. One concerns the level at which inquiry takes place. Mill's picture of the "tissue of connexion" is a picture of nature at its most fundamental level: the level of fundamental physics. Only inquiry in fundamental physics aims at describing that level. Bread baking happens at a different level. Professional bakers use quantitative regularities to guide what they do. But they are regularities about things like flour and water and bread. "Flour," though, is not a precise concept. Although bakers do have quantitative measures of various kinds of flour (bread flour is typically 12–13 percent gluten, as opposed to all-purpose flour, which is 11–12 percent), results depend as well on where the flour was grown, what exactly is in the water, changes in the ambient temperature and air pressure, and so forth. Sometimes the bread comes out great, sometimes not so good. It's unlikely that bread science can get much more precise than that, given that its concepts are fitted to the life of the baker, not the physical scientist.

It is perfectly all right to talk about causes and effects and baking. And there are no perfectly strict laws of baking. The problem is essentially exactly the same as the problem of mental causation: there appears to be a good argument that what makes bread successful is microphysical processes, not items at the level of the concept of bread. Hence settling this problem fully will have to wait until chapter 9.

The second intertwined issue is one of selection. Mill's picture of the "tissue of connexion" says that flour makes things happen only together with the rest of a "cause, philosophically speaking," that is, along with the entirety of the positive producer for the effect. The question then is, why do we say it is the flour rather than all the other things in that positive producer that makes the bread successful? Let's call this "the selection problem": what justifies us in saying that one thing (rather than any of the other parts, or the totality, of the positive producer) is the cause?

Selection is an issue both when we are working at the level of ordinary things and when we are working at the fundamental level. The cause of a particular detector trace from a high-energy collider might be an ion from the beam that was sent through the machine. But that ion only caused the trace in tandem with the rest of the total cause. Why do we say the ion was the cause, rather than, say, one of the magnets that controls the ion beam?

The answer is very often very natural and very obvious. A driver swerves and injures a pedestrian. We would normally, and confidently, say that the cause of the accident was the driver's swerve. We would not normally say that the cause was the presence of the pedestrian. But we might. If the pedestrian shouldn't have been there (for instance, on a high-speed road) and if the driver swerved to avoid an obstacle, we might say the cause was the presence of the pedestrian. Apparently something in the situation makes us confidently give one kind of answer in one situation and another in a different situation. Hence there must be some sorts of principles constraining our choices, and the selection problem is to uncover and articulate what these principles are and how they operate.

Part of what goes into the principles underlying our selection is what we already know, and what we are seeking to discover, and what our purposes are. So there seems to be an element involved in this selection that is not fully objective, since our interests and purposes seem to enter into the selection. Suppose we pick out the cause against a background of things we consider stable (for instance: that there was a road for the speeding automobile to drive on). Call these stable background conditions a "field." John Mackie, following John Anderson, writes, "What is said to be caused, then, is not just an event, but an event-in-a-certain-field, and some 'conditions' can be set aside as not causing this-event-in-this-field simply because they are part of the chosen field, though if a different field were chosen, in other words if a different causal question were being asked, one of those conditions might well be said to cause this-event-in-that-other-field" (Mackie 1974:35; see also 1965:39–42). Mackie's idea allows what counts as a cause to vary with the choice of field.

We cannot count just any part of what happens before an event as the field against which to evaluate the cause. As section 6.1.6 demonstrates, some parts of slices of the light cone for an event don't actually make any difference to it. Only what I called the "positive producer" for the event has causal influence over it. I suggest therefore that Mackie's proposal about different fields should be superimposed only on the parts of the light cone that do have causal influence over the event. That is: a choice of field is a choice to ignore certain parts of the totality of what has causal influence over the event.

That narrows down the range of choice a bit, and in a fully objective way, but it leaves a lot of room for decision. Still, the choice is not arbitrary and perniciously subjective: there are stable principles by which we discover and select causes from the total field of causal influences on an effect.

Hence when we say that one thing causes another, there are two quite different kinds of factors that justify what we say: one is the totality of causal influences on the effect, its positive producers; the other is the principles by which we select out some part of that totality and count that part as *the* cause.

So for a complete solution to the first problem about causation (Mill's total causes don't look like what we ordinarily call causes) two things are needed. One is the subject of this book: how is higher-level causal relevance possible—how is it possible for one event to cause another, both in virtue of the fundamental physical properties it has and in virtue of certain of its higher-level properties, properties such as being flour or being a sensation of warmth? The other—not dealt with in this book—is a satisfactory solution to the selection problem: assuming that when one thing causes another, there is a law of nature linking a positive producer to that effect, what justifies us in saying that only one part of it is the cause?

6.2 Anscombe's Challenge

So far, I have proposed the cause-law thesis as a way to explain how causes could be sufficient for their effects and as an explanation of the motor of the world. I've also argued that the thesis is not trivial and that it has the resources to explain the relation between causation and laws of nature. In this section I'll give a positive argument for the thesis and reply to the most fundamental challenge to its truth.

6.2.1 An Argument for the Cause-Law Thesis

Smoking causes lung cancer, but not for everyone who smokes, and not everyone who gets lung cancer smokes. Just about every general causal claim we make has exceptions. Why are there exceptions? The answer to that question takes us down a level (or down through a series of levels). We don't actually know the full details of the answer for the case of smoking and cancer, but the outlines of the answer look like this: the mechanisms that produce lung cancer in smokers aren't always present or don't always operate, and that's what accounts for those lucky smokers. Those mechanisms, or perhaps different ones, produce lung cancer in the nonsmokers; there is some physiological (or environmental) difference between nonsmokers who get lung cancer and those who do not. Now, these mechanisms are complex systems, and so their operation has exceptions also. (It is remarkable how reliably computers work—so reliably that it is easy to read computer code as a proof that certain things have happened inside the computer. But if you warm a computer up just a little too much, it starts to act erratically.) So what explains these exceptions? Once again, we descend to lower levels. Our explanation for how the mechanism works takes into account its parts and their properties and the regularities that connect these to the behavior of the mechanism. When these regularities have exceptions, we need to look lower down (for instance, to material properties of the parts) to explain the exceptions.

The argument for the cause-law thesis, then, is that this process of explaining the exceptions ends at the fundamental level. That is where things happen without exceptions, or, if there are exceptions, there is a fundamental explanation for why they occur, as there is, for instance, for quantum indeterminacy.

What if there are inexplicable exceptions at the fundamental level? Then the world would behave in a reliable way (or reliably indeterministically) at the fundamental level for the most part. But sometimes it would just not work that way.

I don't know of any conclusive argument that shows that the world doesn't work this way at the fundamental level. But it seems intolerably peculiar to think that it might be that way. The idea is that there can be inexplicable exceptions. But if there are any inexplicable exceptions, it seems reasonable to ask why there are not more: for instance, why do things hang together so well as we go up from the fundamental level? Water keeps on acting like water. But if hydrogen and oxygen might sometimes just not act the way they usually do, why doesn't water sometimes act differently—like the computer that malfunctions when it is too warm, except for no reason whatsover?

6.2.2 Anscombe's Argument

Anscombe famously challenged the idea "that a singular causal statement implies *that there is* . . . a true universal proposition" (1971:104). I'm going to assume that by "true universal proposition" Anscombe means a law of nature. I noted part of her argument in section 6.1.7, above: we do not look for, and we do not find, anything like laws of nature when we look for causes (except perhaps in the special case of fundamental physics). I have no quarrel with that part of the argument, except that I do not believe it entails that the cause-law thesis is false. Here I want to consider whether we can accept the idea that (sometimes, anyway) causes produce their effects, but they aren't connected in any way by laws of nature.

It is not contradictory to suppose that the cause-law thesis is false. There are two ways for it to be false. First, there might be no linkage between causes and laws at all. Causation might be a relation that holds between certain particular individual events, but there is no need for events that stand in that relation to be related by law in any way. Causation would be singular, as philosophers have termed it. In its purest form, the singularist account of causation says that the fact that one event causes another event is ontologically fundamental. It has no analysis; it is not composed of other things; it does not depend on any other facts. Hence, in its purest form, the singularist account of causation says that it is simply misguided to ask in virtue of which of its properties did *c* cause *e*. (Hence the question that generates the mental causation problem—"how can thinking make things happen in virtue of its mental properties?"—would be misguided.)

Second, a more limited version of the cause-law thesis might be true: whenever one event causes another, a law of some sort links the two. It might, for instance, be a mental-physical law. But the law does not need to be a law of nature.

So denying the cause-law thesis is not contradictory. But, I shall argue, neither of the ways it could be false yields a coherent account of how causation actually works. Hence, I conclude, the cause-law thesis is true.

6.2.3 Singular Causation

Consider first singular causation. The claim is that one event can cause another and there is no law of any kind linking the first event to the second. We must ask: what is causation supposed to be, if it is not related to regularity? There is a change; there is another change; the first causes the second. We cannot say: because there is a law connecting properties of the first with properties of the second. We cannot say: there is such a law. If there is no connection, other than the brute, primitive fact of causation, then why is it causation, and not just two events? If it is replied, because the cause made the effect happen (that is a brute, particular fact about the cause), we should ask, and what fact is that?

In section 6.1.6, I distinguished between causal influences on an effect (anything connected by a chain of positive producers with a property of the effect) and things that are not causal influences. If causation were ever singular, in the purest form, then this distinction would collapse. It would be possible for there to be two events, neither of which causally influences an effect (in the sense defined above), yet one of which causes it while the other does not. As I've argued, this is not absurd, in the sense of being logically contradictory. But, I submit, it is false: neither of these events causes the effect, because neither of them is able, by way of its fundamental properties, to make any difference to the effect.

6.2.4 Causation Involves Laws Other than Natural Laws

Consider, next, the idea that causation involves laws, but not necessarily laws of nature. So for mental causation, the idea would look like this: People have various mental properties. There are regular connections between these mental properties and nonmental properties, so that given the same circumstances and the same mental properties, the same kind of effect will ensue. The laws of nature for the most part govern how all the nonmental things operate. But they don't govern how mental things operate, and they don't govern what happens to nonmental systems when minds interact with them. Instead, the effects of things that have mental properties are determined by the mental properties, not the physical ones (or perhaps they work together; in any case, the effects of the physical property differ from what the laws of nature specify). For example: my belief that Vienna is beautiful has various physical properties. On some particular occasion, the laws of nature governing those properties dictate that I do not say, "Vienna is beautiful!" But my belief has mental properties (for instance, the property of being about Vienna). And because of these mental properties I do in fact say, "Vienna is beautiful!"

Call this "sui generis mental causation." Here is a dilemma for sui generis mental causation: either mental properties are physical properties, or they are not. Either way we go, the consequence is unacceptable. Hence we must reject sui generis mental causation.

Mental properties are not physical properties; I argued that in chapter 5, section 5.5, above. But denying the cause-law thesis, while also denying singular causation, directly implies that mental properties are physical properties. When nothing mental is involved, things happen in virtue of the physical properties of causes. But when causes have mental properties, the mental properties can trump the physical ones: what happens is determined by the mental property, and what happens is different from what the physical property would have caused. But now the linkage between instances of mental properties and nonmental properties is a fundamental fact about how the motor of the world works. But that just means that these linkages are fundamental natural laws. Hence mental properties turn out to be physical properties after all, since they are part of the basic motor of the world.

If we insist that mental properties, in this picture, are not physical properties, then sui generis mental causation violates the principle of "the closure of the physical." (Kim states the principle this way: "if a physical event has a cause that occurs at t, it has a physical cause that occurs at t" [2005:43.]) This principle is an essential part of materialism (see below, chap. 8, sec, 8.1.2, for why we cannot deny it). But if sui generis mental causing actually happens, then the effect has a cause, but not a physical cause, and so mental causing would violate closure.

6.2.5 How Anscombe Is Right

So we have good reason to accept the cause-law thesis. The thesis makes a very general metaphysical claim about causes. It does not make any claim about how we think about causes or about how we discover or describe them. Endorsing the thesis is perfectly consistent with denying that we talk about laws of nature when we talk about causes in ordinary life. Endorsing the thesis is perfectly consistent with denying that scientists seek laws of nature when they try to find the causes of things. The cause-law thesis only says that if, for example, a group of scientists finds the cause of AIDS, then in each case of AIDS, there will be a law of nature of the sort described above, connecting the cause with that case. So Anscombe is right that our concepts of causation are not connected with universal propositions. But I don't think she is right that denying that causation involves universal propositions is consistent with materialism (as described in chap. 1, sec. 1.2, above).

6.3 "Only One Thing Does the Causing"

6.3.1 A Damaging Pattern of Reasoning

The cause-law thesis is what makes the mental causation problem hard. I've argued that when one thing causes another (for example: my choice causes me to reach for the ice cream), the cause has fundamental physical properties that are linked by fundamental physical laws to properties of the effect. But then it looks like the fundamental properties are doing all the work. There's no room for any nonfundamental causation.

There is a very general and very damaging pattern of reasoning working here. It goes like this: When one thing causes another, there is something about the cause that makes the effect happen—a power, or a property, or a disposition, or the like. It is not more than one something that does this, since there is only one effect and one cause. Hence for every cause-and-effect pair, the cause has a special sort of something that makes the effect happen. Now, since the world is a physical place, these somethings are physical. Hence if a mental event causes a physical event, it must do so because of one of these somethings. And that something must be a physical thing. If the mental event caused the physical event in virtue of having a mental property, then there would be a second something doing the causing. And that would be too many things.

6.3.2 Who Reasons This Way?

The short answer is: everyone. This pattern of reasoning is easily developed both within a Humean conception of causation and in a variety of non-Humean conceptions.

Humean Accounts of Causation

David Hume's profoundly influential discussion of causes (1978:1.3) begins with an argument against causation as "necessary connexion." We think we have the idea that causes necessitate their effects (make it necessary that they happen). But all that we experience, he says, is one thing after another: there is no basis in experience (no "impression") for the idea of "necessary connexion." Hence, he argues, the idea is empty and meaningless. We do not have the idea of causes. In truth, there really is no such thing as causation.

Strictly speaking, then, Hume says there is no causation. So there is no mental causation, and so there can't be a mental causation problem, either. But Hume certainly writes as though he believes in mental causation; for just one instance: "On the other hand we find, that any impression either of the mind or body is constantly followed by an idea, which resembles it, and is only different in the degrees of force and liveliness, The constant conjunction of our resembling perceptions, is a convincing proof, that the one are the causes of the other; and this priority of the impressions is an equal proof, that our impressions are the causes of our ideas, not our ideas, of our impressions" (1978:1.1.1). So rather than eliminate the category of causation from our metaphysics, we might instead reductively define causation (and related concepts, like that of a law of nature) in terms of constant conjunction (just one thing happening after another). Hume himself may have thought about causation this way; such a position is called a Humean conception of causation.

Mill is Humean about causation. The damaging pattern of reasoning is easily deployed in Mill's Humean framework, and Mill does deploy it. His account of the laws of nature is that they are the component uniformities that make up the uniformities in nature that we actually observe. A uniformity is simply a Humean pattern of constant conjunction. Of the component uniformities, Mill writes that they "according to the stricter acceptation, are called laws of nature; the remainder not" (1973:315, 3.4.1). Hence some uniformities express real causal connection, and others are merely derivative or parasitic: second-class causation.

It is often remarked that a Humean about causation has no difficulty explaining mental causation, since causation is simply a matter of regular succession, and certainly there is regular succession, for instance, of actions upon tryings. But since Humeans make a crucial distinction between fundamental and nonfundamental regularities (and hence causation), this is a mistake.

Non-Humean Causation

Humean accounts of laws and causation are thought to have a multitude of vices (see (Ellis 2001) for a recent catalog). Perhaps the most salient is the thought that a Humean account has no resources to explain how one thing makes another happen: there's no necessitation, just one thing after another; there's no oomph. So in one way or another, non-Humeans add in something to causation and natural law to get the necessitation back in. Perhaps when one thing causes another, the first has a disposition that (together with other things) necessarily leads to the effect happening (Ellis 2001). Perhaps when one thing causes another, the first has properties that are connected to properties of the second by a necessitation relation (Dretske 1977; Armstrong 1983). Perhaps when one thing causes another, the first has properties that bestow causal powers to produce, by necessity, certain kinds of effects— again, in the company of other properties and causal powers (Shoemaker 1984).

Consider, for example, Armstrong's account of laws (1983). When a law of nature, say, "All Fs are Gs" is true, Armstrong tells us, the two properties F and G are related by the necessitation universal, N. Science tells us what universals there are and which ones are connected by the necessitation universal. The world comprises all the first-class states of affairs there are, that is, the instantiations of the genuine universals. There are also (Armstrong 1997b:45) second-class states of affairs, instantiations of all the second-class propertylike things of ordinary life: disjunctive "properties," negative "properties," vague "properties" like the property of being a cat or the property of being bald—or the property of believing that Vienna is beautiful. The necessitation universal connects proper, first-class universals, not these other things. Hence if causal relevance goes with being a proper, first-class universal, then Armstrong's theory pretty much directly entails that there are no causally relevant mental properties. Things happen because they are instances of first-class universals, not because they are instances of so-called universals such as believing that Vienna is beautiful.

6.3.3 How Should We Reason?

To resist the damaging pattern of reasoning, it is crucial to assert that if there is a physical something in virtue of which one event causes another, there can be another something in virtue of which that event causes its effect.

Here is how: As I noted in chapter 5, section 5.1.3, above, it is important to keep track of what exactly we are talking about when we use the philosophical vocabulary of "particulars" and "properties" to talk about things. It is easy to think of properties as things and hence to think that two properties that are not identical are therefore wholly distinct. But properties are not things, and we do not have to say this. We may say instead that properties overlap. There are pairs of properties that are not identical (since there is at least one individual that has one of the properties and lacks the other) yet which are not entirely distinct either (since there is at least one individual that has both). (See Sanford 2005 on why distinctness and nonidentity are different in general, not just for the case of properties.) The property of being red overlaps the property of being scarlet, since all scarlet things are red (but not all red things are scarlet).

So the right response to the damaging line of reasoning is to recognize that even though nonfundamental properties are not *identical* to fundamental properties, they are not entirely distinct from them, either. So when we say that causation happens at the fundamental level, we are not saying that therefore there is no such thing as higher-level causation. The inference from nonidentity to distinctness is invalid, since properties may overlap, and hence properties can be both nonidentical and not distinct. This response about properties is available to both the Humean and the non-Humean.

How a Humean Can Respond

David Lewis's conception of laws of nature (following Frank Ramsay and the picture of laws of nature in Mill described above) is a Humean conception. Lewis holds that "a contingent generalization is a *law of nature* if and only if it appears as a theorem (or axiom) in each of the true deductive systems that achieves a best combination of simplicity and strength" (1973:73). A maximally strong theory of the world would be a list of everything that actually happens. A maximally simple theory wouldn't say anything about what actually happens: "whatever is, is." A theory of the world that says what happens in a simple way, by finding generalizations of the sort that Mill sees as threads in the tapestry of nature, is far stronger than "whatever is, is" and far simpler than a list of all the things that actually happen. A best system of the world is a theory that achieves a maximal balance of strength and simplicity. There will be many systems that achieve a best combination of simplicity and strength. A law of nature, then, is a theorem or axiom that appears in any of these systems.

Lewis's conceptions of properties and laws of nature make it a pretty simple matter to explain what overlap is and how higher-level properties can be causally relevant. If properties just are sets, then property overlap is just set inclusion: the property of being scarlet is a proper subset of the property of being red. If laws of nature just are strongest simplest theories of the world, then causal relevance is what a property has when a strongest simplest theory of the world relates it to another property. Higher-level laws are just strongest simplest theories of the world constructed around higher-level properties. (Lewis 1983a discusses the idea of building up different strongest simplest theories around different starting sets of properties.)

In other words, if there is a reductive account of causation and laws of nature, then causation and laws of nature are built up out of something simpler. And it may be true—as it is in the Lewis system—that building causal relevance out of something simpler will permit us to explain readily how causal relevance can occur both at the fundamental level and at higher levels.

How a Non-Humean Can Respond

All accounts of the laws of nature face what van Fraassen calls "the Inference Problem" (1989:38–39). If it is a law, say, that all swans are white, the Inference Problem is to explain how that law implies that all swans are in fact white. The Humean says that the laws just are the facts and so the explanation is simple: the actual facts imply themselves. The non-Humean says that something more is going on than one fact following another and so the explanation is more difficult. We can think of the Inference Problem as describing a relation between Humean and non-Humean theories of laws: both kinds of theories have to imply the very same (actual) facts. Putting it very roughly, then, non-Humean theories should imply the Humean theories. But the converse implication is not true, since the Humean theories (according to the non-Humeans) don't say enough about the actual facts to deliver oomph. Non-Humean theories add something to the Humean account (causal powers, dispositions, a relation on universals, etc.).

Whatever the anti-Humean account adds to the Humean account, a question must be asked: does all of what matters to causation reside at the fundamental level, or can some of it reside elsewhere? The answer is not obvious. Shoemaker, for instance, has a non-Humean account that permits causal relevance at many levels (1998b). One way to develop Armstrong's universals-based account of laws is to say that the only causal necessitation is at the fundamental level, but one could also say that nonfundamental universals are involved in causation as well.

A trope-based account of properties, laws, and causation might say that there is only one level of tropes and only one level of things making other things happen (Robb 1997). But tropes, and the causal relevance of tropes, could overlap. The causal relevance of a mental trope could then be constituted, but only partly so, by the causal relevance of a physical trope. We can then say that two nonidentical tropes that are not entirely distinct, one overlapping the other, can produce an effect.

The crucial point that needs to be articulated is how exactly causal relevance is distributed across the levels. It cannot be additive, since then we'd have all the causation at the fundamental level and then more of it at other levels. Then there really would be more than one thing involved in every instance of higher-level causation, and that really doesn't seem right. One virtue of the Lewisian account sketched above is that it offers a straightforward means to describe the distribution of causal relevance, and in such a way that it is not additive across levels. The causal powers view also has this advantage, since it can say that causal relevance at higher levels is composed of the same elements—the causal powers—that compose it at the fundamental level (Shoemaker 1998b; Clapp 2001). If causal relevance is, by contrast, taken to be a primitive notion, then it has no structure of the sort that would enable us to work out such principles of causal relevance distribution, and then it may seem as though causal relevance could be located only at one level.

In the chapters that follow I will set out an account of causal relevance according to which both fundamental properties and higher-level properties (like mental properties) can be causally relevant. Causal relevance won't be a primitive notion; instead, it will be based on the idea of laws of nature.

6.4 The Gold Standard

"Causal relevance" is a technical expression; it has no standard meaning in ordinary language or scientific or philosophical discussions of causation. So there are a variety of solutions to the mental causation problem corresponding to different conceptions of what causal relevance is, and hence a variety of different standards against which to decide whether one property is causally relevant to another.

We could say that mental events are causally relevant to physical events if mental events cause physical events. That's a pretty low standard for a solution; it is consistent with saying that the mental properties of the event make no difference to what the event causes.

We could say that mental events are causally relevant to physical events if the agent involved is an "unmoved mover," as libertarian accounts of freedom require (Chisholm 1964). That's a pretty high standard for a solution: it may be that none of us is ever an unmoved mover, and hence it could, according to this standard, turn out that mental causation never happens.

The gold standard I am adopting is pretty high but not so high as that of the libertarian. One property is causally relevant to another when a law of nature links them.

6.5 Framework

6.5.1 Laws of Nature

Let's sum up and present the whole framework for thinking about causal relevance.

Some laws of nature—let us call them "dynamic laws"—describe how one configuration of properties evolves into another. Newton's force laws entail that if two objects with mass have a certain location at one moment in time (and nothing is acting on them other than the force of gravity between them), then they will accelerate toward one another.

Dynamic laws of nature thus relate what properties things have at one place at a certain time with what properties things have a moment later. Putting it a little more formally:

> For all places p and times t, if x is an event that occurs at place p and time t and has property F, then at place p and time $t + \varepsilon$ there will be an event y that has property G.

(The "ε" is a variable for the length of a tiny increment of time. Real laws of physics are expressed as equations relating parameters to change in time and hence don't actually talk about tiny increments of time.) This is a general form for statements of dynamic laws of nature. If two properties F and G are related by a law of nature in this way, let us say that they are "nomic properties." (It is surprisingly difficult to say what it means for an event to "fall under" a law of nature [Davidson 1967]. It is similarly difficult to say what it means for a property to be related by a law of nature to another. See Latham 1987 for a suggestion about how to handle the problem for events.) Sometimes dynamic laws of nature are deterministic and specify that things definitely will evolve in a certain way. Sometimes they are indeterministic and specify an array of probabilities that things will turn out in a range of different ways.

6.5.2 Physical Causal Relevance

The laws of nature are (as Mill put it) the "threads of connexion" out of which the fabric of reality is woven. Any actual instance of a property is positively produced by what we could call a swatch of this total fabric: a structured array of property instances that immediately precede it, that is, what I defined in section 6.1.6 to be a positive producer (there I also called it a "slice of Swiss cheese"). The positive producer is usually much less than a sufficient condition for the instance of the effect property but is much more than a single property. Hence there is a derivative law linking the properties involved in any positive producer with the property of the effect:

> For all places p and times t, if x is an event that occurs at place p and time t and has an array of properties $ABCD\ldots$, arranged in a certain structure S, then at place p and time $t+\varepsilon$ there will be an event y that has property G.

Let's call such a regularity a "swatch law."

If two properties A and G are related by a swatch law in the way just described, then A is causally relevant to G. Property causal relevance is always a relational feature of a property. It makes no sense simply to ask whether a property is causally relevant, but it does make sense to ask of a property whether another is causally relevant to it or whether it is causally relevant to another.

If we make the value of ε large, then there is a lot of time between the cause and the effect and a lot of intermediate steps between the initial positive producer and the effect. So making the value of ε large entails that pretty nearly any property could be causally relevant to any other (since given a large enough interval of time, and enough artifice, we can rig up a causal path between them). Hence the value of ε should be the shortest possible interval of time consistent with the way the laws of nature dictate that the positive producer causes the effect; the value may differ from swatch law to swatch law.

6.5.3 Pragmatics Again

Suppose we take event c to be the creation of a knife, and e to be the event of its rusting. Let's assume that the knife begins to rust at the moment that it is created, so that *c* happens just before *e*. There is a swatch law that connects properties of *c* with properties of *e*; among the properties of *c* will be the property of being iron. It follows, then, that the creation of the knife is causally relevant to its rusting.

This result is counterintuitive but familiar from discussions of causation: it is the selection problem I discussed above, in section 6.1.7. Suppose a short circuit causes a fire. There had to be oxygen present for the fire to start. So oxygen's being present was one of the causes of the fire. Yet we feel some intuitive discomfort in saying this.

The most promising way to deal with this phenomenon focuses on what happens when we talk about causes. If I ask you what caused the fire and you say "oxygen," I will be puzzled. If instead you say "the short circuit," I will be less puzzled. You and I share a certain conception of what things are like, for the most part. Normally there is oxygen around. So we count the presence of oxygen as part of the field of causes. Against the background of that field, adding a short circuit constitutes an explanation of the fire.

The same goes for property causal relevance. We want to say: "the property of dog biscuits in virtue of which they nourish dogs is their chemical makeup." But one thing that causally influences (in the sense defined above in sec. 6.1.6) the nourishing of my dog is the beating of his heart. If I wanted to explain why he is nourished, I wouldn't say, "his heart is beating," since that is part of the normal background that we assume when we consider digestion.

6.6 Conclusion

I give my dog a biscuit, and it makes him happy. My giving it to him causes his happiness in virtue of certain of its physical properties, ones connected by laws of nature. Those properties of my giving him the biscuit are causally relevant to his happiness.

So far, though, I haven't shown how it could be that its being a biscuit is causally relevant to anything, nor have I shown how it could be that the fact that I intended to give him the biscuit was causally relevant to anything. In other words, I've shown how physical properties of the cause are causally relevant to physical properties of the effect, but I haven't shown how ordinary common-sense properties (not described in physical theory) can be causally relevant. That's what I need to do if I am going to solve the mental causation problem.

One tempting solution is to say that my extending my hand is an action only if it is caused by my reasons. That is true, so we may want to go on to say that being a reason is causally relevant to being an action—and necessarily so—because it's necessary that anything that is an action be caused by reasons.

Tempting but incorrect. In the next chapter I'll show why it is incorrect. This will provide the resources to understand why defining mental properties in terms of causes (chap. 2, sec. 2.2.3, and chap. 4, secs. 4.1.1 and 4.3) cannot solve the mental causation problem.

6.7 Further Reading

Sosa and Tooley's *Causation* (1993) is an anthology of papers on a variety of approaches to causation. *Causation and Counterfactuals* (Collins, Hall, and Paul 2004) mainly focuses on David Lewis's program of explaining causation in terms of counterfactuals. Phil Dowe's *Physical Causation* (2000) analyzes causation in terms of causal processes in which conserved quantities (like momentum) are exchanged.

Jonathan Bennett's *Events and Their Names* (1988) discusses different conceptions of events and how they are related to our language for events.

The topic of laws of nature is fundamental in metaphysics. Armstrong's *What Is a Law of Nature?* (1983) criticizes Humean accounts of laws and argues that laws are better understood as relations of universals. David Lewis criticizes this view in his "New Work for a Theory of Universals" (1983a) and proposes a Humean account of laws (there and at Lewis 1973:73), what is usually called the "best system" view of laws of nature. Van Fraassen's *Laws and Symmetry* (1989) includes a useful discussion of Lewis's view. Stephen Mumford's *Laws in Nature* (2004) argues that laws are not the motor of the world.

One of Anscombe's targets in her "Causality and Determination" (1971) was Davidson's "Causal Relations" (1967); Davidson responded in his "Laws and Cause" (1995).

7

Sunburn and Fragile Things

I am asked by the learned doctor for the cause and reason
that opium makes one sleep
To this I reply that there is in it a *virtus dormativa*
whose nature is to make the senses drowsy.
—MOLIÈRE, *LE MALADE IMAGINAIRE*, ACT 3 (CITED IN MUMFORD 1998:136)

IN THE last chapter I argued that one property is causally relevant to another when the two are linked by the laws of nature. That seemed to leave the mental causation problem as severe as ever—for surely the laws of nature don't talk about mental properties, do they?

In chapter 9 I will argue that some mental properties can be causally relevant to other properties. In this chapter, however, I'll show that some could not possibly be. The problem is that these mental properties are connected by necessity with certain things they must cause (or be caused by); that is, they are "causally involved" properties. The aims of this chapter, then, are (1) to set aside a tempting (but incorrect) solution to the mental causation problem and (2) to derive some interesting consequences for metaphysics and philosophy of mind concerning the general category of "causally involved" properties.

I have mentioned the tempting solution to the mental causation problem—and criticized it—several times already (chap. 2, sec. 2.2.3, and chap. 4, secs. 4.1.1 and 4.3). Since at least Aristotle's time, philosophers have noticed, rightly, that some mental states must necessarily stand in certain causal relations. Actions must be caused by reasons; that's what it is to be an action. Memories must be caused by the things they are memories of; that's what it is to be a memory. So why not just say: we already know, just from their nature, that mental properties are causally relevant—for instance, that being a reason is causally relevant to being an action?

The reason why not, as I indicated earlier, is that (putting it roughly) if the nature of one property is that its instances must be causally related to instances of another property, then we really shouldn't call the link between them "causal"; rather, it is a logical relation.

So the work of this chapter is to develop this argument in detail. I'll need to sort out what I will call "independence conditions" on causally relevant properties. These independence conditions show that certain pairs of properties could not possibly be related by causal relevance. These conditions will let us state what I will call the "new logical connections" argument. It's intended to capture what was right about the (old) logical connections argument that was supposed to—but didn't—show that reasons can't be causes (chap. 4, sec. 4.1.1). The upshot of the new logical connections argument is that when a mental property is necessarily related to a particular kind of cause (or effect), then the relation can't be one of causal relevance; for instance, being a reason cannot be causally relevant to being an action.

Independence conditions on causal relevance have at least two other important consequences for metaphysics and philosophy of mind. One central point of dispute about dispositions is whether they are causally relevant: if a glass is fragile and shatters, is its fragility causally relevant to its shattering? Independence conditions show that the answer is "no."

As I discussed above in chapter 4, section 4.3, role or "functional state identity theory" functionalism in the philosophy of mind treats mental properties as functional properties: the property of being a pain, for instance, is the property of being caused by tissue damage and of causing avoidance behavior (in concert with the rest of the things the person believes and wants and feels). Mental properties, as this brand of functionalism understands them, are very much like dispositions. Hence the same arguments, based on independence conditions, apply to role functionalism's properties. This is, I believe, a reason to reject role functionalism. (As I argued above in chap. 4, sec. 4.3, realizer functionalism collapses into the identity theory, in which there are no distinctively mental properties. Since there are distinctively mental properties (chap. 5, sec. 5.5), this brand of functionalism must also be incorrect.)

7.1 The Phenomenon

Suppose Suzy hurls a rock (event a) that hits a window, and the window shatters (event b). Event a caused event b. As chapter 6 discusses, the cause event has physical properties that are causally relevant to the effect event: a causes b because it has, or in virtue of having, these properties.

Suzy's hurling the rock has the following property: the property of causing the window to break. Could this property be causally relevant to the window's breaking? Well: anything that does have the property of causing a window to break will indeed cause the window to break. If you know event *a* has that property, then you know a window got broken.

Suppose, though, we ask: Why did the window break? What explains why Suzy's throwing the rock causes the window to break? Here are two choices:

- the cause event has the property of causing the window to break;
- the cause event gives the rock a certain momentum.

Surely we should choose the second: it states what it is about the collision that made the window break. The first choice offers exactly the following explanation: the first event caused the window to break because it caused the window to break. That's not much of an explanation.

The causal relevance relation between properties is supposed to capture how the world works. Consequently, the causal relevance relation shouldn't involve properties that have causation built in. Putting it metaphorically, properties that have the causation built in don't say *how* the world works. They only say *that* it works.

I'll call properties like the first "causally committed properties." One property is causally committed to another when instances of the first must cause, or be caused by, instances of the second.

Here are more examples of causally committed properties.

7.1.1 Sunburn

Someone who is sunburned has a certain sort of dermal burn, and that burn must have been caused by the sun. You could get that sort of dermal burn in other ways—a sunlamp, for instance—but that wouldn't be *sun*burn. (Reasonable people—and dictionaries—differ about this. Let us agree for the sake of the example that it is impossible to get sunburned except by the sun.) What makes a burn of this kind sunburn is the fact that the burn was caused by exposure to the sun. But this making is logical, not causal. Since it is not causal, we should say that exposure to the sun is not causally relevant to sunburn.

This sounds paradoxical. But it shouldn't, so long as we keep in mind that we are using the expression "causally relevant" in a very particular way.

- We are not using "causally relevant" to talk about any old causal relation between two things. Clearly exposure to the sun causes sunburn; indeed, there is no way to get sunburned other than by being burned by the sun.

We are, rather, using "causally relevant" to talk about a relation between properties, where having one of the properties positively produces the effect event (chap. 6).

• We are not using "causally relevant" to mean "causally explains." Exposure to the sun does causally explain sunburn. Suppose that Suzy doesn't know anything at all about the painful-looking inflammation of Billy's skin. She asks, "What's that?!" I respond (tautologically), "Exposure to the sun caused Billy's sunburn." Since Suzy learns something about the causal history of the condition of Billy's skin, we should say that I have given her a causal explanation. But I give exactly the same information if I say merely, "That's sunburn." The second explanation doesn't specify how the cause makes the effect happen; rather, it simply describes the effect as having a certain kind of cause. Hence causal explanation is not the same thing as causal relevance.

7.1.2 Action

According to the causal theory of action, an event is an action only if it is caused and rationalized by reasons. Hence it is logically necessary that if an event is an action, then it is caused by a reason. What makes an event an action is the fact that it is caused by a reason. But the making here is logical, not causal.

7.1.3 Doing Things Now That Only Happen Later

In doing one thing on a particular occasion (for instance, loosing an arrow), I may be doing other things as well (for instance, hitting a bull's-eye). One way to describe what I did is by reference to one of its effects, as when I speak of hitting a bull's-eye. So my action has a causally committed property, that of being a hitting of a bull's-eye. The commitment in this case is forward looking rather than backward looking.

Hamlet, having been killed by Laertes, goes on to kill him in turn. Laertes, having been killed by Hamlet, says, "Hamlet, thou art slain" (5.2.314). The paradox here evaporates if we think of Laertes' killing Hamlet as a forward-looking causally committed property, one that Laertes' action acquires in virtue of something that happens quite a bit later—Hamlet's actually dying.

7.2 Independence Conditions

Hume argued that events are by nature independent: any pair of events is such that it is logically possible that one or the other fails to occur (or both).

It is straightforward to extend Hume's idea to causal relevance relations among properties.

Several philosophers recently have argued, however, that Hume is wrong about the contingency of causation: Shoemaker (1984, 1998a), Ellis (2001), and Bird (2001) among others. For our purposes, it doesn't matter who is right. In this section I will show how causal relevance is restricted given the assumption that Hume was right. Then in the section following I'll argue for the same conclusion, without the assumption that causation is contingent.

Assume, then, that Hume is right and causation is contingent.

7.2.1 The Independence Condition

Hume's idea applies to particular events: he says that they are by nature independent. What about properties? Just as causation isn't "necessary connexion," causal relevance between properties should not be necessary connection either.

Sunburn has a necessary connection with exposure to the sun: it is logically impossible for someone to have the property of being sunburned if she wasn't exposed to the sun. Now, any case of sunburn is a case of a dermal burn of a certain sort. It is logically possible for someone to have that kind of dermal burn without having been exposed to the sun. It makes sense to say that exposure to the sun is causally relevant to the dermal burn. The cause makes the effect happen in virtue of the connection between exposure to the sun and that sort of dermal burn. But it doesn't make sense to say that the cause makes it happen that the effect is sunburn. That is because being sunburn is logically guaranteed by the fact that the cause is exposure to the sun.

This suggests that the causal relevance relation is restricted in the following way:

If F is causally relevant to G, then it is logically possible for there to be a G-event that is not caused by an F-event.

Let us call this the "independence condition" on causal relevance.

7.2.2 The Superindependence Condition

What makes something sunburn is the fact that it was caused by the sun. There are all kinds of ways for that burn to be caused by the sun: you could sit in the sun for four hours, or at the beach, or standing on your head. . . . Now, the property of sunburn is independent, in the sense just defined, of the property of being exposed to the sun for four hours. That is because it is logically possible for there to be a case of sunburn that is not caused by an exposure to the sun lasting four hours. (Indeed, it is remarkably unlikely that any given case of sunburn was caused by exposure to the sun that lasted exactly four hours.)

Nevertheless, if Suzy sat in the sun for 3 hours and 18 minutes, then, of course, she sat in the sun, and she was exposed to the sun. So being exposed to the sun for 3 hours and 18 minutes entails being exposed to the sun. So there are infinitely many properties that are more specific than exposure to the sun, each of which entails that anything that has it also has the property of being an exposure to the sun. And when there is an event that has any one of these more specific properties that causes a dermal burn, that dermal burn is automatically—by logical necessity—a case of sunburn.

That suggests that the causal relevance relation is restricted still further:

If F is causally relevant to G, then there is no property F' such that if something has G then it must be caused by something that has F', and F entails F'.

We may call this the "superindependence condition" on causal relevance.

So Suzy's property, that she sat in the sun for 3 hours and 18 minutes, can't be causally relevant to the property she now has, of being sunburned, since sunburn isn't superindependent of that property, that is, since (a) any instance of being sunburned must be caused by an instance of exposure to the sun and (b) sitting in the sun for 3 hours and 18 minutes entails being exposed to the sun.

Sunburn is a backward-looking causally committed property, in the sense that sunburn must have a cause (occurring earlier in time) that has a certain property. There are forward-looking causal commitments as well. Laertes kills Hamlet, even though Hamlet doesn't die until well after he himself kills Laertes; thus Laertes' action has the property of being a killing only in virtue of causing, much later, Hamlet's death. There are similar restrictions on causal relevance where the cause property is one that logically looks forward in time to a certain sort of effect (see Dardis 1993 for details).

These restrictions on causal relevance do not, however, mean that causally committed properties can't have any causal relevance relations at all. Sunburn is a backward-looking causally committed property. Its causal commitment involves exposure to the sun. It has no commitment about any other sort of cause, though, and so it would be superindependent of other sorts of causes. Also, sunburn doesn't have any forward-looking causal commitments. That means that it is at least a candidate for being causally relevant to some effect property, since it isn't logically necessary that any case of sunburn must have an effect of some definite particular kind. Dardis 1993 and Block 1990 develop these points in more detail.

7.3 If Hume Was Wrong

Suppose that Hume was wrong. Let's make the argument without assuming that causation is contingent.

The striking thing about causally committed properties is that they are individuated with respect to certain other properties. Necessarily, sunburn is a burn of a certain sort that is caused by exposure to the sun. Necessarily, killing is doing something that causes a death. There is, on the one hand, the totality of the causal relevance facts, "the general tissue of connexion," as Mill put it. And, on the other hand, there are particular selections from this tissue. Let me make this more precise.

When someone is sunburned, that person has a certain sort of dermal burn. That sort of dermal burn can be caused in several ways: by exposure to the sun; by sunlamps; by other sources of the right kind of radiation. Assuming that there are lots and lots of properties (chap. 5), the property of being this sort of dermal burn is represented by a collection of particulars, and the members of the collection have different sorts of causes. But there are also smaller properties (ones that have fewer instances) that are represented by members of the collection that all have the same cause: there is the property dermal-burn-caused-by-sunlamp, the property dermal-burn-caused-by-radiation, and of course the property dermal-burn-caused-by-sun. Call these smaller properties selections of the bigger property.

Now, we could claim that the motor of the world is composed of multiple distinct submotors: the sun-to-dermal-burn-caused-by-sun motor, the sunlamp-to-dermal-burn-caused-by-sunlamp motor, and the others. But there is no reason to say this, that is, no reason from the perspective of saying how the world works. In fact, there is positive reason against doing this: the "multiple motors" account is less simple than the "one motor" view. There is a single mechanism leading from any energetic irradiation of the skin to a certain sort of burn.

So a backward-looking selection has the following characteristic: Any of its instances has a further property, the bigger property from which the smaller is selected. That bigger property's instances can be caused in several different ways. But the backward-looking selection only has instances that are caused in one of these ways.

The reason exposure to the sun isn't causally relevant to sunburn, then, is this: There is a property, the property of being a dermal burn of a certain sort. Various properties are causally relevant to it, and hence it takes its place in the causal relevance relation; this follows from the laws of nature. The property of sunburn is a selection from the property of being that sort of dermal burn: only those instances that have exposure to the sun as their cause. Sunburn is a distinct property from being a dermal burn, since there are dermal burns of that sort that are not sunburn. But the laws of nature do not mention this property. Any regularity expressed using a term for this property is already included in the regularities that refer to the more general property of being a dermal burn.

A forward-looking selection goes the same way, with the directions reversed. Laertes kills Hamlet by nicking him with a poisoned rapier. Moving his arm that way can produce a variety of effects. The laws of nature describe this variety: given these-and-these cooperating factors, you get one kind of effect, given those-and-those cooperating factors, you get another. So moving his arm is one property, which is causally relevant to a variety of types of effect. But there are other properties whose instances are movements of that very kind that produce a certain kind of effect—for instance, the ones that cause deaths, that is, the killing kind.

So a forward-looking selection has the following characteristic, exactly parallel to the backward-looking selection. Any of its instances has a further, bigger property. That property's instances can cause any of several different kinds of things. But the forward-looking selection only has instances that cause things of one of these kinds.

7.4 The New Logical Connections Argument

Either causation is contingent, as Hume argued, or it is not. If it is contingent, the relation between exposure to the sun and sunburn is not contingent, and so it isn't any kind of causal relation. If causation is necessary, we may argue as follows: these causally committed properties are selections from the real causal relevance facts, and hence they are not themselves causal.

In the rest of this chapter I will draw out the consequences of this conclusion for the mental causation problem. In this section I'll show that mental properties cannot be causally relevant to action properties. Next I'll show that dispositions cannot be causally relevant to their manifestations. Finally I'll show that role (as opposed to realizer) functionalism—since it treats mental properties as much like dispositions—also cannot make sense of the causal relevance of mental properties.

Since the main job mental events have in the causation of things in the world is the causation of actions, it seems remarkably natural to suppose that mental properties of mental events are causally relevant to action properties of bodily movement events. So, for instance, it seems remarkably natural to say that my wanting ice cream on some occasion is causally relevant to my reaching for some.

The new logical connections argument shows that this thought is incorrect. The (old) logical connections argument (chap. 4, sec. 4.1, above) held that reasons cannot be causes because they are conceptually connected. The germ of truth in the (old) logical connections argument is that reason properties cannot be causally relevant to action properties because the latter are causally committed with respect to the former—thus the new logical connections argument.

What exactly are the conceptual connections between reasons and actions? The details are philosophically controversial, but the main outlines of the idea go as follows (Davidson 1980a: essays 1–6).

An event counts as an action only if it is something done with an intention. For an action to be performed with an intention is for it to be caused by an intention. In turn, an intention must be caused by a reason. A reason consists of a positive valuation of a certain kind of action (for instance, a desire or a recognition of an obligation), together with a belief that by doing something one can perform an action of this kind.

Action properties are thus causally committed properties. It is logically impossible (if this account of action is correct) for there to be an action (an event with the property of being an action) that is not caused by an intention, a reason, a belief, and a desire.

Hence the property of being a reason cannot be causally relevant to the property of being an action (neither, according to the superindependence condition, can the property of being any particular belief, or desire, or reason). That's not the same as saying that reasons cannot cause actions. They can, and must, according to this theory of action. The point is about the properties of being a reason and being an action, not about the particulars that have those properties.

Moreover, this new logical connections argument leaves open the idea that various mental properties (like the property of being a belief or the property of being a desire for some ice cream) might be causally relevant to properties of actions other than their action properties. Sometimes when I want ice cream, I reach for it. My reaching has the nonintentional property of being an arm's extending in a certain way. That property of my action is not causally committed, and so the property of its cause, that it is a desire for ice cream, may be causally relevant to it.

7.5 Dispositions

A certain wineglass is fragile. That is: it has a disposition to shatter easily. What makes the fragile wineglass shatter (if it does)? Is the fragility—the disposition—causally relevant to the shattering? Or is it something else—for instance, the crystalline structure of glass?

The term "disposition" gets defined in different ways by different philosophers for different purposes: sometimes it is used pick out a linguistic phenomenon; sometimes it is used to characterize a basic metaphysical category. Shoemaker holds that "the term 'dispositional' is best employed as a predicate of predicates, not of properties" (1984:210); in other words, we use the word "disposition" for certain kinds of words, ones that pick out certain ways that things behave. Prior, Pargetter, and Jackson (1982) assert that dispositions are second-order properties (the disposition to B is the property of having a property that causes B under suitable circumstances given a suitable trigger). Their view, then, is that the word "disposition" names a (derived) metaphysical category. Mumford (1998) self-consciously (192) straddles the distinction between linguistic and metaphysical phenomena: "d is a dispositional property if and only if d is a functional role occupying property by definition" (198). Heil (2005) argues that dispositions are intrinsic properties of things possessing them and that dispositions are never higher level (in the sense of Prior, Pargetter, and Jackson 1982). Thus Heil holds that the word "disposition" names a fundamental metaphysical category.

The most thoroughly metaphysical account of dispositions holds that dispositions are a distinctive part of reality, something different from properties. I want to argue that we can gain a perfectly adequate understanding of the nature of dispositions by thinking of them in terms of properties, as I described them in chapter 6, and hence that we should not think of dispositions as a distinctive metaphysical category. Fragile things like wineglasses have various properties that explain what they do, including shattering when struck. Fundamental dispositions (for instance, the way a charged particle is disposed to behave) aren't grounded in this way, but, I'll argue, there is every reason to say fundamental dispositions just are properties.

I am going to make one basic assumption about dispositions, which I'll call the "essential character" assumption. I will argue from the essential character assumption that dispositions (a) cannot be causally relevant to the things they are supposed to be causally relevant to (for example, the fragility of the glass cannot be causally relevant to the glass shattering) and (b) that dispositions are not properties.

These are dire consequences. If we gave up the essential character assumption, we might be able to show that dispositions are causally relevant properties. But, as far as I can see, giving up the essential character assumption means giving up distinction between properties and dispositions, hence giving up any distinctive place for dispositions in the scheme of things.

7.5.1 The Essential Character Assumption

The essential character assumption is that it is essential to dispositions that they have exactly the manifestation types they do.

Each disposition is uniquely identified by a set of trigger/manifestation patterns. For instance: fragility is the disposition to shatter when struck (under ideal circumstances, since fragile things don't always shatter when struck; see Martin 1994 and Mumford 1998: sec. 4.9). Some dispositions have only a single trigger/manifestation pattern, while others have several. For instance, if believing that Vienna is beautiful is a disposition, then it is a disposition to do a variety of things under a variety of circumstances.

The set of trigger/manifestation patterns exhausts the disposition. For example, salt (sodium chloride, NaCl) dissolves in water. It does so because of the interaction of the electrostatic forces between salt and water. The fundamental facts about causal relevance include these facts about the interaction of electrostatic forces. But there are more facts about those interactions than the ones involved in dissolving in water. For instance, when salt is added to bread dough, it toughens the dough and slows the growth of yeast. It is not salt's solubility, however, that causes the dough to toughen, even if it is true that what makes salt dissolve is exactly the same thing that makes it toughen dough.

Stephen Mumford writes: "Dispositions have functional essences in the sense that what it is that makes any particular disposition the disposition it is is the functional role it plays and what it is that makes any property a dispositional property is that it has a functional essence. For example, what it is that makes all things soluble is that they are apt for dissolving when in a liquid. This is a conceptual point: it couldn't be that the property of fragility could have occupied the causal role of solubility instead" (1998:84–85). It is essential to fragility that fragile things are apt to shatter; it wouldn't be fragility if it were aptness for dissolving when in a liquid. The essential character assumption is in the same spirit but slightly stronger than what Mumford writes: not only would it not be fragility if it caused dissolving, but it also would not be fragility if it caused both shattering and dissolving. Dispositions are individuated with respect to their manifestation types; the disposition to shatter is a different disposition from the disposition either to shatter or to dissolve.

7.5.2 The Causal Relevance of Dispositions

"Causally involved" is a generalization of "causally committed": a property is causally involved when it is necessary that its instances have, either actually or potentially, causal relations with instances of some further, definite property. Dispositions thus appear to be forward-looking causally involved properties. Fragility is the disposition to break, as opposed to, say, a disposition to refract light in a certain way. So a fragile thing has some sort of necessary relation to causing breaking. Fragility is unlike, for example, sunburn or killing in that a fragile thing can persist without ever breaking.

If dispositions are indeed causally involved, then they are no more causally relevant to their effects than exposure to the sun is causally relevant to sunburn. Here's another example. The electrostatic character of salt is a physical property. The water solubility of salt is a distinct (smaller) property from the electrostatic character of salt. Since the water solubility of salt is just a particular way of having the electrostatic character of salt (namely: by being soluble in water), the water solubility of salt is not causally relevant to salt's dissolving.

Hence if the essential character assumption is true of dispositions, they are not causally relevant to their manifestation types. We are better off, I suggest, if we say that things that have dispositions have properties that are causally relevant to the manifestation types that are essential to dispositions. In other words, we can explain what we are saying when we talk about dispositions by appealing to the properties that things have. We do not need to say that there are dispositions in addition to properties.

7.5.3 Are Dispositions Properties?

Given my account of properties as correlated with sets of particulars, the property of sunburn turns out to be very simple to describe: the property corresponds to a certain subset of dermal burns, those that were caused by the sun. But this account of properties makes it very difficult to see how, given the essential character assumption, dispositions could be properties.

Table salt has a certain electrostatic character. That is a property. This property is what explains why salt dissolves in water. It is also the property that explains why salt toughens bread dough.

In the case of forward-looking causally committed properties, we could select from the variety of effects that a given property had in order to arrive at the selection, the causally committed property. Causally committed properties are properties the instances of which must stand in certain causal relations, and hence if an instance of one of them exists, then the required cause, or effect, must exist.

The trouble is that dispositions don't have to manifest. So the dispositional property cannot be shared by only those particulars that do in fact manifest the disposition. Some particulars that don't ever manifest the disposition do nevertheless have the disposition.

Nor can we pick out just the disposition by grouping together certain actual things with certain merely possible things. For instance, we might be tempted by the following thought. Suppose that a fragile glass has the disposition to shatter but never shatters. Had things been different, we might say, it would have shattered. So if we group the glass that never shatters with itself as it would have been if it had shattered, then we get a connection with shattering when struck. The trouble is, though, that if fragility is a property, then it groups the fragile things that don't ever shatter both with themselves as they would have been had they shattered and with themselves as they would have been if they had not. Some fragile things break and some do not; all, equally, are fragile, and hence all, equally, are instances of the property of fragility. So we can't pick and choose among the might-have-been-otherwise versions of this actual glass, since they all have to be part of the property of fragility.

That property—the property corresponding to the set of all and only the actual and possible fragile things—is nothing distinct from what makes the fragile things fragile: crystalline structure in glass, thinness and rigidity in porcelain, and so on. Hence the disposition, if it is any property at all, is identical to the disjunction of the causally relevant properties that explain how fragile things behave. But that (perfectly respectable) property violates the essential character assumption, since it explains other things fragile things do.

Something must give. I think that what we must give up is the assumption that dispositions are properties in their own right. So in fact there is a stronger argument to make that dispositions aren't part of the causal relevance relation: they are not properties, so they can't be part of a relation between properties.

Once again, it is simple to talk about the properties of things that have dispositions in order to explain how those things behave. There is no need to say that there are dispositions in addition to properties.

7.5.4 Giving Up the Essential Character Assumption

The arguments that dispositions are not causally relevant to their manifestations and that they are not properties depended on the essential character assumption. Since the word "disposition" doesn't have a standard meaning among philosophers, we could give up the essential character assumption and thereby defuse these arguments. The trouble is that the most plausible way of dropping it removes the distinction between dispositions and properties and hence leaves dispositions with no distinctive job to do.

Suppose dispositions are just regular properties of things capable of producing (in concert with instances of other properties) a variety of effects. Table salt is water soluble, but water solubility can cause dough to toughen and slow the growth of yeast. This wineglass is fragile; its fragility can cause a certain X-ray diffraction pattern.

We have a choice at this point (corresponding to the choice between realizer and role functionalism). We could say that the term "water soluble" picks out that property of salt (the electrostatic character of NaCl molecules) that enables it to dissolve in water, that property of sugar that enables it to do the same, and so forth. Or we could say that disposition words pick out more general properties; for example, both wineglasses and porcelain cups are fragile (have the same disposition), but for different microstructural reasons. Either way, dispositions can be causally relevant to their manifestation types, since denying the essential character assumption means giving up the strong connection between the disposition and its manifestation type. (Assuming, that is, what I will argue for in chapter 9, namely, that higher-level properties can be causally relevant.)

But, equally, either way we go, we are identifying dispositions with certain properties. Denying the essential character assumption means giving up the distinction between properties and dispositions. So denying this assumption seems to leave dispositions with no distinctive metaphysical job to do.

7.5.5 Ungrounded Dispositions

I have been arguing that dispositions are best understood as explicable in terms of properties. A fragile glass shatters when struck because it has an underlying causal structure (the ground of the disposition), that is, a set of properties that can contribute to a positive producer (in the sense defined in chap. 6 above) of shattering. Different fragile things are fragile for different reasons, but in each case the fragile thing has properties that explain its shattering when struck.

The grounding properties have some of the distinctive marks of dispositions: they may never manifest, and they do only manifest in the company of other properties. So we could count the grounding properties as dispositions also. Consider "electric charge: that property of some elementary particles that gives rise to an interaction between them, and consequently to the host of material phenomena known as electrical" (Crane 1996:12). Electric charge—since it is a fundamental force—can't manifest in any way other than is described by the laws of electrical interaction. And, if it really is a fundamental force, then there is nothing further that explains those manifestations: it is an ungrounded disposition. Perhaps, as some philosophers have suggested (Ellis 2001), we should think of the world as fundamentally constituted by ungrounded dispositions like these, rather than by properties.

In the last section I suggested that if a disposition can explain things other than its essential manifestation type, then we might as well call it a property, since there isn't, apparently, any distinction between such a disposition and a property. I suggest we say the same about fundamental dispositions. Such dispositions act exactly as do fundamental properties. We would be better off calling them "properties"; there is no advantage to thinking of them as belonging in a basic metaphysical category that includes higher-level dispositions like fragility and solubility.

7.6 Role Functionalism Can't Explain Most Mental Causation

Functionalism says that what it is to be a pain (for instance) is to be something that is (typically) caused by bodily damage and that (typically) causes avoidance behavior. (This is of course a gross oversimplification.) Particular pains, in this view, are particular things—brain processes, most likely—that have these causal relations.

According to role or "functional state identity theory" functionalism, the property of being a pain is a "generic causal pattern" property. To bring out what this means, consider a particular pain, say, the pain in my knee at the moment. This pain is a physical (bodily) process. It has a variety of microphysical and structural properties. The pain causes things (and was caused) in virtue of its having these properties.

But none of these is the property of being pain. They are not the generic causal property of being caused by bodily damage and causing avoidance behavior. They are the specific properties that enable this pain to stand in these generic causal patterns.

It is traditional to say that generic causal pattern properties are second-order properties (Block 1980c; Prior, Pargetter, and Jackson 1982). The property of being pain is—according to this tradition—the property of having properties that stand in certain causal relations. What exactly this means is not so clear, particularly if we haven't specified any account of what properties are.

According to the framework I set up for properties in chapter 5, properties are represented by sets of particulars. A generic causal pattern property is simply a property that corresponds to a collection of particulars that do in fact stand in certain causal relations. The property of being a pain corresponds to a set of particulars (neurological processes, most likely) that stand in the typical causal relations that pains stand in.

Functional properties understood this way are causally involved properties in the sense discussed in section 7.5. They aren't causally committed properties. Pains can exist that aren't caused by bodily damage, and pains can exist that do not cause avoidance behavior. But since their nature is to stand in these causal relations, they are causally involved. They are very like dispositions, in that their nature is to cause certain things. Unlike most dispositions, their nature is also to be caused by certain things.

The argument of the last section was that dispositions are not causally relevant to their manifestations. Exactly the same arguments go for functional properties understood as generic causal pattern properties. They cannot be causally relevant to the properties they must cause; their causes cannot be causally relevant to them. Worse still, many of them are not properties at all.

7.7 Philosophy of Mind and Causal Involvement

Independence conditions, together with the reasonable demand that mental properties are causally relevant to physical properties, lead to a condition on acceptable theories of mental properties.

> The "*no causal involvement*" *condition*: if a mental property M is causally relevant to a property P, then M has no forward-looking causal involvement with P, and P has no backward-looking causal involvement with M.

The directions are important; the definition leaves open the possibility, for instance, that M has a *backward*-looking causal commitment to P (every M must be caused by a P) but no *forward*-looking involvement and hence might be causally relevant *to* P (Dardis 1993). Role or "functional state identity theory" functionalism defines mental properties in terms of causes and effects their instances have, hence role functionalism fails to meet this condition.

There is a good reason why philosophers have formulated theories of mind that violate this condition. One of the sources of functionalism was the observation (Armstrong 1968) that psychological concepts are very often causal. The concept of memory, for instance, is causal: it is logically impossible to remember a particular matter of fact unless that particular matter of fact is among the causes of the memory. Reasoning seems to be a causal concept. Suppose I come to believe that p. I might have various beliefs that support the belief that p. But I didn't reason from them to my belief that p unless these other beliefs were causes of my belief that p. (There is a parallel here with free action. A free action must not only be caused by the agent's reasons, but those reasons must cause the action in virtue of the mental properties of the reasons. Similarly, an inference must not only be caused by the thinker's reasons, but those reasons must cause the inference in virtue of their mental properties.)

Can a philosophical theory of mind both honor the "no causal involvement" condition and maintain that many psychological concepts are causal concepts? Indeed it can. The main thing is to keep track of precisely how a given concept is causal.

Memory. Remembering that Vienna is beautiful must be caused by the fact that Vienna is beautiful; the "no causal involvement" condition rules that the latter is not causally relevant to the former property.

Reasoning. Reasoning that p must be a causal process with a very special character. Believing that p is not constrained in the same way. Usually one believes that p because one has experienced it or been told about it. But being the belief that p does not require being caused in any particular way. Looking now at effects: there is a range of actions that the belief that p is likely to cause. But it need not result in any of them, or in any action at all. Fragility is not like this: it must cause shattering if it causes anything at all. Also, the range of actions that a belief of a given type can cause is not fixed by the nature of that type: given appropriate new desires, the belief that p may always cause actions unlike any it ever has before.

Functionalism and anomalous monism. Realizer functionalism has no difficulty meeting the "no causal involvement" condition. Any variety of functionalism that can leave open the possibility of nontypical causation can meet this condition. According to Davidson's anomalous monism (via its roots in radical interpretation), thoughts have their intentional contents (what they are about) by virtue of a best fit among causal patterns. I should interpret you as believing things about water when your actions are caused by states that function causally for you the way my beliefs about water function for me. (This is a version of Davidson's "principle of charity.") But the causal pattern isn't logically mandatory. Your beliefs about water aren't going to function causally for you exactly as mine function for me. Hence there is no logical requirement of a certain sort of cause. Both realizer functionalism and anomalous monism thus face no difficulties from the "no causal involvement" condition.

7.8 Conclusion

In chapter 6 I argued that causal relevance is the motor of the world. When one event causes another, it does so in virtue of certain of its properties, ones that are linked to effect properties by laws of nature. These properties are the ones that are causally relevant.

In this chapter I argued that two properties are not related by causal relevance when one is causally involved in the other. One way of being causally involved is to be causally committed: one property is causally committed to another when where the instances of one must necessarily cause (or be caused by) instances of the other. A weaker way of being causally involved is what we see with dispositions: something is fragile if, necessarily, it can shatter when struck (but it may in fact never shatter).

The new logical connections argument exploited the fact that action properties are causally committed: their instances must be caused by reasons. Hence reason properties cannot be causally relevant to action properties.

My argument against the causal relevance of dispositions (and the causal relevance of functional properties as understood by role functionalism) exploited the fact that dispositions and functional properties are causally involved and hence cannot stand in causal relevance relations with those properties that essentially characterize them.

It follows, then, that we cannot solve the problem of mental causation by appeal to the (undoubted) fact that actions must be caused by reasons. The problem of mental causation arises for the causal relevance of properties that do not have this kind of necessary relation to one another. The problem arises, for instance, for the relation between choosing to raise one's arm and one's arm going up. In the next chapter I argue that mental properties, like the property of choosing to raise one's arm, supervene on microphysical properties and are at a higher level than those microphysical properties. Then in chapter 9 I argue that supervening higher-level properties can meet the gold standard for causal relevance: taking their place in laws of nature.

7.9 Further Reading

The literature on causation contains a number of (typically brief) discussions of independence conditions, for instance, Lepore and Loewer's "Mind Matters" (1987), Wayne Davis's "Probability and Causality"(1988), and Ellery Eells's *Probabilistic Causality* (1991).

My "Sunburn: Independence Conditions on Causal Relevance" (Dardis 1993) and Kirk Ludwig's "Causal Relevance and Thought Content" (1994) and "Functionalism, Causation, and Causal Relevance" (1996) present thorough discussions of independence conditions and their consequences in the philosophy of mind. Robert Rupert's "Functionalism, Mental Causation, and the Problem of Metaphysically Necessary Effects" (2006) argues that functionalism cannot explain mental causation since it is committed to "metaphysically necessary effects." Jennifer McKitrick's "Are Dispositions Causally Relevant?" (2005) discusses the connection between independence conditions and the causal relevance of dispositions, as does Stephen Mumford's 1998 book *Dispositions*. George Bealer in "Mental Causation" (2007), develops a solution to the mental causation problem based on "metaphysically necessary" laws of psychology.

8

Supervenience and Levels

Mind-body supervenience *states* the mind-body problem—it is not a solution to it.

—JAEGWON KIM, *MIND IN A PHYSICAL WORLD* (1998:14)

OUR PROBLEM is this: mental events are physical events. Physical events cause their effects in virtue of their physical properties. Mental properties are not identical to physical properties. So—it appears—mental events never cause their effects in virtue of their physical properties.

The issue is about properties: events cause other events in virtue of their microphysical properties but, apparently, never in virtue of their mental properties. Using our terminology, physical properties of events are causally relevant to physical properties of their effects, but mental properties, apparently, aren't ever causally relevant to anything. This is because properties are related by causal relevance when laws of nature link them, and, apparently, mental properties are never linked that way.

The instances of some properties—action properties, for instance—must have mental causes. This won't help us, however, since the connection between the properties isn't causal if it is required by logic.

So far I've said that mental properties are not identical with physical properties, but I haven't said anything else about how the two kinds of properties are related. In this chapter I make two positive proposals about their relation: (1) mental properties supervene on physical properties, and (2) mental properties are higher-level properties relative to physical properties.

Jaegwon Kim has made the point forcefully in recent years (1993a, 1998, 2005) that supervenience is the most fundamental obstacle to the causal relevance of the mental. He is right that there is something intuitively (and intellectually) problematic about supervenient causation. This concern survives even when we argue (as I shall below) that Kim's detailed arguments against supervenient causation don't quite work. Despite this intuitively problematic feel, the intellectual cost of giving up supervenient causation is extremely high. And in fact the supervenience of mental properties on physical properties provides the key to explaining how (in chapter 9) mental properties can meet the gold standard for causal relevance that I articulated in chapter 6 above.

Kim is right that supervenience is not a solution to the mind/body problem, and it is not a solution to the mental causation problem. Two things are needed in addition to supervenience. First, some more substantive relation has to hold between mental properties and physical properties than bare supervenience. Supervenience is a very thin relation. Since it is so easy to supervene (for instance, the property of being either a spoon or a snowflake supervenes on the set of properties {being a spoon, being a snowflake}), lots and lots of clearly causally irrelevant properties supervene on microphysical properties. I'll argue in this chapter that the more substantive relation we need is that mental properties are higher-level properties relative to physical properties.

Second, just because a property supervenes on microphysical properties in this more substantive way doesn't mean it is causally relevant to anything. In chapter 9, I will work out a way to connect higher-level properties to laws of nature: I will work out a leveled conception of property causal relevance. This will permit me to say that mental properties can be causally relevant to other properties—and hence to solve the mental causation problem.

8.1 Supervenience

So: mental properties are not identical to physical properties, but according to materialism, all instances of mental properties are physical things. How then are mental properties related to physical properties? The answer is: they supervene on physical properties.

Donald Davidson was the first to suggest that the right way to understand the dependence of the mind on the body is supervenience: "Although the position I describe denies there are psychophysical laws, it is consistent with the view that mental characteristics are in some sense dependent, or supervenient, on physical characteristics. Such supervenience might be taken to mean that there cannot be two events alike in all physical respects but different in some mental respect, or that an object cannot alter in some mental respect without altering in some physical respect" (1970b:214). The basic idea is that mental facts depend on physical facts, and the physical facts completely determine (or fix, or settle) the mental facts. Given the whole truth about the physical realm, the whole truth about the mental realm is settled: no mental variation is possible. On the other hand, fixing the mental facts permits a great deal of physical variation. A person could have exactly the same mental life even if she were physically slightly different. (For instance, if the core idea of functionalism is right [chap. 4, sec. 4.3], then there can be small physical differences that would make no difference to how mental states causally interact with one another, and perception, and action, and hence would make no difference to a person's mental life.) Much of the world is not mental at all. Lots of nonmental parts of the world could change without any mental changes at all (for instance, tiny bits of rock millions of light-years from any sentient creature).

Davidson argued that supervenience is consistent with irreducibility: we can say that psychology is not reducible to physics, but psychological things are nevertheless still physical things through and through. Davidson's aim in pointing out the compatibility of supervenience and irreducibility was to indicate what we might call "minimal materialism." The concept is designed to answer this question: what is the weakest possible connection between psychology and the physical world, consistent with materialism, that we could describe that would still let us say the many and various things that we think must be true about our minds and behavior? (Kim [1998:15] introduces the expression "minimal physicalism" used in this way.) As I noted in chapter 1, physicalism is the view that everything is physical, including all the properties; materialism is the view that all the things are physical, but not necessarily the properties. The mental causation problem depends on the idea that mental properties are not identical to physical properties. Since physicalism says that all properties are physical, it also says that if there are any mental properties, they are also physical properties—hence identical to physical properties. The mental causation problem thus makes sense given materialism, but it does not make sense if physicalism is true. It is important to see that although materialism concedes that something isn't physical, the concession is very small. Materialism says that all the actual minds are physical things. The fact that a nonphysical thinker is logically possible doesn't mean that the actual world has any nonphysical bits to it—if it did, then materialism would be false.

8.1.1 What Is Supervenience?

There are a lot of different ways to fill in the basic idea of supervenience (McLaughlin and Bennett 2005). There are supervenience relations among sentences, truths, predicates, facts, properties, particulars, and many other things as well. Since I am concerned with the causal relevance of mental properties, I will focus on supervenience relations among properties. People have mental properties, and people have physical properties. Particular mental events, like the event of choosing a raisin muffin rather than a scone, have mental properties, and those particular mental events have physical properties. So the very same things have both mental properties and physical properties. Hence the kind of supervenience I am looking at is local rather than global (Haugeland 1982; Kim 1984). Supervenience is supposed to express the dependence of the mental on the physical. Dependence has to do with not just how actual things are related but how they would be related if things had been different. So, for instance, if I had chosen the scone rather than the raisin muffin, then I would have had different physical properties. Hence supervenience is strong rather than weak (Kim 1984).

Kim's statement of the kind of supervenience we need runs like this: "Mental properties *supervene* on physical properties, in that necessarily, for any mental property M, if anything has M at time t, there exists a physical base (or subvenient) property P such that it has P at t, and necessarily anything that has P at a time has M at that time" (1998:9). The first "necessarily" in this definition demands that every instance of a supervening mental property depends on an instance of a physical property. The second "necessarily" articulates the idea that having the physical property determines having the mental property (Yoshimi 2007).

Contemporary discussions (in the philosophy of mind) of what "necessarily" means center on three kinds of necessity. A proposition is physically (or nomologically) necessary if, given the laws of nature, it has to be true (or: its falsity is inconsistent with the laws of nature). A proposition is logically necessary if, given the relations of the concepts involved in the proposition, it has to be true (or: it is strictly conceptually impossible for it to be false). A proposition is metaphysically necessary if it is impossible for it to be false, period. The standard example of a proposition that is metaphysically necessary but not logically necessary is that water = H_2O. Assuming that it is true, it is not true in virtue of the concepts involved. Yet it is nevertheless impossible for there to be water that is not H_2O (Kripke 1980). The proposition that an aunt has a sibling is logically necessary. The proposition that on Earth I cannot fly unaided is nomologically necessary.

It is logically possible for there to be a nonphysical thinker. (A fiction that begins, "It is a truth universally acknowledged, that a single man in possession of a good fortune, though completely devoid of physical properties, must be in want of a wife," does not immediately contradict itself.) It follows, then, that mental properties are not identical to physical properties. So the necessity of supervenience is not logical or metaphysical. It can't be logical, since that would mean that it is impossible for there to be a nonphysical thinker. Supervenience can't be metaphysically necessary, since if it were, then any thinker would have to be a physical thing—so there couldn't be a nonphysical thinker.

The remaining alternative is physical necessity. So we read Kim's definition of supervenience as saying that it is physically impossible for something to have physical property P and not have mental property M; also, it is physically impossible for something to have mental property M and not have physical property P.

Kim's definition leaves open whether M supervenes on more than one physical property. A token-token identity theory, like functionalism or anomalous monism, will say that in general the instances of a given mental property may have physically different realizations. But given supervenience, if anything has any of the physical realizer properties, then it must have the mental property.

8.1.2 Denying Supervenience Is Costly

Supervenience is supposed to express a minimal materialism. We should ask: is supervenience too much? Can a reasonable philosophy of mind deny supervenience?

The idea of materialism is that everything in the world is physical. The motor of the world is physical also. This means that everything that happens has a physical explanation. In other words, physics is closed: in principle, physics has the resources to explain whatever happens. Here is Kim's statement of the physical closure principle: "if a physical event has a cause that occurs at t, it has a physical cause that occurs at t" (2005:43). Denying supervenience means either denying mental causation altogether or denying physical closure. Here's the proof:

Suppose that the mental does not supervene on the physical. Then the physical facts do not determine (fix, settle) the mental facts. There can be two different persons who are physically completely alike yet differ in some mental respect. Suppose Billy and William are physically completely alike, yet Billy chooses to toss a rock through a window, while William chooses not to.

If what happens is determined exclusively by how things are physically, then both bodies do the same (either throw the rock or not). But then one of the bodies is doing something that doesn't come from what it intends. So mental causation falls by the wayside, since what the bodies do does not depend on their mental properties.

If what happens is (sometimes, at least in part) determined by how things are mentally, then the bodies do different things. But the physical characteristics of their causes are exactly the same. It follows that physical closure would be false.

If we had a strong independent reason to deny that the mental supervenes on the physical, we would then need to decide whether physical closure is false or whether epiphenomenalism is true (or both). Either way the intellectual cost would be very high. The argument for physical closure is essentially a very high level empirical argument deriving from physical theory (Papineau 2001). And I've argued repeatedly that epiphenomenalism is in radical opposition to our conception of ourselves (even if it is logically coherent).

The cost of denying mind-body supervenience is high. As I am about to show, the cost of asserting supervenience is low. Supervenience looks like the way to go.

8.1.3 Supervenience Isn't Much

There are varieties of supervenience (although not the one quoted above) that are compatible with mind/body dualism. The core of supervenience is dependence plus determination: no mental difference without a physical difference, plus how things are physically determines how things are mentally. The core of supervenience is consistent with nonmaterialist conceptions of the world.

Huxley's epiphenomenalism (chap. 3, sec. 3.3), for instance, is a dualist position that involves supervenience. Every change involving a mental property is caused by a physical change in the body. Hence corresponding to each instance of a mental property there must be an instance of a physical property, and the physical change is sufficient for the mental change. According to Huxley's epiphenomenalism, then, mental changes supervene on physical changes.

There are varieties of supervenience that are inconsistent with physical closure (see Horgan 1993:559–560; and McLaughlin 1992 for details). Since the bare idea of supervenience is compatible with such wildly divergent conceptions of the mind-body relation, saying that the mind supervenes on the body isn't saying much.

Horgan (1993) argues that we can't just say, "the mental supervenes on the physical," and be done with it: we have to explain why and how the mental supervenes on the physical. The explanation for supervenience is thus more basic than the fact of supervenience itself. As Kim puts it, "supervenience is not a mind-body theory" (1998:9): "mind-body supervenience *states* the mind-body problem—it is not a solution to it" (14). Kim is right: supervenience does no positive work in explaining the mind-body relation (see Heil 1998 for more on this theme). Nor does it do any positive work in solving the mental causation problem.

But for my purposes it is not necessary to explain how and why supervenience holds, since I am not trying to develop any particular theory of mind in this book. Rather my project is to vindicate mental causation in the context of materialism and physical closure. These two, plus the claim that mental properties are not physical properties, entail that mental properties supervene on physical properties.

The package of these three claims—physical closure, mental properties are not identical to physical properties, and supervenience—provides a particularly crisp way of stating the mental causation problem: Kim's supervenience argument.

8.2 The Supervenience Argument

Jaegwon Kim argues that if mental properties are not identical to physical properties then there is no mental causation (1998:38–47; 2003:153–159; 2005:39–45). Since he believes that there is mental causation, he presents his argument as a good reason to believe that (some) mental properties are reductively identical to physical properties. My job is to show that the argument fails, that we can believe in mental causation and believe that mental properties are not identical with physical properties.

The argument runs as follows: Assume mental properties supervene on physical properties. Assume that a particular mental event c causes another particular event e and that these two events instantiate mental properties M and M^* respectively. (Lowercase letters denote particular events; uppercase letters denote properties.) Assume that c's having M causes e's having M^* or, as Kim writes, that M causes M^*. By supervenience, c and e have physical properties P and P^*. I present all these assumptions in figure 8.1 (for clarity, I leave out the names for the particular events c and e and follow Kim's convention of referring to them by the properties they have: M and M^*, etc.).

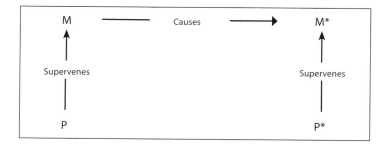

Now, also by supervenience, e's having P^* is sufficient for, and hence fully accounts for, e's having M^*. There are, then, apparently two answers to the question, "How does M^* get instantiated on this occasion?" One is: because it was caused by M. The other is: because P^* is instantiated on this occasion. Kim argues that the latter answer excludes the former. The (seeming) resolution of the seeming tension is to say that M causes M^* by causing P^* (figure 8.2).

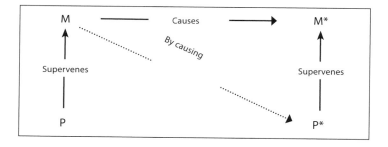

But does M cause P^*? There are again two candidates for what causes P^*: either M or P. As I indicated in chapter 5, section 5.5, mental properties are not identical to physical properties, so $M \neq P$. Now assuming Kim's exclusion principle—"no single event can have more than one sufficient cause occurring at any given time—unless it is a genuine case of causal overdetermination" (2005:42)—either M or P, but not both, causes P^*. But P clearly does cause P^*. So M does not. The argument is fully general, so mental properties are causally impotent. The M–M^* relation (according to Kim) is something like a pseudoprocess, like a causal sequence portrayed in a film (Salmon 1984), determined by the genuine causal process relating P and P^* but not itself causal. Figure 8.3 presents the final picture.

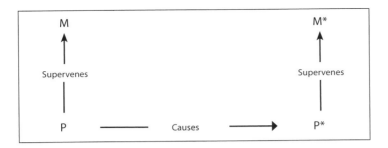

8.3 Supervenience and Causal Relevance

Kim's argument depends on connecting causation and supervenience in a certain way. In a moment, I'll look at the two principles involved in making that connection, the exclusion principle and Edwards's dictum. Both are very plausible principles. They have a firm basis in our understanding of causation and the physical world. I'm not going to argue that Kim's way of treating the relation between causation and supervenience is contradictory or indefensible. There is a consistent overall picture of how the mind and the physical world are related, according to which supervenient properties are never causally relevant to anything. Given that picture, there are only two alternatives: either mental properties are identical to physical properties, so we really can make things happen, or mental properties are not identical to physical properties, so we never make things happen.

There is, however, another consistent overall picture of how the mind, the physical world, and causation are related. Given this picture, we can say that mental properties are not identical to physical properties, that they are irreducible to them and different from them, and also that mental causation happens. Below, in chapter 9, I describe this picture. For the moment I want to dwell on Kim's reasons for adopting his picture.

Traditional discussions of causation and the laws of nature focus on what we may call "the causal connection": that tie or link between events that amounts to causation (see Dowe 2000 for this usage). These discussions do not discuss other kinds of dependency relations. The fact that the internal angles of a triangle sum to 180 degrees depends on its being a plane trilateral figure, but this dependency is not a causal one. Supervenience is another dependency relation that need not be causal and does not show up in traditional discussions. Mill, for example, thinks of nature as a great uniformity or regularity. This uniformity is composed of smaller regularities (1973:315, 3.4.1): "A certain fact invariably occurs whenever certain circumstances are present, and does not occur when they are absent; the like is true of another fact; and so on. From these separate threads of connexion between parts of the great whole which we term nature, a general tissue of connexion un-avoidably weaves itself, by which the whole is held together. . . . these being pre-supposed, the others follow of course. [These] are called laws of nature; the remainder not; because they are in truth mere cases of [the laws of na-ture]; virtually included in them; said, therefore, to *result* from them: who-ever affirms [the laws of nature] has already affirmed all the rest." There is some minimal set of physical properties such that the causal patterns that constitute the progress of the world are a composition of the regularities that obtain among members of that set. These causal patterns determine what is and what is not causally relevant. From this picture of the uniformity of na-ture it is very easy to derive the claim that only the physical properties are the causally relevant ones: those separate threads of "connexion" composed of relations among the properties from the minimal set are the real motor of the world.

Mill does not so much as glance at dependency relations among properties that are not nomic or causal dependencies. He doesn't look at logical depen-dencies; nor does he look at the kind of dependency that holds between expo-sure to the sun and sunburn (chapter 7), a dependency defined logically in terms of causation. He presupposes that some kinds of connection are causal and that other kinds of connection are simply not under consideration. In par-ticular, it appears that he has already presupposed that non–causal depen-dency relations, like supervenience relations, are not under consideration.

Kim's supervenience argument can be seen as a justification for this stance. Kim develops his conception of the way supervenience and causation are re-lated from a marvelous and astonishing passage from Jonathan Edwards's *Doctrines of Original Sin Defended.* Suppose that God directly determines how things are at each moment at every point in the natural world. Then any appearance of causation—any appearance of the causal connection—in the natural world is only an appearance. There is no sense in which earlier things make later things happen, or generate them, or produce them. Again, the re-flections in a glass of the passing scene appear to display the causal connec-tion, but the reflection of a match's being struck does not cause the reflection of the match's lighting. Kim expresses this thought as follows: "*Edwards's dictum.* There is a tension between 'vertical' determination and 'horizontal' causation. In fact, vertical determination excludes horizontal causation" (2005:36). (When an object has its macroproperties in virtue of its parts hav-ing their properties and structural relations, the macroproperties of the ob-ject are "vertically" determined by the microstructure.) Mental properties supervene on physical properties. By the definition of supervenience, when something has one of these subvening physical properties, then, necessarily, it has the supervening mental property. Hence the fact that someone has the mental properties she does is "vertically" determined by her microstructure. Edwards's dictum thus entails that there is no horizontal causation of mental things (provided, that is, that mental properties are not identical to what Kim calls "total micro-based properties," which they will be if they are reducible to physical properties).

What produces the tension Kim describes is the possibility that more than one thing is completely responsible for some phenomenon. Edwards's God is completely responsible for how things are at any time and place, so nothing else can be. Similarly, the microstructural properties of a person at a time are completely responsible for the fact that that person has the mental properties she does, so nothing else can be.

Kim invokes Edwards's dictum only at the first stage of his argument, to rule out supervenient effects. As stated, the dictum would seem to rule out supervenient causes as well: "vertical determination excludes horizontal causation" can be understood to entail not just that something that is "vertically determined" cannot be "horizontally caused" but also that it cannot "horizontally cause" anything. But Kim does not use Edwards's dictum to rule out supervenient causes. Instead he invokes the exclusion principle: "No single event can have more than one sufficient cause occurring at any given time—unless it is a genuine case of causal overdetermination" (2005:42). If M supervenes on P, then if M were to cause something, that effect would have to have a physical cause (either P or some other physical cause). There would then be two causes.

Sometimes it does happen that one event has two (or more) causes, that is, the event is genuinely causally overdetermined. The standard, gory example is that of a firing squad. Suppose three of the shots each by itself would have been sufficient for the death. Then the death was overdetermined. Mills (1996) argues that mental causation is precisely a kind of overdetermination. But that doesn't fit well with experience or with materialism. I move my arm; there do not seem to be two (or more) causes, each of which by itself would have been sufficient for the arm to move. In fact, the conviction that mental causation doesn't involve overdetermination is so firmly held that it is easy to overlook the obligation to demonstrate that a response to Kim's supervenience argument does not involve overdetermination (K. Bennett 2003).

So mental causation does not involve genuine causal overdetermination. So exclusion forces us to select one of the causes, and the best candidate is the physical cause, P. Hence the same tension that underlies Edwards's dictum underlies Kim's exclusion principle: since one thing, the physical cause, is completely responsible for the effect, nothing else can be.

Kim's reasoning concerning causation and supervenience thus depends on the thought that if there were supervenient causation, it would be too much;

it would be redundant. Where there is supervenience, the physical base does all the causing there is to do, and there is therefore no room for the supervening things to do any causing.

But there are difficulties for this thought about causation and supervenience. It has been observed more than once (Loewer 2001; Pereboom 2002) that the exclusion principle does not apply in the case where M supervenes on P, since in that case the two are not independent causes. (Kim doesn't use the word "independent" in this formulation of the exclusion principle, though he does at 1989:239, but the same point can be made about the expression "no single event." If M supervenes on P, there is a sense, to be described in a moment, in which M and P do not add up to more than one sufficient cause.) There is a parallel difficulty for Edwards's dictum. Where M^* supervenes on P^*, Kim says that it is "vertically" determined by P^*. But it is not determined in Edwards's sense. P^* is not an existence distinct from M^* that brings M^* into existence, since P^* cannot exist without M^* (since, by supervenience, necessarily, anything that instantiates P^* at a time instantiates M^* at that time). Hence there would be no redundancy of effects if P were to cause both P^* and M^*, since P^* and M^* do not add up to more than one distinct effect of P. Moreover, because M and M^* are not independent of P and P^*, the $M-M^*$ relation is not relevantly similar to a pseudoprocess in Salmon's (1984) sense.

It may be objected that Edwards's God can make an instance of P^* that is not an instance of M^*, since Edwards's God is omnipotent, and an omnipotent God is not limited by physical necessity. But such an act by Edwards's God in the actual world would be a miracle, in the sense that it would involve breaking the laws of nature. I do not think that we should bring miracles to bear on our theory of causation.

8.3.1 Property Overlap

A key premise in Kim's argument is that $M \neq P$. If this is true, how can M and P fail to be distinct causes of P^*? How can it be that M and P are not more than one sufficient cause of P^*? The answer is that properties overlap: while M and P are not identical, they are not completely distinct properties, either (chap. 6, sec. 6.3, above). I will develop this thought using the abundant ontology of properties I developed in chapter 5. (The idea that mental things are in some respects distinct from and in other respects not distinct from physical things has been made before, in a variety of different ontological settings; see Yablo 1992; Clapp 2001; Watkins 2002; Pereboom 2002).

Kim uses the uppercase letters M, P, and so on, to denote particulars, in this case, property instances. Property instances are individuated with respect to their constitutive objects, properties and times. Kim, I believe, holds that instances of nonidentical properties are always distinct particulars; for example, if the property M is irreducible to physical properties, then every instance of M is a distinct particular from any instance of any physical property P.

I am using the uppercase letters M, P, and so on, to denote properties, not particulars. Two properties may be nonidentical yet not entirely distinct; they can overlap. There are two ways for them to overlap (for ease of exposition I will write as though properties are sets; see above, chap. 5, sec. 5.1):

- one property may be a proper subset of another;
- two properties may share instances but also each have instances that are not instances of the other.

The property {Carnap} overlaps the property {Carnap, Quine} in the first way, and the property {Quine, Davidson} overlaps it in the second way.

When two properties overlap, they are not identical, but neither are they entirely distinct. Similar things may be said about property instances. Consider again the properties {Carnap, Quine} and {Quine, Davidson}. Quine is an instance of both properties. The property instance of Quine's having the first property is not entirely distinct from the property instance of his having the second property. Davidson is an instance of the second property but not of the first, hence the property instance of Davidson's having the second property is entirely distinct from any instance of the first property.

Here's an example using mental properties that supervene on physical properties. Suppose the property of being a red afterimage supervenes on the properties of being in various brain states, say, B_1, B_2, and so on. Then, necessarily, if something has B_1, it is a red afterimage. So the property B_1 is a proper subset of the property of being a red afterimage. But something may be a red afterimage but not B_1. So in this case no instance of B_1 is entirely distinct from an instance of being a red afterimage. Some instances of being a red afterimage are entirely distinct from any instance of B_1. And no instance of being a red afterimage is entirely distinct from every instance of every property on which being a red afterimage supervenes.

Kim's supervenience argument, and the justification I am imputing to him of the traditional practice of ignoring supervenient properties in accounts of laws of nature and causation, depends on supervenient causes and effects being too much causing. But they are too much only if they are completely distinct from their supervenience bases. But they are not. So the argument, and the justification, doesn't succeed.

Now, various complaints may be made against this critique of Kim's argument. We might decide to reject supervenient causes on the ground that doing so yields a simpler, cleaner, clearer picture of what causation is. We may feel that the whole avenue of inquiry is obviously closed off from the start. For if supervenient causes (effects) are not distinct from their supervenience bases, then they aren't anything new. Kim writes, concerning supervenient causation, "This is only a gimmick with no meaning; . . . inserting a dotted arrow and calling it 'supervenient causation,' or anything else (how about 'pretend' or 'faux' causation), does not alter the situation one bit. It neither adds any new facts nor reveals any hitherto unnoticed relationships. Inserting the extra arrow is not only pointless; it could also be philosophically pernicious if it should mislead us into thinking that we have thereby conferred on M, the mental event, some real causal role" (2005:62). It's important to avoid a real danger here (Sider 2003). Kim is right that there is a powerful intuition that there's something fishy about supervenient causation; I'll take this up in a moment. But it's easy to mistake the intuition for a real argument that there is something wrong with supervenient causation. It is worth noting, for instance, that this passage expresses a new argument against supervenient causation, not the supervenience argument at all. The supervenience argument was that supervenient causation would be too much. The claim of this passage is rather that supervenient causation isn't anything at all. But that's not correct: since the mental properties are not identical with the physical properties, there are new facts and new relationships (see below, chap. 9, especially sec. 9.5).

8.3.2 Which Conception?

In any event, Kim offers a coherent conception of causal relevance and supervenience that entails that irreducible supervenient properties are never causally relevant. Kim is right that there is a tension here, and it is important to acknowledge that.

But there is another coherent conception of causal relevance and supervenience. It makes room for supervenient properties to be causally relevant. Hence it makes room for mental causation even if mental properties are not reducible to (and not identical to) physical properties.

Both conceptions are consistent, coherent pictures of how causation works. Kim's picture respects an intuition for minimalism: the exclusion principle and Edwards's dictum compact the collection of putative causes down into the ones that are really doing the work.

But Kim's picture demands that mental properties are identical to physical properties if they are involved in mental causation. This violates an intuition flowing from our conception of ourselves and how we make things happen. When I move my arm, it's important that the cause should be my choice and that my choice should be something distinctive about the world. It has been easy (for philosophers and nonphilosophers alike) to inflate this sense of distinctiveness into a conviction that minds occupy a fundamentally different kind of reality from physical things. And it has been easy to counter this inflated sense of self-importance by insisting on reductionist physicalism. But there is a middle way. Mental properties are not identical to physical properties, but they also are not completely distinct from them. Our conception of ourselves as not just atoms swerving in the void is vindicated, but at the same time we can say we are not more than atoms swerving in the void. Hence I think the alternative conception is better grounded in our ordinary thinking about ourselves as making things happen.

In the next chapter I articulate the alternative conception: the leveled account of causal relevance. The account says that properties at the fundamental level are causally relevant and that properties at higher levels, perhaps including psychological properties, can also be causally relevant. The picture is in some respects less clean than just banning supervenient causation would produce. But it allows for the causal relevance of supervenient properties. And it does so in a way that honors the fundamental picture of causation and law that we get from Mill: that causal relevance is a matter of being related by laws of nature.

8.4 Levels

The leveled account of causal relevance says that properties at higher levels can also be causally relevant. What are levels? Can philosophical critiques of the idea of levels be overcome?

The idea of levels is a familiar one. We say that the liquidity and transparency of water are higher-level features and the charge and geometry of molecules of H_2O are lower level. Macroeconomic trends are high level; individual economic transactions are low level. A computer application (such as emacs or Microsoft Word) is high level; how the chips in the computer work is low level. There are high-level programming languages (Lisp), and there are low-level programming languages (assemblers, perhaps C). The fitness of a particular animal is high level; the detailed physical microstructure of the animal that (for instance) enables it to see a bit more clearly is low level. Thoughts and feelings seem to be high-level features of people, while action potentials in single neurons are lower-level features. The picture of reality dividing into a hierarchy of levels is standard in science and science education. Physics, chemistry, biology, anatomy, psychology, and political science pick out successively higher levels of beings in the natural world: particles, atoms, molecules, cells, organisms, groups of organisms. The picture constitutes a metaphysical view about what the world is like (Oppenheim and Putnam 1958; Wimsatt 1974, 1986).

The idea of levels is closely related to that of supervenience. Roughly speaking, levels imply supervenience, but supervenience doesn't imply levels. Take the liquidity of water as an example. Liquidity is a higher-level property of water. It supervenes on lower-level properties of water. This means that any sample of water that is liquid has these lower-level properties and that any set of molecules of H_2O that has these lower-level properties will be liquid. So higher-level properties supervene on lower-level properties.

But supervenience doesn't imply levels. The supervenience relation is far less specific than the relation of levels. For instance, identity is a supervenience relation. Here's Kim's definition of mental/physical supervenience again: "Mental properties *supervene* on physical properties, in that necessarily, for any mental property M, if anything has M at time t, there exists a physical base (or subvenient) property P such that it has P at t, and necessarily anything that has P at a time has M at that time" (1998:9). If we put in the same property for both P and M, this statement will be true. But clearly no property is at a higher (or lower) level than itself. For another example, the property of being either a spoon or a snowflake supervenes on the set of properties {being a spoon, being a snowflake}, yet the former property isn't at a higher level than either of the latter. And, more troubling for our purposes, we wouldn't want to say that being either a spoon or a snowflake is a causally relevant feature of things that have that property. Suppose we are comfortable with the idea that spoons make things happen because they are spoons and snowflakes make things happen because they are snowflakes. We are not likely to be comfortable with the idea that having the additional property of being either a spoon or a snowflake makes things happen.

So if we want to defend the idea that supervening mental properties are causally relevant, we need more than the bare idea of supervenience. Now, we could at this point turn to the project of building up from idea of supervenience to the idea of levels. The project would be to say what it is, in addition to supervenience, we need in order to have something that satisfies our commonsense idea that we have something higher level. Alternatively, we could just assume that some idea or other of levels is perfectly acceptable.

Either strategy is open to a very general philosophical critique: that there is something badly wrong with the very idea of levels. Kim 2002 and Heil 2003a, 2003b, for instance, sharply criticize leveled or layered accounts of reality.

SUPERVENIENCE AND LEVELS   147

There are several kinds of complaints. Perhaps the most pressing is that a leveled account of properties implies that only the fundamental level has any causal relevance. If things at the fundamental level do the causal work, how could anything at any higher level make any difference? This is my main concern in this book: to explain how higher-level properties could have causal relevance. The full explanation comes in the next chapter; so let me set this complaint aside for the moment.

Another kind of complaint is that adding levels beyond the fundamental level is adding extra unnecessary things to our ontology. Levels are supposed to bloat our ontology. This isn't a worry for the abundant conception of properties that I described above in chapter 5, since I've already said that for every set of actual and possible entities there is a property.

Yet another set of complaints revolves around the ideas of supervenience and multiple realization. Higher-level things supervene on lower-level things and, often, are multiply realized by them. Both supervenience and multiple realization have been argued to be problematic (Heil 1998, 1999; Shapiro 2000). The main problem with supervenience is supposed to be that it doesn't explain anything; as I argued above, that's right, but that doesn't show that mental properties do not supervene on physical properties, and, indeed, there is a good reason to think that they do (sec. 8.1.2, above). Gillett 2003 and Aizawa 2006 argue that the supposed difficulties for multiple realization are only apparent.

But there is another and more serious problem. We don't have a well-defined conception of what levels are. Consider again the familiar claim that the following sciences are arranged according to increasing level: physics, chemistry, biochemistry, biology, psychology, sociology. What principle governs dividing things into levels: Is it size? How much energy goes into interactions at a level? Some of the principles people have suggested have absurd consequences (Kim 2002). Some properties of things are shared at every level: protons and hearts and people and galaxies all have mass. Further, the hierarchies are local. The heart is an organ and so sits at a certain level relative to organisms. But does it make sense to say that it is at the same level as or at a different level from a part of a mountain or a part of a car? The problem is that it is doubtful that there is "a single hierarchy of connected levels, from higher to lower, in which every object and phenomenon in the natural world finds its 'appropriate' place" (Kim 2002:16). There is no monolithic conception of levels, in the sense that for every pair of things in the world, the conception tells us that these two items are on the same level or that one is higher than the other. It seems quite likely that there are several distinct conceptions of levels that divide various portions of reality in different ways for different purposes. For instance, the sense in which the heart is high level relative to its valves is certainly distinct from the sense in which the Lisp programming language is high level relative to the C programming language.

These are serious and interesting problems. But they do not amount to a fundamental problem for the very idea of levels. Rather, they mean that when we talk about levels, we need to be clear about what kind of level we are talking about.

Craver (2007: chap. 5) argues that many or most of the things that people have wanted to say about levels come out true if we take them to be talking about levels of mechanisms. The "levels of mechanisms" conception is not monolithic: many things are not mechanisms or parts of mechanisms or composed of mechanisms at all, and so they get no level in this conception. And even when two things are parts of the same mechanical system, it may not make sense to ask whether they are at the same or different levels. For instance, it might make sense to say that a particular valve is lower level relative to the fuel-mixing mechanism of an automobile engine and that a particular chip is lower level relative to a control computer in the same automobile, but it doesn't make sense to say that the valve and the chip are higher or lower level relative to one another.

Craver argues that explanation in neuroscience integrates explanations from many levels. Neuroscience aims to understand the brain. Understanding the brain requires many strategies, techniques, methods that explore mechanisms of the brain at different levels. Hence neuroscience presupposes the existence of real levels of mechanisms in the brain and body.

There are two philosophical dangers here. One is arguing from the practice of science to metaphysical conclusions. Just because well-established sciences use the idea of levels doesn't show that the world actually has levels; it might be that the idea is a convenient way to talk about a world devoid of levels. The second danger is arguing from claims about levels and explanation to metaphysical conclusions about how the world actually is. Again, it might be that there are different ways to explain things and that we tend to think of these ways in terms of levels of things, yet nevertheless reality itself doesn't actually have levels.

These are serious concerns. Again, just because they are possible worries about whether there really are levels of properties, independent of what people (including scientists) say or think about them, doesn't mean that we should give up on the very idea of levels of properties, that is, the metaphysical idea that in addition to the fundamental properties there are also properties at many levels.

Mechanisms, for instance, are objective features of reality. They have parts, which interact, and when they do, the entire mechanism exhibits particular behaviors. Mechanisms in turn interact with other mechanisms, and when they do, the larger mechanisms of which they are a part exhibit their own distinctive—higher-level—behaviors. The history of the life sciences, and the history of neuroscience, is full of research that explains the behavior of complex entities by revealing the mechanisms that produce that behavior. When a photon hits a cone cell, it can cause a nerve impulse. How does it do this? The first step is that the added energy of the photon causes a molecule of rhodopsin to change from the 11-cis to the 11-trans form. This is part of the mechanism by which cone cells turn light into nerve impulses. There is a higher-level mechanism that takes light as input and produces representations of the world; one of its parts is the mechanism that generates nerve impulses from photons in cone cells.

Hence the levels of mechanisms conception shows how the things that we do (for instance, speaking or acting) can be explained in terms of mechanisms at a lower level. The behavior of these mechanisms in turn is explained in terms of the behaviors and causal powers of the mechanisms that compose them. It may be, for instance, that speaking involves a computational mechanism that looks up words in a lexicon given a semantic representation. This mechanism will be composed of further mechanisms that do simpler things. And so forth.

The idea that there are levels and that things at various levels have causal powers does not depend on any particular account of how the world actually works. It is to be expected that we will change our thinking about the sciences of the mind and the brain as we learn more. But we aren't going to outgrow the idea that the behavior of complex things can be explained by the composition of the behavior of their simpler parts. And so we aren't going to outgrow the idea of thinking of reality in terms of levels.

So the very general philosophical complaints against the idea of levels can, I suggest, be answered. I am about to turn to the most serious, the worry that higher-level properties would be causally irrelevant. For present purposes, I need not do further work on the idea of levels. There is every reason to think that there is some reasonable conception of levels, such that mental properties are higher-level properties than microproperties of the brain.

8.5 Conclusion

Mental properties are different (but not entirely distinct) from physical properties. If we do make things happen—if mental causation is real—and if physics is causally closed, then mental properties have to supervene on physical properties.

The most basic reason for thinking that mental causation is impossible stems from the claim that when a property supervenes on a causally relevant property, it is not itself causally relevant. The argument for this claim is that if the supervenient property were causally relevant, it would be too much: supervenient causation would be overdetermination.

As I've shown, when one property supervenes on another, they overlap and hence are not entirely distinct. Consequently, the supervening property and its supervenience base cannot overdetermine their effect; so supervenient causation would not be too much causation.

I argued that supervenience is necessary for mental causation (given physical closure and the nonidentity of mental properties and physical properties). It is not sufficient. Supervenience is a very weak relation, and many supervening properties are causally irrelevant. We want a stronger relation: mental properties are higher-level properties relative to their supervenience bases.

If mental properties are higher-level properties, and higher-level properties can be causally relevant, then we can solve the mental causation problem. The remaining difficulty, then, is to show how a higher-level supervening mental property may be causally relevant, to show how such a property—like the physical properties on which it supervenes—can stand in the right relation to the laws of nature to count as causally relevant (the gold standard).

8.6 Further Reading

Supervenience is almost exclusively a technical term in philosophy—mainly in the philosophy of mind but widely used in many other areas of philosophy as well. Terry Horgan's "From Supervenience to Superdupervenience" (1993) is an excellent account of the history, character, and usefulness of the supervenience relation. Jaegwon Kim wrote many of the seminal papers on supervenience; they are collected in his *Supervenience and Mind* (1993a). McLaughlin and Bennett's "Supervenience" (2005) is a comprehensive account of varieties of supervenience and their relations. John Heil's "Supervenience Deconstructed" (1998) and his *From an Ontological Point of View* (2003a) argue that supervenience explains nothing; consequently, we should avoid its use in working on the metaphysics of mind.

Oppenheim and Putnam's "Unity of Science as a Working Hypothesis" (1958) is an early exposition of a leveled account of reality. William Wimsatt's papers "Complexity and Organization" (1974) and "Forms of Aggregativity" (1986) characterize levels somewhat differently. Jaegwon Kim's "The Layered

Model: Metaphysical Considerations" (2002) argues that none of the standing conceptions of levels is completely coherent. Carl Craver argues persuasively in his *Explaining the Brain: Mechanisms and the Mosaic Unity of Neuroscience* (2007) that there are coherent conceptions of levels and that neuroscience makes use of the concept of levels of mechanisms.

The Causal Relevance of Mental Properties

IN CHAPTER 8 I showed that causation in virtue of (supervenient, irreducible) mental properties would not be too much, or overdetermined causation. But I didn't show that mental properties can meet the gold standard that physical properties meet, namely, being linked by the laws of nature (chap. 6). That is the task of the present chapter: to give a positive account of the causal relevance of mental (and other higher-level) properties.

Here's the broad outline of the solution. What seems to disconnect mental (and other higher-level) properties from laws of nature, and causal relevance, is exceptions. If I want a glass of water, I may reach for it, or I may not, depending on what else is going on. The laws of nature (operating together) are supposed to be exceptionless. This is so even if they are probabilistic: a probabilistic law doesn't have exceptions; rather, it just specifies the probabilities of a fixed range of alternatives. Now, an event never causes its effect in virtue of a single property; property instances always work in concert with other property instances to cause their effects. This is true even at the level of fundamental physics. Suppose we could fill in or qualify the conditions under which instances of higher-level properties act, in order to take care of the exceptions. And suppose that the filling-in isn't simply reverting to the physical laws; that is to say, it's not a matter of providing the physical properties of the event that has the higher-level property (which would be conceding that it's really the physical properties that matter). We would then have a system of laws of nature expressed from the perspective of the higher-level properties. Then higher-level properties would be tied to laws of nature just as physical properties are. And mental properties could be just as causally relevant to effect properties.

9.1 Recapitulation

Here's a brief review of the ingredients we need for the solution.

9.1.1 Chapter 4: Physicalism

The world is physical. This means that the world is a system of things and properties interacting according to the laws of nature. So minds are physical. This just means that thinking and feeling and desiring and being conscious are all physical phenomena. Minds are not things distinct from bodies; minds are not things distinct from the physical world.

Since everything is physical, and since physical laws determine what causes what, causation obeys the principle of physical closure: "if a physical event has a cause that occurs at t, it has a physical cause that occurs at t" (Kim 2005:43).

9.1.2 Chapter 5: Properties

Properties are abundant: to every grouping of the particulars, actual and possible, there corresponds a property. The most basic, and most important, job for properties is to provide all the commonalities, and all the distinctions, among things. There are enough properties for any possible difference between any two things.

Mental properties are not identical with physical properties. This follows from the logical possibility of a nonphysical thinker. We can also derive their nonidentity from the proposition that mental properties are not reducible to physical properties. Various arguments have been offered for this proposition. For instance, it is supposed to follow from functionalism (Block 1980c), the failure of functionalism (Putnam 1988), and the anomalism of the mental (Davidson 1970b).

9.1.3 Chapter 6: Causation

Causation involves generality. When one event causes another event, it does so in virtue of, or because it has, certain properties, which are shared by other events and which must stand in certain relations to properties of the effect. This is the motor of the world.

Mill conceived of the motor of the world as a set of laws of nature, where the laws make up "threads of connexion" that weave together to produce the "general tissue of connexion" of the natural world, or the fabric of the world. If we focus on a single property of a single occurrence, there is a swatch of that fabric that produces that occurrence. So a swatch law is a complete specification of a positive producer (chap. 6, sec. 6.1.6) for an effect of a certain type. The form of such a law is as follows:

> For all places p and times t, if x is an event that occurs at place p and time t and has an array of properties $ABCD$ . . . arranged in a certain structure S, then at place p and time $t+\varepsilon$ there will be an event y that has property G.

Whenever a swatch law of this form is true, then each of the properties mentioned in the antecedent condition is causally relevant to the property mentioned in the consequent condition.

The Causal Connection

One event makes another happen because it has certain properties. The first event is thus connected to the second event by causation. Different theories of causation give very different answers to the question, what is the nature of the causal connection? A purely Humean account would say: constant conjunction. A "laws of nature" account would say: succession by virtue of the laws of nature. An account based on counterfactuals such as David Lewis's would say: the fact that if the cause had not happened, the effect would not have, either. A probability-raising account says: the cause raised the probability of the effect. A conserved quantity view says: a causal process occurred that transferred a conserved quantity from the cause to the effect. A dispositional account says: dispositions manifesting with reciprocal disposition partners necessitate their effects.

Whatever is the right account, let us call what it describes "the causal connection." What matters for our purposes is that there is such a connection, not the details of its character.

9.1.4 Chapter 7: Causally Involved Properties

The instances of action properties must, by definition, be caused by instances of mental properties. But causal relevance is not logical connection. All instances of sunburn must be caused by exposure to the sun. But this is a logical fact that stems from our selecting something of interest out of the total fabric of what is causally relevant to this sort of burn. Hence the property of being exposure to the sun is not causally relevant to the property of being sunburn. Nor is the property of being a reason causally relevant to the property of being an action. According to (role) functionalism, all mental properties are causally involved with specific types of causes and so (role) functionalism must be rejected, as it cannot explain mental causation. If there are any dispositional properties, like the property of being fragile, they cannot be causally relevant to their manifestation types (like shattering, for fragility), since the connection between the dispositional property and the manifestation type is logical and hence not causal.

9.1.5 Chapter 8: Supervenience

Mental properties must supervene on physical properties, if we are to keep the causal closure of the physical world and mental causation. Causation in virtue of both mental properties and physical properties is not too much causing, since mental properties supervene on (and hence overlap) physical properties.

So the situation is this. If we can make things happen, that is, if there is mental causation, then mental events have to be able to cause things in virtue of their mental properties. That is to say: mental properties must be causally relevant to some properties of the effects of mental events. Mental properties supervene on and are not identical with physical properties (although they are not entirely distinct from physical properties, either). When something happens in the world, it is a physical event, and it has physical causes. The event's having those physical properties (governed by the physical laws) is causally sufficient to produce the effect. Now, if mental properties were entirely distinct from physical properties, then, since the physical properties already are enough to produce the effect, there would really be nothing for the mental properties to do, and they really would be causally irrelevant. (That is why dualism is ruled out: it would make mental properties entirely distinct from physical properties, since the mental particulars would be entirely nonphysical.) But even if they are not entirely distinct from the physical properties, there is a mystery: if causal relevance is a matter of being linked by laws of nature, how can the mental properties be causally relevant? For, surely, isn't it so that only physical properties are linked by laws of nature?

What we need, then, is to show how mental properties can be causally relevant, by showing how they can stand in the same relation to the laws of nature as do the physical properties.

9.2 Causal Relevance Within Levels

Consider for a moment why physical properties are causally relevant. The causal connection is exclusionary: some properties of an event are causally relevant to properties of its effects, while others are not. Methods for discovering causes seek out the properties that matter by seeking to exclude the ones that do not. For instance, Mill's second canon reads, "If an instance in which the phenomenon under investigation occurs, and an instance in which it does not occur, have every circumstance in common save one, that one occurring only in the former; the circumstance in which alone the two instances differ, is the effect, or the cause, or an indispensable part of the cause, of the phenomenon" (1973:391, 3.8.2). We can think of Mill's methods as a kind of competition: many properties enter, and only one prevails, by virtue of best exemplifying the causal connection. (Mill's methods are about how we can know or justify a claim about causes. But we are not talking now about knowledge or justification. Rather, we are talking about the metaphysics of causation. There is in fact no competition; rather, the causally relevant properties are the ones that fit the pattern of the causal connection better than any of the alternatives.)

But the argument of chapter 8 that supervening properties are not causally relevant is not based on this image of properties competing for their place in the causal connection. There is no question of their losing the competition; the arguments are designed to show that they were never in the competition to begin with. Supervenient causation was supposed to be too much. Supervenient properties are supposed to be instantiated by virtue of supervenience, not by virtue of causation.

Moreover, the idea that supervening properties could compete with their supervenience base properties for causal relevance is incoherent (Dardis 2002). Competition requires independence: each competitor must be such that it is logically possible for it to cross the finish line ahead of the rest of the pack. But when one property supervenes on another, this can't happen: the supervenience base property will of necessity carry the supervening property along with it (like Aeneas carrying Anchises from Troy). This metaphysical fact has a familiar consequence for finding out causes: when we test for causal relevance, we vary independent variables in order to determine what depends on them. But a supervening property and its supervenience base are not independent and cannot be varied independently.

The competition for causal relevance thus takes place within a family of properties that are independent of one another. What family of properties will this be? Kim's metaphysical arguments that supervening properties are not causally relevant in effect demand that the competition for causal relevance must take place entirely at the lowest level of the hierarchy of levels of properties. As I noted in chapter 8, Kim's two principles (Edwards's dictum and exclusion) compact all causal relevance down to the lowest level.

We could, however, think of competitions for causal relevance as happening within levels. Physical properties then would be causally relevant at the physical level. And properties at higher levels would compete for causal relevance at their own level. In fact, this suggestion fits quite neatly with a conviction that many philosophers share: that causation happens at levels (Hardcastle 1998; Block 2003).

How does this suggestion mesh with the gold standard for causal relevance?

9.3 Higher-Level Laws

The gold standard for causal relevance (chap. 6) is that one property is causally relevant to another when a swatch law entailed by the laws of nature connects them.

On the face of it, higher-level properties, like mental properties, aren't connected by laws of nature and hence cannot pass muster according to this austere standard. One difficulty derives from causal closure. Recall Kim's statement of closure (2005, 43): "if a physical event has a cause that occurs at t, it has a physical cause that occurs at t." The set of fundamental laws of nature should be closed in this sense. But levels other than the physical aren't, apparently, closed. In fact, it seems virtually definitive of being a nonphysical level that sufficient causes of events at that level involve properties from lower levels. If a mental event has a cause that occurs at t, it may well not have a mental cause that occurs at t; for instance, seeing an apple typically has only nonmental causes, namely, the presence of the apple. And the presence of the apple causes the perception only with the assistance of light, which arguably is not at the mental level.

Another difficulty is that instances of higher-level properties may be physically different in various ways. Instances of physical properties, the ones that show up at the bottom of the level hierarchy, don't come in varieties and flavors that differ in their ability to produce further states of affairs. By contrast, instances of most nonphysical properties, the properties that show up at higher levels, differ physically, sometimes subtly, sometimes more grossly. The instances of the property of being a cup differ widely: some are porcelain, some are glass, some are wood, and some cups are made of ice. These different kinds of cups differ correspondingly in what they can do.

The issue is more general than that of multiple realizability, although the two are closely related. As discussed in chapter 4 above, the idea that mental properties are multiply realizable motivated the move from identity theory to functionalism. Multiple realizability has recently come under considerable critical scrutiny (Bechtel and Mundale 1999; Heil 1999; Lawrence Shapiro

2000; for some responses, see Gillett 2003; Aizawa 2006). The core difficulty is that philosophers haven't clearly articulated the difference between physical differences that are irrelevant and physical differences that are enough for a real difference in realization. We don't need to settle the difficulty for our present worry: even tiny physical differences can be enough to make a difference to what an instance of a higher-level property can do, even if we shouldn't count the differences as multiple realizations.

9.3.1 Form and Matter and Higher-Level Laws

So linking higher-level properties to laws of nature faces two hard problems. Both encourage us to think of the real work of higher-level things as being done at a lower level. Since the psychological level isn't closed, and psychological things are realized by physical things, we think that things at the physical level must be doing the work. So the problem is to connect higher-level properties of causes with properties of effects, in such a way that (1) closure is preserved and (2) differences among realizations are compensated for. And we can't do this by simply reverting to the physical properties of the causes. In this section I will describe the structure of the solution using the example of a cup of tea. In the next section I will apply the structure to a real example from biology.

Cups that are made of porcelain are good for holding hot tea. Those made of ice are no good for holding hot tea but are really good for making messy puddles. For the property of being a cup to be causally relevant to these kinds of effects, that property has to be qualified in a certain way, so that having that property, qualified one way, is causally sufficient (as always, in the company of an array of other properties) for holding hot tea, while having that same property, qualified another way, is causally sufficient for making messy puddles. What should that qualification look like?

Suppose that at the level of the physical properties there are several laws of nature, each making up a thread in Mill's fabric of nature, and that they combine into a swatch of the fabric—a swatch law—that looks like this:

> For all places p and times t, if x is an event that occurs at place p and time t and has an array of properties $ABCD\ldots$ arranged in a certain structure S, then at place p and time $t+\varepsilon$ there will be an event y that has property G.

To keep the discussion uncluttered, let's express the swatch law this way, leaving the structure, time, and place in the background:

> If x has $ABCD\ldots$, then y has G.

For the purposes of my example, let's suppose that any event that has *ABCD* . . . is an event of pouring hot Earl Grey tea into a porcelain teacup. *A*, *B*, *C*, *D*, and so on are physical properties, and each of them is causally relevant to *G*, another physical property. Let's suppose further that *T* is the property of being a cup and that it supervenes on the property *A*, so that anything that has *A* is a cup—as it happens, a porcelain cup. There are other ways for something to have property *T* (being a tin cup, being a cup made completely of ice, and so forth). Hence *T* supervenes on a set of properties that properly includes *A*. Suppose that any event that has *BCD* will be an event of pouring hot Earl Grey tea into the cup. Finally, let instances of *G* be instances of holding hot tea.

Now consider the swatch law:

If *x* has *TBCD* . . . , then *y* has *G*.

This is identical to the first swatch law but with *T* taking the place of *A*. Since the instances of *T* differ physically, this statement is false; sometimes *TBCD* . . . isn't followed by a *G*. To make it true, we will have to ensure that we have the right kind of cup of tea. We do that by adding more properties to the structured array that includes *T*. We could qualify *T* with the original *A*, giving us this condition, which is true if and only if the original condition is true:

If *x* has *TABCD* . . . , then *y* has *G*.

But this qualification is redundant: since being an *A* is a way to be a *T*, there is no difference between there being an instance of *A* and being an instance of *T* and an instance of *A* at the same place and time (except for the difference between *T* and *A*, which is the *T*s that are not *A*s—but this particular cup is not one of them). It's also, intuitively, a cheat: this regularity is just the physical regularity, with an irrelevant extra bit added.

Mackie considers the same sort of problem when describing causes as a special sort of sufficient condition: "*ABC* is a *minimal* sufficient condition: none of its conjuncts is redundant: no part of it, such as *AB*, is itself sufficient for *P*" (1974:62). Since in our case *T* supervenes on *A*, the structured collection *TABCD* isn't redundant in quite the same way, because by supervenience it's not possible to produce *G* with that collection without *T* (since it is not possible to produce any instance of the collection *ABCD* that is not also an instance of *T*). Nonetheless, whatever an *A*-type *T* can do is exactly what *A*-type things can do, so the objection stands.

So we need some property other than *A* to put together with *T* (and the other elements of the structured array), so that when that collection of properties is instantiated in that structure, the result is an instance of G and so that the collection isn't redundant.

Something similar to Aristotle's distinction between form and matter will help us out. This particular cup of Earl Grey tea is some porcelain in a certain shape. There are two properties here, one for the form, one for the matter. The form property—T—is the property of being a cup of tea, that is, the property corresponding to the set of all possible cups of tea, made of porcelain, wood, glass, cardboard, titanium, ice, and so on. The matter property for this particular cup of tea—call it H—is the property of being of this kind of stuff, that is, the property corresponding to the set of all actual and possible arrangements of the exact amount and kind of porcelain of which this cup is made. These arrangements will include ones that are cup shaped, cube shaped, thin films, and so forth.

Is H itself a physical property? The causal relevance of mental properties is threatened by the physical properties of things that figure in the fundamental laws of nature. H is not one of those physical properties. H is the property shared by all and only the actual and possible individuals that are arrangements of a certain amount of a certain kind of physical stuff (for instance, the porcelain of this cup). This is a collection of very heterogeneously formed clumps of stuff. What happens at the physical level depends on how the components of these clumps, in their structure, behave. Hence H will not figure in the laws of nature that constitute the motor of the world. Hence it is not a physical property. Hence there is no threat that, by invoking H, we will be reverting to the underlying physical causes of G. (There are broader conceptions of physical properties that count H as a physical property: for instance, properties represented by arbitrary collections of only nomologically possible individuals. But these physical properties are no threat to the causal relevance of mental properties.)

Also, T does not supervene on H, since many of the particulars that have H are not cups. (Indeed, it's hard to think of any familiar, or scientific, classification of things that supervenes on H, other than perhaps "some porcelain.")

If T and H are instantiated together in the same thing at the same time, that thing will also instantiate the conjunction of those two properties. Something that has the conjunction of those two properties is something with the form of a cup of Earl Grey tea, a cup that is moreover made of porcelain: that is, the conjunction of T and H is exactly the original property A. (For this to work, H must be porcelain in any of the shapes it can take. It cannot be just any arrangement of the ultimate constituents of a porcelain cup, since those could be rearranged to yield something that is not porcelain.)

Then the regularity

If x has $THBCD \ldots$, then y has G

is true if and only if the original

If x has $ABCD \ldots$, then y has G

is true.

A similar maneuver can be performed on G. Some higher-level property, like the property of holding tea, supervenes on this physical property. It, like T, can have instances that differ physically. But there are swatch laws that generate each of the variations, once the variation is made explicit in the way sketched above.

Finally, the collection of all these laws expresses the laws of nature at the level of the higher-level properties. For all the non–higher-level parts of the world, the laws are just the physical laws. For the parts of the world that do have higher-level properties, the laws relate suitably qualified higher-level properties.

9.3.2 A Real Example

The question of the causal relevance of higher-level, irreducible, supervening properties is the question of whether the properties of the "special sciences" (Fodor 1974, 1975) are causally relevant. If the properties of a given special science, for instance, biology, are not reducible to physical properties, but they do supervene on physical properties, then Kim's argument would show that they are all causally irrelevant.

A recent discussion in the philosophy of biology uses several of the moves that I have just discussed. Beatty (1995) offers two reasons why biology contains no laws. One is that the fact that there are any biological organisms at all, and that there are biological laws at all, is contingent on the special sort of initial and background conditions that obtained and presently obtain on Earth. Change those conditions, and the laws cease to work. Second, the biological laws have exceptions. Mendel's first law says that "diploid sexual organisms form haploid gametes by a 'fair' 50/50 meiotic division" (Sober 1997: S460). But this is not always true, since there are genes that cause segregation distortion. Moreover, Rosenberg (1994) argues that the properties of biology (like fitness) are multiply realized, and hence there can't be laws governing such properties.

Sober (1997) responds to Beatty's first reason by pointing out that even if some putative law of biology is contingent on initial conditions, we can make the law noncontingent by including the initial conditions. Following the pattern described in the last section, we can make the same response to Beatty's second objection: even if some diploid sexual organisms don't form haploid gametes by a 50/50 meiotic division, there is a difference between those that do and those that don't. To get exceptionless laws, we just need to include the full characterizations of the differences. The same goes for the worry about multiple realization: to get an exceptionless law, the higher-level property needs to be qualified by additional properties. If we simply reverted to a complete physical description of each particular variant realization, we would be characterizing the causes redundantly, as above. But there do exist appropriate matter properties that dovetail with the biological properties to yield exceptionless laws.

Let's abbreviate Mendel's first law as follows: if x has DA, then y has F, where D refers to the property of being a diploid sexual organism, A refers to the property that such an organism has that leads it to form gametes, and F refers to the property of the process of the formation of the gamete that it is a "fair" 50/50 meiotic division. This law clearly has exceptions: if the organism is struck by lightning, it doesn't get to the point of being an instance of F. To get an exceptionless generalization for the organisms that do form genes by a fair division, we need to add two things:

- the properties of the initial situation of the world on which this law is contingent (call this I); and
- the properties of things that are DA that ensure that there are no genes that cause segregation distortion (call this U).

So now we have this law: if x has $IDAU$, then y has F. Now suppose that D and A are multiply realized. We'll need to add in a variety of H_D and H_A properties—matter properties—to dovetail with D and A to suffice for a complete existing diploid sexual organism. And, to get a truly exceptionless law, we'll have to add in some more of the background and the structured arrangement of all these things, which we've been abbreviating with an ellipsis (. . .). So the final form of the higher-level swatch laws is: if x has $IDH_D AH_A U \ldots$, then y has F.

Given these laws, then, our theory of causal relevance permits us to say that DA is causally relevant to F. (Equally, it permits us to say that the initial condition property I is causally relevant to F. This may seem odd, but it is a difficulty familiar from Mill, as I noted in chapter 6. Perhaps the best way to handle it is to focus on our explanatory interests. Since the property I is the background for everything that happens on the face of the earth, we would tend not to count it as explanatory.)

9.3.3 Objections Answered

I can now respond to the two difficulties with which I began this section.

First, for each level there is a set of laws governing properties at that level. The set of laws is causally closed in the sense that the physical laws are closed: if an event that has a property referred to by a higher-level system of laws has a cause, then the cause has a property linked to the effect property by the set of higher-level laws appropriate to the effect property. Since a higher-level set of laws must govern some parts of the world that contain no instances of higher-level properties, there will be laws in the set that are identical to the physical laws. The rest of the set will be laws that involve the higher-level properties.

Second, even though different instances of higher-level properties will differ in what exactly they can do, since they are physically different, the higher-level set of laws will include laws that cover each of the variations.

9.4 Supervenient Causation

The rest of this chapter will be concerned with various extensions, clarifications, and possible difficulties for the leveled account of causal relevance.

The leveled account is a version of a supervenient causation theory of causal relevance. Kim (1983) endorsed the idea that supervenient causation removes the threat of property epiphenomenalism but soon came to think that this is incorrect (Kim 1993b); he now calls the idea a "gimmick with no meaning" (2005:62). There are two difficulties. The basic intuitive difficulty with supervenient causation is that it seems like an irrelevant redundancy: not a real kind of causation, just a sort of pretend or faux causation. This complaint can take various forms; I will return to it in section 9.8 below.

There is a more technical difficulty that can be made in various forms. The basic idea is that supervenient causation lets too many things count as causally relevant. Suppose, just for the sake of the example, that being a raven is causally relevant to croakings of "Nevermore!" and that being a writing desk is causally relevant to producing dents in carpets. The property of being a raven or a writing desk supervenes on the set of properties {being a raven, being a writing desk}, since if anything has the former property, it has one of the latter properties, and if it has one of the latter properties, then necessarily it has the former property. Yet the property of being a raven or a writing desk seems to be causally irrelevant to anything.

But the leveled account of causal relevance says more is required for causal relevance than supervening on causally relevant properties. A property only counts as causally relevant at its level if it wins the competition for causal relevance at its level (sec. 9.2 above). Suppose, for instance, that causal relevance at a level is connected with what mechanisms operate at level (Craver 2007). Then a property at a level is causally relevant only if it is referred to by an account of the mechanisms operating at that level. Being a diploid sexual organism is causally relevant to forming haploid gametes by a fair 50/50 meiotic division, because that is the mechanism of gamete formation. Assuming that wanting ice cream is causally relevant to moving one's body in a way that would be appropriate to getting some, that will be because the mechanism for explaining bodily movements in creatures who have desires will refer to properties like this one.

It is critically important to acknowledge that whether mental properties are causally relevant depends on what the facts about the causal mechanisms really are. If the eliminativists are right (Churchland 1981), we have good empirical reason to hold that old-fashioned or folk psychology is simply not a good explanatory theory. Then we have reason to say that there are no beliefs or desires. If there are no such things, then clearly they are not causally relevant. Again, if Libet (2005) is right, then (much) action is caused by unconscious brain processes that also cause the conscious decision to perform the action, and hence the conscious decision to act is not the cause of the action but a causal by-product of the unconscious brain processes. The argument of this chapter is that higher-level property causal relevance isn't ruled out a priori; whether a given higher-level property actually is causally relevant to some effect type depends on how the world actually works.

9.5 Some Puzzles

9.5.1 Are There Too Many Higher-Level Laws?

One might worry that, since the higher-level laws must have distinct versions for every possible material difference in the instances of the higher-level properties, there must be enormous numbers of qualified laws like these—and that this doesn't feel like what we thought laws of nature are supposed to be like.

The concept of a law of nature answers to a number of different and probably incommensurable demands (this helps explain why theories of laws of nature differ so wildly). One thing we might want the concept for is to pick out is laws as we formulate and use them. Another thing we might want the concept for is to describe how the past determines the future. What actually happens in any concrete situation—although a product of all the laws—is hardly ever expressible, since there is so much going on (chap. 6, sec. 6.1.3). The first concept concerns laws that we could come to know and use; the second concept concerns laws that in principle can account for everything that happens (even if we couldn't know them and couldn't use them). I am focusing on the metaphysics of laws and causal relevance, not on their epistemology, and hence on the second concept.

In this context, it is worth explicitly noting (as I did above in chap, 6, sec. 6.2, discussing Anscombe) that the metaphysical claim that what happens is governed by laws of nature has next to no consequences for how the sciences (do or ought to) describe and explain the world. It may be that much explanation in the sciences works by finding mechanisms by which phenomena are produced and that these explanations do not cite or work with laws of nature. It would not follow, if this is right, that there are no laws, in the metaphysical sense described above in chapter 6, governing the actions of each instance of these mechanisms.

9.5.2 Are Higher-Level Laws Too Easy to Come By?

One might worry that any exception can be compensated for. Exceptions to Mendel's law were fixed by adding enough properties to guarantee that the exceptions didn't happen. So why can't we claim that any property whatsoever—suitably qualified so as to yield a sufficient condition—is causally relevant?

Physical laws are those regularities that account for everything that happens. Physical properties are groupings of things that facilitate the best possible accounts of what happens. Higher-level laws are those regularities that account for what happens at their levels. Higher-level properties are groupings of things at the higher levels that facilitate the best possible accounts of what happens at that level. The reason Mendel's first law is a law is that at the level of the mechanisms of inheritance (as they have evolved in our particular context, i.e., on Earth) the basic mechanism of sexual reproduction involves diploid organisms producing haploid gametes by a 50/50 meiotic division. The exceptions are law driven as well, but the fundamental mechanism is the fair division. So it would not be legitimate to pick just any grouping of things at some level and then build a system of laws around that. Rather, we start with the best explanations at a given level. Then we build exceptionless higher-level laws around the properties from those explanations.

The laws at higher levels pick out real patterns that aren't visible from the perspective of the laws at lower levels. The physical laws have the various supervenience bases for T (our example of the property of being a cup) showing up along with various structural configurations of various properties. But those various supervenience bases don't group together: the property T would group them, but the property T doesn't appear in the fundamental laws. At its level, T shows up in place of the supervenience bases, paired with various matter properties. So in places of occurrences of members of the set A, A', A'' ... (on which T supervenes), we have occurrences of members of the set TH, TH', TH'' .... There is a sacrifice in a certain kind of simplicity, for in the first level regularity we have n properties whereas at T's level we have $n+1$. But there is a gain in strength, since at T's level there is a grouping of things—namely, the Ts—that is absent at the first level. T, then, is a "thread of connexion" that draws a different line through the general "tissue of connexion" that is the laws of nature from the line drawn by the physical property A.

Notoriously, simplicity and strength are vague criteria for picking competing theories of the world. Simplicity might be thought in the present context to cut decisively against the leveled account of causal relevance, since, after all, the laws at the fundamental level capture all the facts and regularities of the world as well as they can be captured. But there are real patterns at nonfundamental levels—increases in strength—that come along with the further levels in the leveled account.

9.5.3 How Can There Be More than One Causally Sufficient Condition?

A swatch law is a sufficient condition for a type of effect. The set of all such sufficient conditions for a given type of effect makes up a condition that is both sufficient and necessary for that kind of effect.

But, one might object, if some physical condition V is sufficient for an effect property W, then it can't turn out that something other than V is necessary for W. There cannot be more than one complete and independent condition that is necessary and sufficient for some effect. But the leveled account claims that there is more than one nonidentical necessary and sufficient condition for a given type of effect.

This objection is a relative of objections based on Kim's exclusion principle: how could there be more than one complete and independent set of the laws of nature? If there is one set of laws that exhaustively specifies the motor of the world, how could there be another?

The reply to the objection is that the laws of nature at the fundamental level are not independent of the laws of nature expressed at higher levels. The laws of nature expressed at higher levels involve properties that are supervenient on lower levels, and where there is supervenience we do not have independence.

Suppose that the physical condition V is sufficient for a physical property W. And suppose there is a higher-level property O that (apparently) is causally relevant to W-type effects. If V and O are entirely distinct, then V can produce W by itself (without O). That is because V is sufficient for W, and consequently O couldn't be necessary for W. But if O is not entirely distinct from V, it may be that when V produces W, O is already included. That is exactly the situation with respect to the first-level system and higher-level systems. A higher-level system is obtained from a lower-level system by taking higher-level properties and conjoining them with matter properties in such a way that the combination amounts exactly to one of the lower-level properties. So whenever the lower-level system is instantiated in a particular case, that particular is also an instantiation of the higher-level systems.

9.6 Cross-Level Causal Relevance

Kim's argument, in brief, went like this (chap. 8, sec. 8.2): assume, for reductio, that M causes M^*. But (1) Edwards's dictum entails that nothing causes M^*, and (2) the exclusion principle entails that the physical cause P, on which M supervenes, is the cause, not M.

The leveled account of property causal relevance replies as follows (chap. 8, sec. 8.3): (1) Edwards's dictum does not apply in the case in which the vertical determination relation is supervenience; (2) the exclusion principle does not apply in the case in which one of the causes supervenes on the other, since the two properties are not independent of one another.

So M can cause M^*: what is required is that M and M^* be related by laws of nature at their level.

Can M be causally relevant to P^*, M^*'s supervenience base? We no longer have Kim's motivation to say that M causes M^* by causing P^*. Kim's argument suggested that the nonreductive physicalist will want to say this when forced to acknowledge that M cannot simply cause M^*. If the foregoing argument is correct, we are no longer forced to acknowledge this. But there are advantages for the leveled account if it is possible for M to cause P^* (that is, for the property M to be causally relevant to P^*). One is that it allows avoiding the appearance (even if it is only an appearance) that the leveled account has causation going on autonomously in causally isolated layers. Another is that as a matter of actual fact the right sort of connection needed for causal relevance may well hold across levels as well as within levels.

So we have the following situation. Suppose the following is a physical swatch law: if x has $ABCD \ldots$, then y has P^*. So P^* is a physical property. Let M supervene on some set of properties $A, A', A'' \ldots$. As indicated in section

9.3 above, simply replacing A with M or adding M to the structured arrays of properties in which A occurs would either falsify the regularity or qualify it redundantly. But a suitable property H exists such that anything that has both M and H also has A and such that replacing A in this regularity with M and H would neither falsify it nor render it redundant. Hence M would be causally relevant to P^*.

9.7 Drainage

What if (Block 2003) there are levels and there is no lowest level—what if matter divides infinitely or analytically decomposes in some other way, and there is no best level? (Perhaps the explanations of one level in terms of the next lower level improve asymptotically, or perhaps at each level there is a trade-off, where some parts of the world get stronger simpler explanations and others end up with worse explanations.) If causal relevance at a given level depends on causal relevance at lower levels, then if there is an infinite hierarchy of levels, causal relevance apparently drains away.

According to the leveled account of property causal relevance, for a property to be causally relevant to another, a swatch law at its level must refer to it. To get swatch laws at a given level, higher-level properties have to be qualified by other properties. But this isn't causal relevance bubbling up from the lower levels. It is not a matter of importing causal relevance from lower levels. The claim is not that the higher-level properties count as causally relevant because they supervene on causally relevant properties. The claim is, rather, that the higher-level properties count as causally relevant because they figure in laws of nature (at their level). So the leveled account is not open to the concern that causal powers might drain away.

9.8 Is Supervenient Causation a Gimmick?

There are two substantial intuitive difficulties for the leveled account of causal relevance. One is to get the number of causes right. As I argued in chapter 6, section 6.3, if we say that only one thing produces the effect, we immediately get the conclusion that causation only happens at the lowest level. But we don't want more than one thing, that is, overdetermination (chap. 8, sec. 8.3) or dualism (chap. 3, sec. 3.1.3). The solution is that mental properties overlap, so it is true neither that we have one thing or that we have more than one thing.

The other intuitive difficulty is that it still may appear that supervenient causation is redundant, faux, a gimmick.

First: is it redundant? No, it is not. The leveled account of causal relevance doesn't hold that when a mental event causes another mental event, there are two independent causal powers operating. The leveled account is consistent with causal closure. For whenever a nonfundamental property is causally relevant, its instances also have fundamental causally relevant properties. So every event happens in virtue of instantiating fundamental physical properties. In this sense, the supervenient properties don't add anything. The leveled account does not entail that mental causes overdetermine their effects. The leveled conception does not entail emergentism, if by "emergentism" we mean that supervening causally relevant properties contribute causal powers that are not already contributed by the distribution of fundamental properties (McLaughlin 1992). So if the leveled account doesn't hold that there are extra causes in any of these senses, then it cannot be accused of introducing redundant causes.

Nor is it true that supervenient causation is nothing at all, faux, an empty name. Supervening properties are not identical with the properties on which they supervene. The causal connections among supervening properties are not identical with the causal connections among the properties on which they supervene.

Is supervenient causation a gimmick? The objection might be that, really, only the physical properties are doing the real causal work. We must ask what exactly we are supposing "causal work" to be (Loewer 2001, 2002). Clearly the phrase is metaphorical, since properties do not cause anything; only particulars stand in causal relations, and only particulars do causal work. It is difficult to see that the metaphor helps indicate a real problem for the leveled account. Perhaps causal work is only done at the fundamental level. Or perhaps there is a way to see properties, laws of nature, and causal relevance according to which causal work can be done at the fundamental level and at higher levels as well. As I argued above in chapter 6, section 6.3, seeing things this way requires getting the number of causes right.

I have not yet, perhaps, got to the heart of the objection. For Kim, it lies in Edwards's picture of God's determination of the world. By supervenience, the supervenient mental effect is determined to be as it is by its supervenience base, and, given the supervenience base, it would be that way no matter what happened before. By supervenience, the supervenient mental cause produces something that is already produced by the supervenience base. "Supervenient causation" is a mere empty name for instances of nonsupervenient causation.

I've already noted (sec. 8.3, above) that some of the force of this thought is dissipated by the fact that supervenient causes are not fully distinct from their supervenience bases. What remains, I think, is the possibility of treating causation and supervenience as Kim recommends: accord causal relevance only to fundamental properties and to those reductively identical with them. That is one possibility. There is another. It is not ontologically extravagant. It is more complex than Kim's proposal. But it fits well with our conception of ourselves: that the mental is not reductively identical with the physical, and yet it is not causally impotent either.

We might, finally, wonder whether there is a real dispute between Kim's conception of causation and the leveled account of causal relevance. Suppose someone asks, "We seem to have here two different concepts expressed with the words 'causal relevance,' on one of which it makes sense to say 'mental properties are causally relevant' and on the other of which it does not make sense. Is this a substantive dispute, or is it merely verbal, everyone agreeing on the underlying facts and how the different concepts are to be deployed?" The underlying facts are the motor of the world. The leveled account says that the power of the motor is expressed at many levels. The "no supervenient causation" view holds that that power is purely physical. From that point of view, the dispute looks substantive: it concerns fundamental issues about what makes things happen. From the point of view of the leveled account, the dispute looks verbal. There are differences between the power of a physical property and the power of a nonphysical property. But they are both powers. We could decide to call the physical properties "causally relevant" and call the nonphysical ones something else. That is a verbal issue. But there is no metaphysical reason to honor only one of them with the title "causally relevant."

9.9 Conclusion

The argument of this book is now complete. Let me now summarize where I have got to and how I got there.

The mental causation problem—like the problem of free will—stems from our dual nature. We experience ourselves as acting in the world and consciously making things happen. But we also know that we are material beings, part of the natural world. Thus a conflict: since the matter of material beings is causally responsible for what they do, it seems impossible that we, as we experience ourselves, could have any causal responsibility, could ever make anything happen.

Plato and Descartes interpret the duality of our nature as so drastic that they make the experiencing self into something distinct from the material body. Plato argued that our ability to know the Forms shows that the soul is more akin to the Forms than it is to the body. Descartes argued that no material, mechanical body is capable of speech or reason, and he argued that no material substance has the attribute of thought. Both thus argue for mind/body dualism, separating the mind and the body into distinct ontological realms.

Huxley's sense of our dual nature, together with his respect for mechanical explanation, led him to hold that consciousness is an epiphenomenon, caused by the workings of the body yet incapable of causing anything. A similar configuration of allegiances continues to lead contemporary writers (Jackson 1982; Chalmers 1996) to epiphenomenalism.

Our nature is dual—we are material beings and we are conscious—yet too much respect for the way we are different from material reality takes us too far out of the causal order. If we are entirely distinct from material reality, or if we are a mere causal by-product of it, then we are unable to make anything happen. If we cannot make things happen, then we are not free agents; indeed, arguably, we are not agents at all. It is no help to say (as did Huxley and some of Descartes's dualist followers) that when I choose to do something, my body happens to do the thing I chose. Freedom and agency demand the ability to make things happen, and if our choices are not part of the material causal order, then we cannot have that ability.

A large part of twentieth-century philosophy of mind was about how to fit the mind into the material causal order. The most direct and straightforward way to do this is to say that physicalism is true, that is, that absolutely everything is physical: all the things and all the properties. Yet this path gives too little respect to our dual nature. Physics is competent to explain how every material thing works (in principle, at any rate). But that does not mean that every property is physical, and that does not mean that physics can explain, say, picnics as picnics (rather than as a structured swarm of atoms). Nor is physics competent to explain our conscious choices as mental or as conscious.

Materialism is the view that everything is physical but that only some of the properties are physical. Materialism doesn't say that nonphysical properties are spooky or otherworldly. Properties are distinguishers, not ontological admission tickets. My watch and my pen share a nonphysical property (namely, being one or the other of them), yet for all that both are perfectly physical objects.

Materialism can respect our dual nature as far as the distinction between physical and mental properties goes, but it has long seemed powerless to explain how mental properties could make any difference to anything. Mental events are physical events, according to the materialist, but physical events make things happen because they have the physical properties they do. As D'Holbach wrote, "Man is a being purely physical; in whatever manner he is considered, he is connected to universal nature, and submitted to the necessary and immutable laws that she imposes on all the beings she contains, according to their peculiar essences or to the respective properties with which, without consulting them, she endows each particular species" (2001:1.11.97–98). What room is there in this picture for mental properties to make any difference to anything?

Physical properties make a difference to things because they are linked by what D'Holbach called "the necessary and immutable laws" of universal nature: the laws of nature. The laws of nature say which properties generate which properties through time. The material world progresses as it does through time because the laws of nature dictate how one configuration of property instances develops into another. One property, then, is causally connected to another—or, as I put it above, causally relevant to another—when the laws of nature say that instances of the one will always (or will probably) be followed by instances of the other.

If the mental properties of things were fully independent of the physical properties of things, then it really would be impossible—consistently with materialism—to explain how mental properties could be causally connected to anything. The laws of nature would dictate the progression of all the material natural properties, while the mental properties could appear in any old distribution over the physical objects.

But mental properties are not fully independent of physical properties. All mental things are physical things (as they must be, if, as materialism says, everything is physical). And two things that are physically just alike will be mentally just alike as well. While we cannot pretend that we know this for certain, we have an enormous amount of evidence to believe that it is true. In short: mental properties supervene on physical properties.

Mental properties are at a higher level than physical properties. The natural world falls into levels. Fundamental physics seeks to describe the world at the lowest level. Things at the fundamental level explain what things at higher levels do. Things at higher levels behave in various characteristic ways and in their turn explain how things at yet higher levels work. Atoms make up molecules; organic molecules make up cells of various kinds; cells, interacting with one another and with things of higher and lower levels, make up living beings. Often properties at higher levels are less specific than physical properties, that is to say, their instances can differ physically. These physical differences must, according to the laws of nature, lead to different effects. Hence mental properties (and higher-level properties in general) make a heteroge-neous pattern in the progression of time, at least as viewed from the perspec-tive of physical laws and physical properties.

The differences are all physical. Hence the heterogeneity of the pattern of mental properties can be fully described and explained in purely physical terms. We could then claim that mental properties make the pattern in na-ture required for a law: the mental properties, when bolstered by all the physical properties with which they work, generate the pattern of what actu-ally happens. But this is a cheat. The work is all being done by the physical properties and the physical laws.

But there is another way to think of how mental properties make things happen. Mental properties dovetail with matter properties custom-made to supplement their work. Mental properties are like Aristotle's form proper-ties. A form needs matter to constitute a complete being. A mental form property dovetails with a correlative matter property in order to constitute a mental event. Matter properties are not physical properties. A matter prop-erty specifies exactly what is needed for one way that a mental property con-stitutes a mental event. Since that specification is geared to the mental prop-erty in question, it will appear heterogeneous from the perspective of physics. Being a diploid sexual organism is a form property; one way to be such an organism is to have the material constitution that, for instance, I have, yet simply having matter exactly similar to mine is consistent with doing very different things than I do. Only when the form and the matter are combined do we have one diploid sexual organism like me.

So a mental property instantiated along with a nonphysical matter prop-erty, these two instantiated along with an appropriate context, will produce an effect property precisely as regularly as do the physical properties. Hence there are laws that link mental properties with other properties, laws exactly as robust as the laws of physics. Hence mental properties can be causally rel-evant to other properties just as much as physical properties are causally rel-evant to other physical properties.

Materialism had a problem explaining how the nonphysical properties of things could be causally relevant because it seemed that the progress of na-ture could only depend on the way physical property instances generate one another. Yet once we put nonphysical matter properties together with higher-level nonphysical properties, we find exactly the same pattern of property instances generating property instances, all together generating exactly the same rich and complex total fabric of reality.

We may feel some residual intuition that really only the progression of the instances of the physical properties is what determines the course of the world. But why should we feel that? The mental properties are just as real as the physical properties. Instances of mental properties generate instances of other properties just as robustly as any physical cause. Mental properties are linked to laws just as securely as are the physical properties. The system of higher-level laws is not independent and distinct from the system of physical laws, since the higher-level properties supervene on and hence are not independent or distinct from physical properties. Hence there is no concern that somehow higher-level laws are autonomous from physical laws, out there making things happen on their own. If there were something special about the fundamental physical laws, some additional linkage between physical properties connected by physical laws, that is absent from the linkage between mental properties and others connected by higher-level laws, that would indeed be a fatal obstacle to mental causation. But what linkage is that?

So materialism can explain how one event can cause another because it has the mental properties it does; it can explain how mental causation is possible, while both respecting our dual nature and acknowledging that the world is, and that we are, physical through and through.

9.10 Further Reading

Kim's *Mind in a Physical World* (1998) and *Physicalism, or Something Near Enough* (2005) are the best comprehensive discussions of the mental causation problem. His statement of the supervenience (or exclusion) argument is particularly useful, as are his criticisms of a variety of attempted responses to the problem, particularly responses that treat the problem not as metaphysical but rather as a problem about relating different areas of scientific inquiry. Glymour (1999) argues that Kim's problem is not a genuine problem.

Two recent monographs on the mental causation problem are Corbí and Prades (1999) and De Muijnck (2003).

Heil and Mele (1993) is a useful collection of essays from a variety of perspectives on the problem, beginning with Donald Davidson's reply (1993) to criticisms of his anomalous monism (Davidson 1970b) that it has a difficulty to do with epiphenomenalism. Two more recent collections of essays are Slors and Walter's *Mental Causation, Multiple Realization, and Emergence* (2003) and Walter and Heckmann's *Physicalism and Mental Causation* (2003).

Frank Jackson's "Mental Causation" (1996) is a comprehensive survey of the field. What follows is a very selective list of contemporary articles representing the main alternative approaches that have been taken to the problem.

Several approaches construct conceptions of causal relevance according to which mental properties are causally relevant in some sense other than the way physical properties are causally relevant; for instance, Dretske (1988) and Allen (1995). Jackson and Pettit (1990) present a way that higher-level properties are related to fundamental, really causally relevant properties. Bieri (1992) considers the arguments to type epiphenomenalism sound and tries to work out what it would be like for that to be true. Kazez (1995) argues that arguments based on counterfactuals, such as Horgan (1989) and Heil and Mele (1991), do not succeed; she notes (89) that any account of causal relevance needs to say something about supervenient properties. Lepore and Loewer (1987) work out an account based on laws and counterfactuals; Fodor (1989) and Lepore and Loewer (1989) pursue this strategy. Antony (1991) criticizes these proposals. Loewer (2001), responding specifically to Kim (1998), notes its reliance on a particularly strong notion of causal relevance and suggests a counterfactual analysis of causal relevance. Yablo (1992) argues that determinables and their determinates cannot compete for causal efficacy (see also Yablo 1998). Clapp (2001), using elements from Yablo (1992) and Shoemaker (1984), argues that the right kinds of multiply realized properties have causal powers, namely, the intersection of the causal powers of their realizers; Shoemaker (1998b) gives essentially the same account, citing Michael Watkins (2002).

References

In references to works of which both the original and a reprint are cited here, the page citations always relate to the reprints, even when the original year of publication is cited.

Aizawa, Kenneth. 2006. "The Biochemistry of Memory Consolidation: A Model System for the Philosophy of Mind." *Synthese* 155 (1): 1–34.

Alighieri, Dante. 1975. *The Divine Comedy: Paradiso*. Trans. Charles S. Singleton. Princeton: Princeton University Press.

Allen, Colin. 1995. "It Isn't What You Think: A New Idea About Intentional Causation." *Noûs* 29 (1): 115–126.

Anscombe, Elizabeth. 1957. *Intention*. 2d ed. Ithaca: Cornell University Press.

——. 1971. "Causality and Determination." An inaugural lecture delivered at Cambridge and published by the Cambridge University Press. Reprinted in Sosa and Tooley 1993, 88–104.

Antony, Louise. 1991. "The Causal Relevance of the Mental: More on the Mattering of Minds." *Mind and Language* 6 (4): 295–327.

Aristotle. 1941. *The Basic Works of Aristotle*. New York: Random House.

——. 1996. *Introductory Readings*. Trans. Terence Irwin and Gail Fine. Indianapolis: Hackett.

Armstrong, David Malet. 1968. *A Materialist Theory of the Mind*. London: Routledge and Kegan Paul.

——. 1978a. *Universals and Scientific Realism: Nominalism and Realism*. Vol. 1. Cambridge: Cambridge University Press.

——. 1978b. *Universals and Scientific Realism: A Theory of Universals*. Vol. 2. Cambridge: Cambridge University Press.

——. 1983. *What Is a Law of Nature?* Cambridge: Cambridge University Press.

——. 1989. *Universals: An Opinionated Introduction*. Boulder, Colo.: Westview.

——. 1997a. "Smart and the Secondary Qualities." Chap. 3 in Byrne and Hilbert.

——. 1997b. *A World of States of Affairs*. Cambridge: Cambridge University Press.

Bacon, John. 1995. *Universals and Property Instances*. Oxford: Basil Blackwell.

Bealer, George. "Mental Causation." Philosophical Perspectives 21 (2007): 23–54.

Beatty, John. 1995. "The Evolutionary Contingency Thesis." In Gereon Wolters and James G. Lennox, eds., *Concepts, Theories, and Rationality in the Biological Sciences: The Second Pittsburgh-Konstanz Colloquium in the Philosophy of Science*, 45–81. Pittsburgh: University of Pittsburgh Press.

Bechtel, William and Jennifer Mundale. 1999. "Multiple Realizability Revisited: Linking Cognitive and Neural States." *Philosophy of Science* 66 (2): 175–207.

Bedau, Mark A. 1986. "Cartesian Interaction." *Midwest Studies in Philosophy* 10: 483–502.

Bennett, Jonathan. 1988. *Events and Their Names*. Indianapolis: Hackett.

Bennett, Karen. 2003. "Why the Exclusion Problem Seems Intractable, and How, Just Maybe, to Tract It." *Noûs* 37 (3): 471–497.

Bieri, Peter. 1992. "Trying Out Epiphenomenalism." *Erkenntnis* 36 (3): 283–309.

Bird, Alexander. 2001. "Necessarily, Salt Dissolves in Water." *Analysis* 61 (4): 267–274.

Block, Ned, ed. 1980a. *Readings in Philosophy of Psychology*. Vol. 1. Cambridge: Harvard University Press.

——. 1980b. "Troubles with Functionalism." In Block 1980a: 268–306.

——. 1980c. "What Is Functionalism?" In Block 1980a: 171–184.

——. 1990. "Can the Mind Change the World?" In George Boolos, ed., *Meaning and Method: Essays in Honor of Hilary Putnam*, 137–170. Cambridge: Cambridge University Press.

——. 2003. "Do Causal Powers Drain Away?" *Philosophy and Phenomenological Research* 67 (1): 133–150.

Bobonich, Chris. 1994. "Akrasia and Agency in Plato's *Laws* and *Republic*." *Archiv für Geschichte der Philosophie* 76 (1): 3–36.

Bok, Hilary. 1998. *Freedom and Responsibility*. Princeton: Princeton University Press.

Brogaard, Berit. 2007. "A Puzzle About Properties." *Philosophy and Phenomenological Research* 74 (3): 635–650.

Broughton, Janet. 2002. *Descartes's Method of Doubt*. Princeton: Princeton University Press.

Broughton, Janet and Ruth Mattern. 1978. "Reinterpreting Descartes on the Notion of the Union of Mind and Body." *Journal of the History of Philosophy* 16 (1): 23–32.

Burge, Tyler. 1979. "Individualism and the Mental." In Peter A. French, Theodore E. Uehling, Jr., and Howard K. Wettstein, eds., *Midwest Studies in Philosophy*, 4:73–121. Studies in Metaphysics. Minneapolis: University of Minnesota Press.

Byrne, Alex and David R. Hilbert, eds. 1997. *Readings on Color: The Philosophy of Color*. Cambridge, Mass.: MIT Press.

Byrne, Christopher. 1989. "Forms and Causes in Plato's *Phaedo*." *Dionysius* 13:3–15.

Campbell, John. 1993. "A Simple View of Color." In John Haldane and Crispin Wright, eds., *Reality, Representation, and Projection*, 257–268. Oxford: Oxford University Press. Reprinted in Byrne and Hilbert 1997: 177–190.

Campbell, Keith. 1981. "The Metaphysic of Abstract Particulars." In Peter A. French, Theodore E. Uehling Jr., and Howard K. Wettstein, eds., *Midwest Studies in Philosophy*,

6:477–488. Studies in Metaphysics. Minneapolis: University of Minnesota Press. Reprinted in Mellor and Oliver 1997, 125–139.

Campbell, Neil. 2003. *Mental Causation and the Metaphysics of Mind*. Peterborough, Ontario: Broadview.

Carnap, Rudolf. 1959. "Psychology in Physical Language." In A. J. Ayer, ed., *Logical Positivism*, 165–198. Glencoe, Ill.: Free Press. Translation of "Psychologie in physikalischer Sprache," *Erkenntnis* 3 (1932–1933): 107–142.

Chalmers, David J. 1996. *The Conscious Mind: In Search of a Fundamental Theory*. New York: Oxford University Press.

——. ed. 2002. *Philosophy of Mind: Classical and Contemporary Readings*. Oxford: Oxford University Press.

Chisholm, Roderick. 1964. "Human Freedom and the Self." Lindley Lecture at the University of Kansas, Lawrence, Kansas. Reprinted in G. Watson 2003: 26–37.

Churchland, Paul. 1981. "Eliminative Materialism and the Propositional Attitudes." *Journal of Philosophy* 78 (2): 67–90.

——. 1984. *Matter and Consciousness*. Cambridge, Mass.: MIT Press.

——. 1985. "Reduction, Qualia, and the Direct Introspection of Brain States." *Journal of Philosophy* 82 (1): 8–28.

——. 1996. "The Rediscovery of Light." *Journal of Philosophy* 93 (5): 211–228. Reprinted in Chalmers 2002: 362–370.

Clapp, Lenny. 2001. "Disjunctive Properties: Multiple Realizations." *Journal of Philosophy* 98 (3): 111–136.

Cohen, S. Marc, Patricia Curd, and C. D. C. Reeve, eds. 1995. *Readings in Ancient Greek Philosophy: From Thales to Aristotle*. Indianapolis: Hackett.

Collins, John, Ned Hall, and L. A. Paul, eds. 2004. *Causation and Counterfactuals*. Cambridge, Mass.: MIT Press.

Corbí, Josep E. and Josep L. Prades. 1999. *Minds, Causes, and Mechanisms: A Case Against Physicalism*. Oxford: Blackwell.

Crane, Tim, ed. 1996. *Dispositions: A Debate*. London: Routledge.

Craver, Carl. 2007. *Explaining the Brain: Mechanisms and the Mosaic Unity of Neuroscience*. Oxford: Clarendon.

Daly, Chris. 1997. "Tropes." In Mellor and Oliver, 140–159. Specially rewritten version of a paper first published in *Proceedings of the Aristotelian Society* 94 (1994–1995): 253–261.

Dardis, Anthony. 1993. "Sunburn: Independence Conditions on Causal Relevance." *Philosophy and Phenomenological Research* 53 (3): 577–598.

——. 2002. "A "No Causal Rivalry" Solution to the Problem of Mental Causation." *Acta Analytica* 17 (1): 69–77.

Davidson, Donald. 1963. "Actions, Reasons, and Causes." *Journal of Philosophy* 60 (23): 685–699. Reprinted in Davidson 1980a: 3–19.

——. 1967. "Causal Relations." *Journal of Philosophy* 64 (21): 691–703. Reprinted in Davidson 1980a: 149–162.

——. 1970a. "How Is Weakness of the Will Possible?" In J. Feinberg, ed., *Moral Concepts*. Oxford: Oxford University Press. Reprinted in Davidson 1980a: 21–42.

——. 1970b. "Mental Events." In L. Foster and J. W. Swanson, eds., *Experience and Theory*. Amherst: University of Massachusetts Press. Reprinted in Davidson 1980a:240–260.

——. 1973. "The Material Mind." In P. Suppes, L. Henkin, G. C. Moisil, and A. Joja, eds., *Proceedings of the Fourth International Congress for Logic, Methodology and*

Philosophy of Science. Amsterdam: North-Holland. Reprinted in Davidson 1980a: 245–260.

———. 1974. "Psychology as Philosophy." In S. Brown, ed., *The Philosophy of Psychology.* London: Macmillan. Reprinted in Davidson 1980a: 229–243.

———. 1980a. *Essays on Actions and Events.* New York: Oxford University Press.

———. 1987. "Knowing One's Own Mind." *Proceedings and Addresses of the American Philosophical Association* 60:441–458.

———. 1993. "Thinking Causes." In Heil and Mele, 3–17.

———. 1995. "Laws and Cause." *Dialecta* 49 (2–4): 263–279. Reprinted in Donald Davidson, *Truth, Language, and History,* 201–219. New York: Oxford University Press, 2005.

Davis, Wayne. 1988. "Probability and Causality." In James Fetzer, ed., *Probabilistic Theories of Causation,* 133–160. Dordrecht: Reidel.

De Muijnck, Wim. 2003. *Dependencies, Connections and Other Relations: A Theory of Mental Causation.* Dordrecht: Kluwer Academic Publishers.

Descartes, René. 1964. *Oeuvres de Descartes.* 12 vols. Ed. Charles Adam and Paul Tannery. Paris: Librairie Philosophique J. Vrin.

———. 1984. *The Philosophical Writings of Descartes.* 3 vols. Trans. John Cottingham, Robert Stoothoff, and Dugald Murdoch. Cambridge: Cambridge University Press.

Devitt, Michael. 1980. " 'Ostrich Nominalism' or 'Mirage Realism'?" *Pacific Philosophical Quarterly* 61 (4): 433–439. Reprinted in Mellor and Oliver 1997: 93–100.

Dowe, Phil. 2000. *Physical Causation.* Cambridge: Cambridge University Press.

Dretske, Fred. 1977. "Laws of Nature." *Philosophy of Science* 44 (2): 248–268.

———. 1988. *Explaining Behavior: Reasons in a World of Causes.* Cambridge, Mass.: MIT Press.

D'Holbach, Paul-Henri Thiry (Baron). 2001/2003. *The System of Nature* (1868). Trans. H. D. Robinson. Kitchener, Ont.: Batoche. Reprint (as electronic book), Palo Alto, Calif.: eBrary. Originally published as *La système de la nature* in 1770.

Eells, Ellery. 1991. *Probabilistic Causality.* Cambridge: Cambridge University Press.

Ellis, Brian. 2001. *Scientific Essentialism.* Cambridge: Cambridge University Press.

Fahrbach, Ludwig. 2005. "Understanding Brute Facts." *Synthese* 145 (3): 449–466.

Feynman, Richard. 1965. *The Character of Physical Law.* Cambridge, Mass.: MIT Press.

Field, Hartry. 1986. "The Deflationary Conception of Truth." In Graham MacDonald and Crispin Wright, eds., *Facts, Science and Value,* 55–117. Oxford: Blackwell.

Fine, Kit. 1975. "Vagueness, Truth and Logic." *Synthese* 30 (3–4): 265–300.

Fodor, Jerry. 1968. *Psychological Explanation.* New York: Random House.

———. 1974. "Special Sciences (or the Disunity of Science as a Working Hypothesis)." *Synthese* 28 (2): 97–115. Reprinted in Block 1980a: 120–133.

———. 1975. *The Language of Thought.* New York: Crowell.

———. 1987. *Psychosemantics.* Cambridge, Mass.: MIT Press.

———. 1989. "Making Mind Matter More." *Philosophical Topics* 17 (1): 59–79. Reprinted in *A Theory of Content and Other Essays.* Cambridge: MIT Press, 1990.

Frege, Gottlob. 1892. "Über Sinn und Bedeutung." *Zeitschrift für Philosophie und Philosophische Kritik* 100: 25–50. Translated as "On Sense and Reference" in Peter Geach and Max Black, eds., *Translations from the Philosophical Writings of Gottlob Frege,* 56–68. Oxford: Blackwell, 1980.

Garber, Daniel. 1982. "Understanding Interaction: What Descartes Should Have Told Elizabeth." Proceedings of the Spindel Conference, "The Rationalist Conception of Consciousness." *Southern Journal of Philosophy* 22 (supp.): 15–32.

Gillett, Carl. 2003. "The Metaphysics of Realization, Multiple Realizability and the Special Sciences." *Journal of Philosophy* 100 (11): 591–603.

Glymour, Clark. 1999. "A Mind Is a Terrible Thing to Waste—Critical Notice: Jaegwon Kim, *Mind in a Physical World*." *Philosophy of Science* 66 (3): 455–471.

Goodman, Nelson. 1954. *Fact, Fiction and Forecast.* 4th ed. Cambridge: Harvard University Press.

Hardcastle, Valerie Gray. 1998. "On the Matter of Minds and Mental Causation." *Philosophy and Phenomenological Research* 58 (1): 1–25.

Hardin, C. L. 1988. *Color for Philosophers.* Indianapolis: Hackett.

Harman, Gilbert. 1977. *The Nature of Morality.* New York: Oxford University Press.

Haugeland, John. 1982. "Weak Supervenience." *American Philosophical Quarterly* 19 (1): 93–104.

Heil, John. 1998. "Supervenience Deconstructed." *European Journal of Philosophy* 6 (2): 145–155.

——. 1999. "Multiple Realizability." *American Philosophical Quarterly* 36 (3): 189–208.

——. 2003a. *From an Ontological Point of View.* Oxford: Oxford University Press.

——. 2003b. "Levels of Reality." *Ratio* 16 (3): 205–221.

——. 2005. "Dispositions." *Synthese* 144 (3): 343–356.

Heil, John and Alfred Mele. 1991. "Mental Causes." *American Philosophical Quarterly* 28 (1): 61–71.

——, eds. 1993. *Mental Causation.* Oxford: Clarendon.

Hempel, Carl. 1935. "The Logical Analysis of Psychology." In Block 1980a: 14–23. Translation of "Analyse logique de la psychologie," *Revue de Synthese* 10:27–42.

——. 1966. *Philosophy of Natural Science.* Englewood Cliffs, N.J.: Prentice-Hall.

Hilbert, David R. 1987. *Color and Color Perception: A Study in Anthropocentric Realism.* Stanford: Center for the Study of Language and Information.

Honderich, Ted. 1993. *How Free Are You?* Oxford: Oxford University Press.

Horgan, Terry. 1989. "Mental Quausation." In James Tomberlin, ed., *Philosophy of Mind and Action Theory*, Philosophical Perspectives, no. 3, 47–76. Atascadero, Calif.: Ridgeview.

——. 1993. "From Supervenience to Superdupervenience: Meeting the Demands of a Material World." *Mind* 102 (408): 555–586.

Horwich, Paul. 1980. *Truth.* New York: Oxford University Press.

Hume, David. 1978. *A Treatise of Human Nature* (1739). Ed. L. A. Selby-Bigge, rev. ed. Peter H. Nidditch. Oxford: Oxford University Press.

Huxley, Thomas H. 1874. "On the Hypothesis that Animals Are Automata and Its History." *Nature*, September 3, 362–366. Revised and reprinted in *Methods and Results*, vol. 1 of *Collected Essays*. 9 vols. New York: D. Appleton, 1896–1897.

Jackson, Frank. 1982. "Epiphenomenal Qualia." *Philosophical Quarterly* 32 (127): 127–136.

——. 1986. "What Mary Didn't Know." *Journal of Philosophy* 85 (5): 291–295.

——. 1996. "Mental Causation." *Mind* 105 (419): 377–413.

——. 1998. *From Metaphysics to Ethics: A Defence of Conceptual Analysis.* Oxford: Clarendon.

Jackson, Frank and Robert Pargetter. 1987. "An Objectivist's Guide to Subjectivism About Colour." *Revue Internationale de Philosophie* 41 (160): 127–141. Reprinted in chap. 6 of Byrne and Hilbert 1997: 67–79.

Jackson, Frank and Philip Pettit. 1990. "Program Explanation: A General Perspective." *Analysis* 50 (2): 107–117.

James, William. 1879. "Are We Automata?" *Mind* 4 (13): 1–22.

Jubien, Michael. 1989. "On Properties and Property Theory." In Gennaro Chierchia, Barbara H. Partee, and Raymond Turner, eds., *Properties, Types and Meaning*, 1:159–175. Dordrecht: Kluwer.

——. 1997. *Contemporary Metaphysics*. Malden, Mass.: Blackwell.

Kant, Immanuel. 1929. *Critique of Pure Reason*. Trans. Norman Kemp Smith. New York: Macmillan.

——. 1964. *Groundwork of the Metaphysics of Morals*. Trans. H.J. Patton. New York: Harper and Row.

Kazez, Jean R. 1995. "Can Counterfactuals Save Mental Causation?" *Australasian Journal of Philosophy* 73 (1): 71–90.

Keefe, Rosanna and Peter Smith, eds. 1997. *Vagueness: A Reader*. Cambridge, Mass.: MIT Press.

Kelsey, Sean. 2004. "Causation in the *Phaedo*." *Pacific Philosophical Quarterly* 85 (1): 21–43.

Kim, Jaegwon. 1971. "Causes and Events: Mackie on Causation." *Journal of Philosophy* 68 (14): 426–441. Reprinted in Sosa and Tooley 1993, 60–74.

——. 1983. "Epiphenomenal and Supervenient Causation." In Peter A. French, Theodore E. Uehling, Jr., and Howard K. Wettstein, eds., *Midwest Studies in Philosophy*, 9:257–270. Studies in Metaphysics. Minneapolis: University of Minnesota Press.

——. 1984. "Concepts of Supervenience." *Philosophy and Phenomenological Research* 45 (2): 153–176. Reprinted in Kim 1993a: 53–78.

——. 1985. "Psychophysical Laws." In LePore and McLaughlin, 369–386.

——. 1989. "Mechanism, Purpose, and Explanatory Exclusion." In James E. Tomberlin, ed., *Philosophy of Mind and Action Theory*, Philosophical Perspectives, no. 3, 77–108. Atascadero, Calif.: Ridgeview. Reprinted in Kim 1993a: 237–264.

——. 1993a. *Supervenience and Mind*. Cambridge: Cambridge University Press.

——. 1993b. "Postscripts on Mental Causation." In Kim 1993a: 358–367.

——. 1996. *Philosophy of Mind*. Boulder, Colo.: Westview.

——. 1998. *Mind in a Physical World*. Cambridge, Mass.: MIT Press.

——. 2002. "The Layered Model: Metaphysical Considerations." *Philosophical Explorations* 5 (1): 2–20.

——. 2003. "Blocking Causal Drainage and Other Maintenance Chores with Mental Causation." *Philosophy and Phenomenological Research* 67 (1): 151–176.

——. 2005. *Physicalism, or Something Near Enough*. Princeton: Princeton University Press.

Kitcher, Philip. 1986. *Abusing Science*. Cambridge, Mass.: MIT Press.

Kripke, Saul. 1980. *Naming and Necessity*. Cambridge: Harvard University Press.

——. 1982. *Wittgenstein on Rules and Private Language*. Cambridge: Harvard University Press.

Kuhn, Thomas. 1957. *The Copernican Revolution*. Cambridge: Harvard University Press.

Latham, Noa. 1987. "Singular Causal Statements and Strict Deterministic Laws." *Pacific Philosophical Quarterly* 68 (1): 29–43.

Leibniz, Gottfried Wilhelm. 1989. *Philosophical Essays*. Trans. Roger Ariew and Daniel Garber. Indianapolis: Hackett.

Lepore, Ernest and Barry Loewer. 1987. "Mind Matters." *Journal of Philosophy* 84 (11): 630–642.

——. 1989. "More on Making Mind Matter." *Philosophical Topics* 17 (1): 175–191.

LePore, Ernest and Brian McLaughlin, eds. 1985. *Actions and Events: Perspectives on the Philosophy of Donald Davidson*. Oxford: Basil Blackwell.

Levine, Joseph. 2001. *Purple Haze: The Puzzle of Consciousness*. Oxford: Oxford University Press.

Lewis, David. 1966. "An Argument for the Identity Theory." *Journal of Philosophy* 63 (1): 17–25.

——. 1970. "General Semantics." *Synthese* 22:18–67. Reprinted in Lewis 1983c: 189–232.

——. 1973. *Counterfactuals*. Cambridge: Harvard University Press.

——. 1979. "Scorekeeping in a Language Game." *Journal of Philosophical Logic* 8:339–359. Reprinted in Lewis 1983b: 233–249.

——. 1983a. "New Work for a Theory of Universals." *Australasian Journal of Philosophy* 61 (4): 343–377. Reprinted in Mellor and Oliver 1997: 188–227.

——. 1983b. *Philosophical Papers*. Vol. 1. Oxford: Oxford University Press.

——. 1986. *On the Plurality of Worlds*. Oxford: Basil Blackwell.

Libet, Benjamin. 2005. *Mind Time: The Temporal Factor in Consciousness*. Cambridge: Harvard University Press.

Locke, John. 1975. *An Essay Concerning Human Understanding* (1700). Ed. Peter H. Nidditch. Oxford: Clarendon.

Loewer, Barry. 2001. "Review of *Mind in a Physical World: An Essay on the Mind-body Problem and Mental Causation*." *Journal of Philosophy* 98 (6): 315–325.

——. 2002. "Comments on Jaegwon Kim's *Mind and the Physical World*." *Philosophy and Phenomenological Research* 65 (3): 655–662.

Lucretius. 1969. *The Way Things Are*. Trans. Rolfe Humphries. Bloomington: Indiana University Press.

Ludwig, Kirk. 1994. "Causal Relevance and Thought Content." *Philosophical Quarterly* 44 (176): 334–353.

——. 1996. "Functionalism, Causation, and Causal Relevance." *Psyche* 4 (3). Electronic journal available at psyche.cs.monash.edu.au.

——, ed. 2003. *Donald Davidson*. Contemporary Philosophers in Focus. Cambridge: Cambridge University Press.

Mackie, John L. 1965. "Causes and Conditions." *American Philosophical Quarterly* 2/4 (October): 245–255 and 261–264. Reprinted in Sosa and Tooley 1993: 33–55.

——. 1974. *The Cement of the Universe: A Study of Causation*. Oxford: Oxford University Press.

McKitrick, Jennifer. 2005. "Are Dispositions Causally Relevant?" *Synthese* 144 (3): 357–371.

McLaughlin, Brian. 1985. "Anomalous Monism and the Irreducibility of the Mental." In LePore and McLaughlin: 331–368.

——. 1989. "Type Epiphenomenalism, Type Dualism, and the Causal Priority of the Physical." In James E. Tomberlin, ed., *Philosophy of Mind and Action Theory*, Philosophical Perspectives, no. 3, 109–135. Atascadero, Calif.: Ridgeview.

——. 1992. "The Rise and Fall of British Emergentism." In Ansgar Beckerman, Hans Flohr, and Jaegwon Kim, eds., *Emergence or Reduction?* 49–93. Berlin: De Gruyter.

McLaughlin, Brian and Karen Bennett. 2005. "Supervenience." In Edward N. Zalta, ed., *Stanford Encyclopedia of Philosophy*. plato.stanford.edu/archives/fall2006/entries/supervenience/.

Makin, Stephen. 1991. "An Ancient Principle About Causation." *Proceedings of the Aristotelian Society* 91: 135–152.

Martin, Charles. 1994. "Dispositions and Conditionals." *Philosophical Quarterly*, 44 (174): 1–8.

———. 1996. "Properties and Dispositions." In Crane, 71–87.

Matthews, Gareth and Thomas Blackson. 1989. "Causes in the *Phaedo.*" *Synthese* 79 (3): 581–591.

Matthews, Robert J. 1994. "The Measure of Mind." *Mind* 103 (410): 131–146.

Meerbote, Ralf. 1984. "Kant on the Nondeterminative Character of Human Actions." In William A. Harper and Ralf Meerbote, eds., *Kant on Causality, Freedom, and Objectivity*, 138–163. Minneapolis: University of Minnesota Press.

Melden, Abraham Irving. 1961. *Free Action.* London: Routledge and Kegan Paul.

Mellor, David Hugh and Alex Oliver, eds. 1997. *Properties.* Oxford: Oxford University Press.

Melzack, Ronald and Patrick Wall. 1988. *The Challenge of Pain.* 3d ed. London: Penguin.

Mill, John Stuart. 1973. *The Collected Works of John Stuart Mill.* Vol. 7, *A System of Logic Ratiocinative and Inductive.* Toronto: University of Toronto Press.

Mills, Eugene. 1996. "Interactionism and Overdetermination." *American Philosophical Quarterly* 33 (1): 105–117.

Moore, George Edward. 1925. "A Defence of Common Sense." In J. H. Muirhead, ed., *Contemporary British Philosophy*, 193–223. London: Allen and Unwin.

Muir, John. 1911. *My First Summer in the Sierra.* Boston: Houghton Mifflin. Reprint, San Francisco: Sierra Club Books, 1988.

Mumford, Stephen. 1998. *Dispositions.* Oxford: Oxford University Press.

———. 2004. *Laws in Nature.* New York: Routledge.

Nassau, Kurt. 1980. "The Causes of Color." *Scientific American* 243 (4): 124–154.

Nelkin, Dana. 2000. "Two Standpoints and the Belief in Freedom." *Journal of Philosophy* 97 (10): 564–576.

Nussbaum, Martha and Amélie Oksenberg Rorty, eds. 1992. *Essays on Aristotle's De Anima.* Oxford: Clarendon.

Oliver, Alex. 1996. "The Metaphysics of Properties." *Mind* 105 (417): 1–80.

Oppenheim, Paul and Hilary Putnam. 1958. "Unity of Science as a Working Hypothesis." In Herbert Feigl, Michael Scriven, and Grover Maxwell, eds., *Minnesota Studies in the Philosophy of Science*, vol. 2, *Concepts, Theories, and the Mind-Body Problem*, 3–36. Minneapolis: University of Minnesota Press.

Papineau, David. 2001. "The Rise of Physicalism." In Carl Gillett and Barry Loewer, eds., *Physicalism and its Discontents*, 3–36. Cambridge: Cambridge University Press.

Pereboom, Derk. 2002. "Robust Nonreductive Materialism." *Journal of Philosophy* 99 (10): 499–531.

Place, Ullan T. 1956. "Is Consciousness a Brain Process?" *British Journal of Psychology* 47:44–50. Reprinted in Chalmers 2002: 55–60.

Plato. 1935. *Plato's Theory of Knowledge: The Theatetus and the Sophist.* Trans. Francis Macdonald Cornford. Reprinted as *Sophist* in Plato 1961: 957–1017.

———. 1952. *Plato's Phaedrus.* Trans. R. Hackforth. Cambridge: Cambridge University Press. Reprinted as *Phaedrus* in Plato 1961: 475–525.

———. 1961. *The Collected Dialogues.* Ed. Edith Hamilton and Huntington Cairns. Princeton: Princeton University Press.

———. 1977. *Phaedo.* Trans. G. M. A. Grube. 2d ed. Indianapolis: Hackett.

———. 1992. *Republic.* Trans. G. M. A. Grube, rev. C. D. C Reeve. Indianapolis: Hackett.

Priest, Graham. 1998. "What's So Bad About Contradictions?" *Journal of Philosophy* 95 (8): 410–426.

———. 2005. *Towards Non-Being.* Oxford: Clarendon.

Prior, Elizabeth W., Robert Pargetter, and Frank Jackson. 1982. "Three Theses About Dispositions." *American Philosophical Quarterly* 19 (3): 251–257.

Putnam, Hilary. 1960. "Minds and Machines." In Sidney Hook, ed., *Dimensions of Mind*. New York: Collier, 138–164. Reprinted in Putnam 1975b: 362–385.

——. 1967. "Psychological Predicates." In William H. Capitan and Daniel Davy Merrill, eds., *Art, Mind and Religion*, 37–48. Pittsburgh: University of Pittsburgh Press. Reprinted as "The Nature of Mental States" in Block 1980a: 223–231.

——. 1975a. "The Meaning of 'Meaning.'" In K. Gunderson, ed., *Language, Mind and Knowledge*. Minnesota Studies in the Philosophy of Science VII. Minneapolis: University of Minnesota Press, 1975. Reprinted in Putnam 1975b: 215–271.

——. 1975b. *Mind, Language and Reality: Philosophical Papers Volume 2*. Cambridge: Cambridge University Press.

——. 1988. *Representation and Reality*. Cambridge, Mass.: MIT Press.

Quine, Willard van Orman. 1960. *Word and Object*. Cambridge, Mass.: MIT Press.

Radner, Daisy. 1971. "Descartes' Notion of the Union of Mind and Body." *Journal of the History of Philosophy* 9:159–170.

Ray, Greg. 1992. "Modal Identities and De Re Necessity." Ph.D diss., University of California, Berkeley.

Robb, David. 1997. "The Properties of Mental Causation." *Philosophical Quarterly* 47 (187): 178–194.

Rosenberg, Alexander. 1994. *Instrumental Biology or the Disunity of Science*. Chicago: University of Chicago Press.

Rosenthal, David. 2006. *Consciousness and Mind*. New York: Oxford University Press.

——, ed. 1991. *The Nature of Mind*. New York: Oxford University Press.

Rozemond, Marleen. 1998. *Descartes's Dualism*. Cambridge: Harvard University Press.

Rupert, Robert. 2006. "Functionalism, Mental Causation, and the Problem of Metaphysically Necessary Effects." *Noûs* 40 (2): 256–283.

Russell, Bertrand. 1912–1913. "On the Notion of Cause." *Proceedings of the Aristotelian Society* 13:1–26. Reprinted in *Mysticism and Logic*, 174–201. New York: Doubleday Anchor, 1957.

——. 1912. *The Problems of Philosophy*. London: Williams and Norgate. Reprint, New York: Oxford University Press, 1997.

Ryle, Gilbert. 1949. *The Concept of Mind*. London: Hutchinson. Reprint, Chicago: University of Chicago Press, 2000.

Salmon, Wesley. 1984. *Scientific Explanation and the Causal Structure of the World*. Princeton: Princeton University Press.

Sanford, David H. 2005. "Distinctness and Non-identity." *Analysis* 65 (4): 269–274.

Schiffer, Stephen. 2003. *The Things We Mean*. Oxford: Oxford University Press.

Searle, John R. 1983. *Intentionality*. Cambridge: Cambridge University Press.

——. 1992. *The Rediscovery of the Mind*. Cambridge, Mass.: MIT Press.

Shapiro, Lisa. 1999. "Princess Elizabeth and Descartes: The Union of Soul and Body and the Practice of Philosophy." *British Journal for the History of Philosophy* 7 (3): 503–520.

——. 2007. *The Correspondence Between Princess Elisabeth of Bohemia and Rene Descartes*. Chicago: University of Chicago Press.

Shapiro, Lawrence A. 2000. "Multiple Realizations." *Journal of Philosophy* 97 (12): 635–654.

Shoemaker, Sydney. 1984. "Causality and Properties." In *Identity, Cause and Mind: Philosophical Essays*, 206–233. Cambridge: Cambridge University Press.

———. 1998a. "Causal and Metaphysical Necessity." *Pacific Philosophical Quarterly* 79 (1): 59–77.

———. 1998b. "Realization and Mental Causation." *Proceedings of the Twentieth World Congress of Philosophy* 9:23–33.

Sider, Ted. 2003. "What's So Bad About Overdetermination?" *Philosophy and Phenomenological Research* 67:719–726.

Siewart, Charles. 1998. *The Significance of Consciousness*. Princeton: Princeton University Press.

Skinner, B. F. 1953. *Science and Human Behavior*. New York: Macmillan.

Slors, Marc and Sven Walter, eds. 2003. *Mental Causation, Multiple Realization, and Emergence*. Amsterdam: Rodopi.

Smart, J. J. C. 1959. "Sensations and Brain Processes." *Philosophical Review* 68 (2): 141–156.

———. 2004. "The Identity Theory of Mind." In Edward N. Zalta, ed., *The Stanford Encyclopedia of Philosophy*. plato.stanford.edu/archives/sum2007/entries/mind-identity/.

Sober, Elliot. 1997. "Two Outbreaks of Lawlessness in Recent Philosophy of Biology." *Philosophy of Science* 64 (4): S458–S467.

Sosa, Ernest and Michael Tooley, eds. 1993. *Causation*. Oxford: Oxford University Press.

Sturgeon, Nicholas. 1985. "Moral Explanations." In David Copp and David Zimmerman, eds., *Morality, Reason and Truth*, 49–78. Totowa, N.J.: Rowman and Allenheld.

Swoyer, Chris. 1982. "The Nature of Natural Laws." *Australasian Journal of Philosophy* 60 (3): 203–223.

Taylor, Barry. 1993. "On Natural Properties in Metaphysics." *Mind* 102 (405): 81–100.

van Fraassen, Bas. 1989. *Laws and Symmetry*. Oxford: Clarendon.

van Inwagen, Peter. 2004. "A Theory of Properties." In Dean Zimmerman, ed., *Oxford Studies in Metaphysics*, 1:107–138. Oxford: Oxford University Press.

Vlastos, Gregor. 1969. "Reasons and Causes in the *Phaedo*." *Philosophical Review* 78 (3): 291–325.

Walter, Sven and Heinz-Dieter Heckmann, eds. 2003. *Physicalism and Mental Causation*. Exeter, UK: Imprint Academic.

Watkins, Michael. 2002. *Rediscovering Colors: A Study in Pollyanna Realism*. Philosophical Studies, vol. 88. Dordrecht: Kluwer Academic Publishers.

Watson, Gary, ed. 2003. *Free Will*. 2d ed. New York: Oxford University Press.

Watson, John. 1924. "Talking and Thinking." In *Behaviorism*. New York: Norton. Excerpt reprinted in W. G. Lycan, ed., *Mind and Cognition: A Reader*, 14–22. Oxford: Basil Blackwell, 1990.

Weinberg, Steven. 2001. "Can Science Explain Everything? Anything?" *New York Review of Books*, May 31, 50.

Williams, Donald Cary. 1966. *Principles of Empirical Realism*. Springfield, Ill.: Charles C. Thomas.

Williamson, Timothy. 1994. *Vagueness*. London: Routledge.

Wilson, Margaret Dauler. 1978. *Descartes*. London: Routledge and Kegan Paul.

Wilson, Robert A. 1993. "Against A Priori Arguments for Individualism." *Pacific Philosophical Quarterly* 74 (1): 60–79.

Wimsatt, William. C. 1974. "Complexity and Organization." In Kenneth F. Schaffner and Robert S. Cohen, eds., *Boston Studies in the Philosophy of Science*, 20:67–86. Dordrecht: Reidel.

———. 1986. "Forms of Aggregativity." In Alan Donegan, Anthony N. Perovich, Jr., and

Michael V. Wedin, eds., *Human Nature and Natural Knowledge*, 259–291. Dordrecht: Reidel.

Winch, Peter. 1958. *The Idea of a Social Science and Its Relation to Philosophy*. London: Routledge and Kegan Paul.

Wittgenstein, Ludwig. 1953. *Philosophical Investigations*. New York: Macmillan.

———. 1958. *The Blue and Brown Books*. New York: Harper and Brothers.

Yablo, Stephen. 1992. "Mental Causation." *Philosophical Review* 101 (2): 245–280.

———. 1995. "Singling Out Properties." In James E. Tomberlin, ed., *AI, Connectionism and Philosophical Psychology*, Philosophical Perspectives, no. 9, 477–502. Atascadero, Calif.: Ridgeview.

———. 1998. "The Seven Habits of Highly Effective Thinkers." *Proceedings of the Twentieth World Congress of Philosophy* 9:35–45.

Yoshimi, Jeffrey. 2007. "Supervenience, Determination and Dependence." *Pacific Philosophical Quarterly* 88 (1): 114–133.

Index

Non-Humean response, 107–8
Nonmental properties, 102
Nonphysical properties: of choice, 5; materialism and, 173–74; of soul, 22; of thoughts/mind, 2, 84–85
Nonphysical thinker, 135
Noumenal world, 37

Objective articulation, 79
Overdetermination, 141, 152, 168

Particle behavior, 3
Particulars, 65; concrete, 88; distinct nature of, 69; events as, 55, 88; Locke on, 66; philosophical vocabulary of, 68–69, 106; possible, 71; properties and, 65–66, 124–25, 142–44; repeatability of, 65, 67–69; theory of, 78
Philosophical dangers, 148
Photons, 34, 95–96, 149
Physical causal relevance, 110
Physical event(s): causal relevance of, 108–9; mental events and, 56, 131; properties of, 63
Physical heterogeneity, 81–82
Physical indeterminacy, 55, 89, 100
Physicalism, 2, 133, 153
Physical laws, 101, 109–10, 165–66
Physical necessity, 135
Physical properties, 63, 160, 165–66, 172; causal relevance of, x, 108–10, 160, 170; of events, 87; as mental properties, 50; mental properties and, x, 61, 84–85, 102, 137–38
Physics: consciousness and, 85; laws of, 2, 58; mental causation and, 7; mind control and, 4, 6; see also Metaphysics
Physiology, 38
Picture theory of language, 82–83
Pineal gland, 30, 32
Placebo effect, 7
Plato: on dualism, 17, 171; on forms, 17; on immortality, 10–18; on mental causation, xi, 10–12, 14–17, 25–26; on properties vs. property instances, 66; on soul, 11–12, 22, 25
Positive producer, 95, 98
Possibilia (possible particulars), 71
Pragmatics, 97–99, 110–11, 162

Predicates, 80–82
Primitive notions, 30–31, 33
Problem from below, 60–61
Problem from without, 60–61
Problem of one over many, 69
Properties, 48–49, 64–80, 84–85, 106–8, 127–28, 147–48, 153, 158; of actions, 131, 154–55; backward-looking, 118–20; causal relevance and, 87–88, 111, 115, 154–55; causation and, 54, 63; collective work of, 93–94; dispositions as, 122, 125; of effects, 158; forward-looking, 120; functional, 127–28; grounding, 126–27; higher-level, 157, 161, 172–73; intrinsic, 79–80; language and, 80–84; laws and, 93, 109–10, 163; leveled account of, 158–61, 167–68; levels of, 148–49, 158–59; naming of, 83; natural, 74, 77; nonmental, 102; nonphysical, 2, 5, 84–85, 173–74; overlap of, 106, 142–44; particulars and, 65–66, 124–25, 142–44; predicates and, 82; reason, 121; special science, 161–62; supervenience of, 132, 134–35, 150, 169; see also Mental properties; Physical properties
Property instances, 66, 95, 152–53
Psyche, 11
Psychiatry, 6–7
Psychological struggle, 12
Psychology: constitutive laws of, 56–57; Davidson on, 54–57, 85; language of, 81, 84; mental causation and, 7
Psychosemantics, 22
Putnam, Hilary, 50–51, 59

Rationality, 11, 56–57
Realizer functionalism, 52–54, 114, 126, 129
Realm division, 33
Reasons: actions and, 5, 16–17, 111–12, 121; as cause, xi, 46–47
Relevance; see Causal relevance
Response dependence, 81
Role functionalism, 52, 64, 114, 154–55; mental causation and, 53–54, 127–28
Russell, Bertrand, 89–91
Ryle, Gilbert, 44–47

Scientific realism, 74
Second actuality, 20